CAS

U.S. NATIONAL SECURITY

CONCEPTS AND PROCESSES

—■—

DONALD M. SNOW

UNIVERSITY OF ALABAMA

ROWMAN &
LITTLEFIELD

Lanham · Boulder · New York · London

Executive Editor: Traci Crowell
Assistant Editor: Mary Malley
Senior Marketing Manager: Amy Whitaker

Published by Rowman & Littlefield
An imprint of The Rowman & Littlefield Publishing Group, Inc.
4501 Forbes Boulevard, Suite 200, Lanham, Maryland 20706
www.rowman.com

6 Tinworth Street, London SE11 5AL, United Kingdom

British Library Cataloguing in Publication Information Available

Library of Congress Cataloging-in-Publication Data

Names: Snow, Donald M., 1943– author.
Title: Cases in U.S. national security : concepts and processes / Donald M. Snow, University of Alabama.
Description: Lanham, MD : Rowman & Littlefield, [2019] | Includes bibliographical references and index.
Identifiers: LCCN 2018039887 (print) | LCCN 2018042857 (ebook) | ISBN 9781538115671 (electronic) | ISBN 9781538115657 (cloth : alk. paper) | ISBN 9781538115664 (pbk. : alk. paper)
Subjects: LCSH: National security—United States—Case studies. | United States—Military policy—Case studies. | United States—Foreign relations—Case studies.
Classification: LCC UA23 (ebook) | LCC UA23 .S5246 2019 (print) | DDC 355/.033073—dc23
LC record available at https://lccn.loc.gov/2018039887

∞™ The paper used in this publication meets the minimum requirements of American National Standard for Information Sciences—Permanence of Paper for Printed Library Materials, ANSI/NISO Z39.48-1992.

Printed in the United States of America

Contents

Preface

Public discussions about matters of American national security have been democratized greatly since terrorism broke onto the American scene following the September 11, 2001, Al Qaeda attacks against New York and Washington, DC. There was not much public discussion of national security during the Cold War, because there was a consensus about the enemy and the policy to deal with the peril that enemy represented. During the decade between the last lowering of the Soviet hammer and sickle flag from the Kremlin in 1991 and the airplanes slamming into the Twin Towers and the Pentagon, national security receded into the political landscape, with what discussion there was focused on what the outcome of the breakup of European communism would look like and some passing concern for developing unrest in places like the Balkans and Africa. There did not seem to be a lot to talk about when the subject was national security.

9/11 changed that perception. The country arguably overreacted to the degree of peril under which religious terror placed the United States, but the sneak attacks personalized, frightened, and in some cases paralyzed Americans. I personally remember meeting my national security class the day of the attack, and one of the first questions students asked was whether they were personally safe; some even asked if it was safe to walk across the quadrangle by Denny Chimes at the University of Alabama. I tried to assure them there was almost certainly no terrorist hiding behind a tree who would jump out and harm them. Most of the students believed me; I am pretty sure some of them did not.

Reaction to the terrorist attacks reenergized interest in national security. In an abstract sense, this was beneficial, but not entirely so. People were suddenly more interested in national security affairs, but they were no more knowledgeable than they were before. They turned to opinion leaders in the government and the electronic and print media for assistance, but unfortunately, many of those to whom they turned were hardly any more knowledgeable than they were. The result was that almost all public figures became "experts" and propounded analyses and recommendations they were, by dint of knowledge, too inexpert to express. People listened to them anyway. That situation largely continues today.

This situation creates a problem for the lay citizen trying to form reasoned opinions on national security matters and judging the veracity of those officials and others advocating one American policy or another. In 2018, two examples stand out. The first is the relocation of the American embassy in Israel from Tel Aviv to Jerusalem. The action, completed in mid-May 2018, had enormous consequences for the stability of the Middle East, and especially for the Israelis and Palestinians. The solution strongly favors the Israeli government of Benjamin Netanyahu, who could have dictated President Trump's argument for making the move, and virtually precludes progress on a settlement of the Palestinian crisis. The president's defense was that it fulfilled a 2016 campaign promise. But it was much more than that, as chapter 8 tries to convey. The second is the U.S.-DPRK (North Korea) relationship. It is an enormously complex situation that goes well beyond the personalities of Kim Jong Un and Donald J. Trump and even the disposition of the North Korean nuclear arsenal. Before agreeing with one position or another, it is very helpful to know at least something about those innuendos and competing undercurrents. Chapters 6 and 12 explore the situation.

Cases in U.S. National Security is my modest attempt to provide a vehicle by which readers (primarily students) can gain enough information and perspective on national security policy areas and dynamics to make more reasoned judgments than they could if they did not read the book. It does not provide a definitive, exhaustive treatment of any of these problems, an impossible task given the six-thousand-word parameter set for each of the chapters. It is designed to be a supplement for courses in national security, foreign policy, and international relations to provide a platform for the reasoned discussion of current, important matters affecting American national security. It could also serve as a core text for a course in issues in security or foreign policy. The student who reads and studies this book will not walk away as an authority in the important policy subjects that are covered; he or she will know more than before reading it and may, in the process, discover how relaxed the public criteria for being considered an "expert" have become.

Cases in U.S. National Security is a book I have wanted to write since the early 2000s, when I got in the casebook "business" with the publication of the first edition of *Cases in International Relations*, scheduled to go into its eighth edition in 2020. *Cases in IR* started a process and format with which I have become comfortable through the years, and particularly with the idea of compiling a collection of personally written articles about subjects that I thought germane to the subject of the book. The virtues of this approach, in my opinion, are that the result is a more uniform book in terms of how the subjects are presented, and that creating a common framework within which to examine each subject facilitates comparisons among subjects. The alternative approach is to compile a compendium of scholarly or policy articles published in journals. The advantage is that these tend to be written by acknowledged experts; the disadvantage is they are rarely written specifically as educational materials for student audiences. I extended my approach to foreign policy with *Regional Cases in U.S. Foreign Policy*, now in its second edition. The publication of this volume completes the circle of subject matters in which I feel I have enough knowledge for a complete volume.

Content and Features

Each of my casebooks features a model around which the individual cases are built, but each has a different organizational structure. The IR book, for instance, follows the format of offering a basic or applied principle of international politics illustrated by a substantive examination of the principle in action. The foreign policy book concentrates on American policy toward different countries in different regions, with each section containing two chapters on regional examples examined in historical and current policy terms, the underlying rationale being that foreign policy is in application foreign *policies* toward different places and regions.

This volume follows that tradition. It consists of eighteen chapters. Chapter 1 presents basic concepts for thinking about national security and develops a model for thinking about that process and its outcomes originally designed for the U.S. Air Force by Col. (ret.) Dennis M. Drew and myself for use in Air Force professional military education. It provides a rational approach to organizing national security concerns and is presented both for its coherence and for its frequent violations in practice.

This framework forms the basic intellectual thread that binds the substantive chapters, which are divided into three parts. Part I, Strategic Dynamics, consists of six chapters devoted to basic problems facing American national security policy illustrated by prominent ongoing cases. It begins, in chapter 2, with the generic problem of asymmetrical warfare, the major form of violent conflict in the developing world, which is the locus of most ongoing international violence that might engage the United States. Chapter 3 deals with the continuing problem of terrorism since the essential defeat of the Islamic State and the dispersion of terror to other developing world locations; it features the difficulty of devising a coherent strategy for containing the terrorist threat. The following four chapters focus on revived aspects of nuclear weapons strategy. Chapter 4 is devoted to the theories of nuclear deterrence that have new relevance in the contemporary environment. Chapter 5 analyzes a parallel revival of concern with nuclear proliferation that has arisen because of actual and alleged efforts by countries like North Korea and Iran to obtain nuclear weapons in the face of international prohibitions on doing so. Chapter 6 looks more specifically at the conflict and maneuverings by the United States and the DPRK over North Korea's nuclear arsenal, while chapter 7 addresses the nuclear relationship with Iran, including the agreement between six countries and Iran for Iran to eschew the weapons (the JCPOA), the Trump withdrawal of the United States from the arrangement, and the repercussions of that action.

Part II, Geographic Spotlights, is more territorially oriented. It consists of six cases, three from the Middle East and three others. The Middle Eastern chapters begin with chapter 8, which explores the national security implications for the United States, and the region, of the American decision to move its embassy to Jerusalem, a de facto recognition of that holy city as the capital of the country, and the impact on the Palestinians and the peace process. Chapter 9 explores the "Afghanistan trap," the circumstances that have prevented the United States from either achieving its goal of an antiterrorist Afghan state or from extricating itself from "America's longest war." Chapter 10 looks at the long, bloody Syrian civil war, focusing on atrocities (chemical weapons use) and geopolitical concerns (Russian and Iranian influence) and the inability or unwillingness of the United States to take on a decisive role in ending the carnage.

The other cases in Part II look at different U.S. relationships. Chapter 11 examines the increasingly adversarial relations with Russia, focusing on Russian expansionism in its geographical domain and interference in the 2016 American presidential election as national security problems for America. Chapter 12 examines the complex subject of Sino-American relations, both in terms of the geopolitics of the Asia-Pacific region and increasingly adversarial economic relations. Part II concludes with chapter 13, which looks at emerging national security concerns with Africa, including the 2017 incident where four American Special Forces personnel were killed in an apparently unauthorized attack against a terrorist leader.

Part III, Political Context, consists of four chapters that discuss constraints on and opportunities for policy and strategy based in the broader political environment. It begins with chapter 14, which raises the familiar question of "how much is enough?" in terms of both the physical and monetary effort of the country in the national security area, emphasizing the budgetary and monetary factors that affect the national security effort. Chapter 15 looks specifically at the question of military personnel recruitment and retention in the context of an extensive pattern of overseas deployment since 2001 and raises the possibility that there may be circumstances in which the All-Volunteer Force (AVF) concept for military procurement that has been in effect since 1972 might prove inadequate and create the need either for alternative forms of recruitment like conscription or a reduced commitment of American forces. Chapter 16 explores the idea of cybersecurity both as it arose in the Russian election hacking of 2016 and in terms of the use of computers and information technologies as parameters in future national security. Chapter 17 looks specifically at one technology, drone warfare, as a technological "fix" for some national security problems but also as a potential source of concern. The book concludes with chapter 18, which asks the question *quo vadis*, a Latin phrase meaning roughly "where are we going?" It attempts to provide some conceptual tools deriving from the rest of the text to aid the reader in reaching opinions about answers to the question.

To promote reasonable coherence among the diverse subjects in the text, each chapter is organized in the same manner. The framework derives from the set of concepts and constructs introduced in the first chapter. It has two basic purposes. The first is to create order and some sense of comparability among the topics considered. The second is to promote an active learning of individual topics and national security more generally. It does not tell readers *what* to think about issues, but it *does* attempt to help the reader develop the more important skill of *how* to think of these problems. To this end, each chapter begins with a general overview, followed by designated sections on "Perspectives on the Problem," "Policy Options," and a concluding "Consequences: What to Do?". Each chapter contains a set of study/discussion questions and a bibliography of cited works and other materials that may assist in conducting more concentrated inquiry into the chapter's subject.

Rejoinder: What This Book Is and Is Not About

This casebook is distinguished from other books in the field in several ways. First, it is—as noted earlier—a set of original essays rather than a conglomeration of articles and papers written for other purposes, reasons, and outlets (like journals). The purpose is to add continuity and comparability between the subjects. Second, it is more contemporary in the subjects covered than is typically the case in a "reader." The reason is simple: I did not have to wait for journals to publish articles before I could add them to the table of contents. The "middle man" of a review and publication in another source is avoided. They are all up-to-date as of the latter part of 2018. Third, the writing style and pedagogy are purposely student friendly. My purpose is to write in a manner that engages the undergraduate student who is this book's primary target; it is not to impress colleagues with my mastery of the arcane language and concepts of the field. Fourth, single-author composition makes it easier to update materials than is possible when one is dealing with the publication schedules of journals, even those which seek currency in their articles. This has proven advantageous in my other casebooks, and I trust the same will be true with this one.

A word about what this book is *not* is also appropriate. It is not a comprehensive textbook, but rather a series of essays about individual aspects and dynamics of a large, complex, and diverse field of study. It does not seek to replace core texts for a National Security or Defense Policy course; there are other books available for that (I favor, of course, my own *National Security* book). It can be used, particularly in courses where the text is more oriented toward the American politics of national security, as a supplement, and it can serve as a core or supplementary text in national security problems and related courses. It is not a systematic overview and theoretical examination of the entirety of the field; rather, it is a collection of essays on interesting and important policy matters affecting national security. There is no grand theory of international relations or national security in these pages; rather, there is a set of essays designed to help students think about and hone their views on some important national security matters of the day.

Bibliography

Drew, Dennis M., and Donald M. Snow. *Making Twenty-First Century Strategy: An Introduction to Modern National Security Processes.* Montgomery, AL: Air University Press, 2006.

Snow, Donald M. *Cases in International Relations: Principles and Applications.* Seventh Ed. Lanham, MD: Rowman & Littlefield, 2018.

———. *National Security.* Sixth Ed. New York and London: Routledge, 2017.

———. *Regional Cases in U.S. Foreign Policy.* Second Ed. Lanham, MD: Rowman & Littlefield, 2018.

Acknowledgments

No book is an entirely individual effort, and this one is no exception. I am indebted to colleagues who read and commented on the manuscript, including Gary Donato, Tom Moriarty, Azmat Sakiev, Jordan Tama, and Matthew Zierler. As always, I have enjoyed the unstinting and generous assistance of the editorial team at Rowman & Littlefield. Special thanks go to Traci Crowell, my senior editor who provided valuable advice on cases for inclusion and exclusion. A fellow University of Colorado graduate, she has always provided a sympathetic ear to my numerous ideas, some good and some maybe not so good. Sainthood should be bestowed on Mary Malley, my assistant editor and day-to-day contact on things computer, which is not, shall we say, my strongest attribute. I (and hopefully she) have long since lost count of the number of times she picked up the phone to my salutation, "Have I ever told you I hate computers?" after which she remedied the current crisis for me. The sincerest of thanks to you both. I would also be remiss if I did not offer similar thanks to Alden Perkins for her cheerful and efficient guidance of this enterprise from manuscript to bound book. Finally, thanks to my wife Donna, who accommodated my mood swings as this book progressed. She is a veteran and a trooper in these enterprises. Finally, our white German shepherd/Labrador Toby made sure there was not so much peace and quiet around the house that concentration was not broken from time to time.

Donald M. Snow
Professor Emeritus
University of Alabama

1

Starting at the Beginning
Basic Dynamics and Concerns

Most people have only a very general idea about national security as a political dynamic and as it affects their individual lives. That general condition is understandable, because the idea of national security is outside the general realm of most people's personal and even academic experience. One can, for instance, take any number of courses in political science and never confront more than fleeting glances of this subject, and there are relatively few students or faculty with specialized expertise. National security studies, as they are known, are a hybrid of American national politics and international relations, and most of the people who mine the subject matter have their intellectual feet in either American politics or IR. As a result, national security specialists often have difficulty even talking to one another!

If you feel a certain level of inadequacy or discomfort thinking about this subject, you have a good deal of company, and it is the purpose of this text to try to strip away some of your misgivings and feelings of inadequacy about it. The process of doing so is important to you and your country: national security is about national safety, even survival, and it is vitally imperative that those who manage and make decisions about what serves national security matters be held in the closest account and scrutiny. Getting to that point requires recognizing that the subject, while foreign and initially forbidding, is not inscrutable.

There are several reasons that people are typically overwhelmed when questions of national security are raised, and especially when their views on specific issues are solicited. The first problem is the nature of the policy area itself. National security is a "special" policy domain that is somehow different and aloof from other areas of domestic or foreign policy. Unless one has some special background such as having veterans in the family, it has a generally unfamiliar content and is enshrouded in a kind of mystique and aura of seriousness and consequence that does not adhere to many policy areas, making people reluctant to opine on matters that are important but about which they have little informed background. For many, this condition is reinforced by an aversion to the most applied aspects of the concept, prominently including war and personal violence and killing.

Second, it is difficult to obtain all the information one might want or need to make the most reasoned possible judgments about national security matters, a point often emphasized by "experts" if one voices an opinion at odds with theirs. Part of the problem is the technical nature of many of the factors that go into making decisions. Military factors such as the performance of weapons systems go beyond the capacity of most people to pass judgment upon or incorporate into operational considerations of policy options. Much of the information is secret for good, security-related reasons, but secrecy can often be excessive, and it can be used to stifle criticism or debate about policy. The haughtily dismissive response to questioning policy that begins with the admonition "if you knew what I knew, you would understand and agree with me," is emblematic of this tendency. The point of technical complexity and the need for secrecy is not invalid; it can, however, be overdone and used to stifle disagreement with policy considerations.

Third, the debate over policy alternatives is often distorted and misleading because it is conducted by people whose expertise and authority is presumed due to their positions when that presumption of superior knowledge or perspective is suspect. This observation is particularly true of two groups that the prevalence of electronic media has thrown into an unflattering spotlight. One group is elected officials, and especially rank and file members of the Congress. Hardly any members of Congress are elected because of their expertise in national security affairs unless their districts/states house large military bases or major defense contractors. Historically, they were judged on how well they understood and represented those issue areas most salient to their constituents—farm issues in the Midwest or public land usage in the West, for instance. On other matters, they were not expected to be experts and were rarely asked for their opinions on matters where they lacked expertise. Instead, they deferred to the ranking member of their party on the appropriate Senate or House committee. Thus, if you wanted to know what your representative thought about national security, it was probably what the ranking party member of the House or Senate armed services committee believed, and your representative would defer to that individual. This arrangement both insulated members of Congress from being embarrassed by being asked questions they could not answer in front of television cameras and contributed to some discipline within the parties.

This situation stands in stark contrast to the present. Television and print reporters are ubiquitous fixtures on Capitol Hill, and members of the Congress are regularly beseeched to offer their opinions on a broad range of subjects, including areas where their knowledge base may be quite limited. They can, however, no longer hide from public scrutiny, and as a result, are often placed in the uncomfortable position of commenting on matters about which they know very little to avoid the appearance of ignorance. Their positions as elected officials cast an aura of knowledge and wisdom to the viewer or reader that may not be deserved and thus may distort the views that members of the public adopt. National security affairs represents one of the policy areas where this distortion occurs, because so few members of Congress really understand the issues involved. The same general comments apply to most of those in the media who collect and report national security news.

This critique may seem harsh, and some of its implications are damning. This does not mean that either group is venal or wishes to prejudice or distort the debate on specific national security issues (although in some cases that may be their purpose). What it does suggest is that the implicit (and sometimes explicit) claims to superior knowledge, perspective, and thus judgment that officials or commentators make about sensitive, important policy areas should not automatically be accorded the sanctity and authoritativeness that they are sometimes accorded and which those in such positions may claim or imply. The informed citizen may have as valid a perspective on policy matters as the purported expert. It is one thing to listen to and respect the views of those with apparently superior credentials; it is quite another matter to accept those positions simply because they are asserted.

Reaching reasoned, informed judgments on national security affairs is not easy. For one thing, the nature and language of national security is specialized, technical, and initially forbidding, as already suggested. Thus, a first challenge to the neophyte in this area is working your way through the thicket of confusing, sometimes obfuscating language in which the arguments are couched, and this problem is compounded by the gravity and severity of national security outcomes. Using terms like national "survival" to describe policy may be true, but it is also intimidating, sometimes on purpose. Second, the process is complex, involving multiple institutional and individual actors at different levels and locations in that process. Understanding the dynamics can be thought of as a two-step process. The first step is coming to grips with key concepts and dynamics of national security, what we will call perspectives on the problem. The second step involves coming to grips with how responses at various levels of specificity are made by the political process, an area we will call policy options.

Perspectives on the Problem

Developing a perspective and framework within which to understand national security generally and from which to reach judgments on individual policy areas is aided by understanding the basic ideas and processes by which the policy process operates. I have attempted to lay out some of these dynamics in other works, some of which are cited in the bibliography. What follows is a skeletal version of those concepts.

The heart of American national security is what keeps the United States safe and protected from those countries and other entities like terrorist groups that wish to deny the country those conditions. The conceptual discussion of national security thus begins with the determination of what those interests are, what conditions or forces seek to compromise or deny those aspirations, and what the United States should try to do to protect its interests. These concepts form a kind of progression:

$$\text{Interests} \longrightarrow \text{Security} \longrightarrow \text{Threat} \longrightarrow$$
$$\text{Power/Capability} \longrightarrow \text{Risk and Risk Management}$$

Interests

The first and most fundamental concept is interests. The term has multiple meanings and applications in normal usage, but in political dialogue, it generally refers to the things normally expressed in terms of preferred or necessary conditions of existence. These are not always compatible with one another, and this incompatibility forms the basis of animosity, competition, and the need to resolve the differences that exist. Because some of these interests and their incompatibility can be attached to values that countries feel are very important to them, interests thus serve as the foundation for the consideration of security.

Although there are more elaborate depictions of their hierarchy (see, for instance, Snow, *Cases in International Relations*, Seventh Edition, especially chapter 2 for an elaboration), basic interests of states can be divided into two categories that provide a bridge to other elements in the security chain. The first category is *vital interests* (VIs), conditions a country deems so important to its existence or well-being that it will not willingly compromise on their achievement. The second category is *less-than-vital* (LTV) *interests,* which refers to those conditions a country values and the failure to realize would affect it adversely but where non-realization would not endanger the most important values. The LTV designation covers a broad range of conditions of varying importance from near-vital to relatively unimportant.

There are three qualifications to the concept of vital interests. The first arises from the word *willingly* in the definition of a vital interest. It is a qualification that says in effect that while all states will do what they can to secure vital interests, they will not always succeed, normally because they lack the power to protect all their interests. The qualification suggests a hierarchy between the powerful and the less powerful in achieving goals. It can also refer to the relevance of power in specific situations, e.g., the United States was clearly more powerful than North Vietnam, but it could not assert its will over the DRV.

The second qualification refers to the objectivity of the notion of various gradations of interests. While people agree in principle that there are conditions vital to countries that must be pursued with maximum efforts, they do not always agree what those interests are and how vigorously they should be pursued. Political dialogue often obscures this distinction, because advocates on various sides of any issue will normally depict the position they promote as "vital" to the national interest as a means of adding gravitas to that advocacy. The notion of vitality and its applicability in given situations is not an empirical matter of fact, but represents the opinion of whoever is propounding it. Some matters may be so overwhelmingly important that there is essential agreement on their vitality, but that reflects unanimity of opinion. One should always view claims of vitality with some caution.

The third qualification flows from the second and refers to the boundary between VIs and LTV interests. It is a critical distinction in national security affairs because it is often considered the boundary between situations that do and do not justify the employment of force to realize them: protecting a VI potentially justifies the use of force, whereas pursuing LTV interests normally does not. The location of the boundary generally or in specific situations is, however, subjective, a matter of honest disagreement among observers and policy makers. In the contemporary international environment, only massive nuclear threats unambiguously threaten the most basic vital interest—

survival—and all other threats fall somewhere closer to or across the frontier between VIs and LTV interests.

Security

The second link in the chain is security. It is a subcategory of interests, since some interests have an effect on the security of the country and others do not. What is distinctive about national security threats is the severity of the consequences of non-realization, which is why national security represents a distinctive area of concern. Unfortunately, like interests, the concept of security is also shrouded in some level of uncertainty and ambiguity. It is also non-intersubjective. What this awkward philosophy of science term means is that views on interests and security are opinions, not facts, and that different people can and do hold different views about their content and, as a result, what consequences and actions apply to different situations.

Security is a variable condition. Dictionary definitions tend to ascribe two attributes to the term: safety and a *feeling* of safety. All people want to be safe or secure, which has as its core a physical condition of safety. A roof over one's head in a rainstorm provides security from getting wet, for instance, and this is a physical, objective situation everyone can observe and experience by standing under the roof while it is raining. The feeling of safety, on the other hand, is a psychological state based on what makes the individual believe that he or she is safe, and this can and does vary among individuals based on their beliefs or opinions. Roofs, after all, can be constructed of different materials, and the safety they provide to people depends to some degree on what kind of roof is over their heads when the rain starts falling.

This may seem an unimportant distinction, but it is not. The question of national security revolves on the degree of endangerment to achieving or maintaining interests in given situations. People can disagree about what conditions are in the national interest and how important various conditions are. These are sources of division on policy preferences, since different people feel endangered by very different conditions. When both interests and effects on security are entailed, the meanings and interpretations of events and conditions can, and do, vary greatly. Thus, if someone says a national interest is imperiled and that national security is compromised as a result, that person is expressing what is at least partially a subjective judgment, not a "fact." If you hold and express a contradictory view on the same issue, you are also voicing your opinion on the facts.

Threat

The third link in the chain, and in some ways the critical distinguishing of national security compared to other policy areas, is threat, and specifically threats that may be resolved by the prospect or actual application of military force. Threats enter the equation when countries (or non-state groups) profess interests at odds with our own and demand that their interests be honored, even if doing so requires the threatened party to abandon or dilute an interest of its own. In these frequent situations, one side or the other (or both) must be persuaded to do the other's bidding. The most frequent vehicle for gaining such compliance is through the issuance of threats.

A threat is a promise to do something harmful to the threatened party if it does not accede to the threatening party's demands. Threats cover a wide range of situations and severity of threatened actions, and only dire threats promising the most harmful impacts on the country's interests become matters of general national security concern. The threats that are issued can make matters better or worse and can inflame national egos in addition to creating fears of the consequences of threats being carried out. The brouhaha between the United States and North Korea, described elsewhere in this volume, exemplifies threat interaction at its most virulent.

Three distinctions about threats are important. The first is between "good" and "bad" threats, and it is based on instrumental definitions of value. A good threat is one that causes compliance by the threatened party without having to be carried out, and a bad threat is one that must be carried out; it is bad because carrying out threats (especially military ones) normally entails costs to the threatening as well as the threatened parties. The party issuing a threat "wins" if the other accepts the demanded terms; if that party does not accede, both parties lose in varying degrees.

The second distinction is the expansible nature of threat. Not all threats are made explicitly by one party to another. Many are implicit and represent threatening situations that the parties infer. As a result, some of the structure of threat a country faces results from the calculation of parties about what does and does not threaten them. The idea of threat thus enters the chain of non-intersubjective calculations that begins with interests and security. Put simply, some people feel threatened by situations and conditions that others find tolerable. Because of human ingenuity, the list of possibly threatening conditions is almost infinitely expandable and what is and is not threatening becomes part of the general disagreement about national security.

The third distinction is what to do when one is confronted with threats. Some threats (to VIs, for instance) are clearly compelling and must be dealt with to maintain national integrity, while LTV interests command lesser efforts. The state, however, must have the ability to counter some or all of the threats it faces, and to do so, it must have available the means to resist, including counter-threaten, its opponents. The mechanism for doing so is the possession of power.

Power/Capability

The fourth link in the conceptual link is thus power or capability. The need for power to achieve national goals is the result of an anarchical international order in which all authority is invested in the sovereign states. Power is conventionally defined as the ability to get someone to do something that party would not otherwise do. In a situation of threat, one or both parties must back away from demands they have of the other, which means they must do something they would prefer not to do. The party that succeeds in a power relationship is the one that has the relevant capability to bring about this compliance.

Power is a relationship between a threatening and a threatened party. For power to act as a credible threat against an adversary, it must possess two characteristics. The first is a belief by the object of a power threat that the threatening party has both the physical capacity to carry out the action threatened (capability) and the will to do so (credibility). Both can be questionable: states frequently try to hide their physical capabilities, and since carrying out these capabilities often entails counter actions, it is not always clear threats will be carried out. It is largely the burden of the threatened party to determine both capacity and will. Second, power is situation-specific. It is not enough to know which party in a power situation has the most power, but whether that party can or will bring it to bear. The United States, for instance, has more power by most measures than any other country, but it is not always effective because it may not apply to specific situations, e.g., the United States has the power to destroy Niger (see chapter 13) with nuclear weapons, but no one would believe the U.S. government would use them against that African state, despite the attack on American Special Forces there in October 2017.

What makes power a uniquely important element of national security is that the use of military force is an important element in threatening and implementing force in conflict situations. Military force is considered key to national security, but this fact also creates a limitation on the ability of any country, including the United States, to realize all its interests. Military force is expensive, and its availability is finite. In a world where there are many claimants to the need for force due to the expandability of worthy interests and threats to security, it will always be true that possible needs for capability will exceed the amount of threat-reducing force available to satisfy all claimants. The heart of national security policy is how to reconcile claims on capability to gain compliance with demands with the resources available.

Risk and Risk Management

The fifth and final link in the conceptual chain is thus risk and risk management, and the heart of much national security policy is how to approach this problem. Simply put, risk as a national security matter represents the difference between the threats to interests and the capability it possesses to deflect or defeat those threats. It can be depicted in a simple, suggestive formula: Risk equals threat minus capability ($R=T-C$). As a practical matter, the volume of threats that a country feels it faces will always exceed its capability to deal with all the challenges its members believe it faces. Those threats for which there are inadequate capability represent risks the country faces; much of the task of national security planning and policy is risk management, the attempt to deal with those problems that cannot routinely be managed with existing resources.

Both threats and capabilities are, as noted, variable. They can be expanded or contracted based on policy determinations and resource allocations. Since threats are especially vulnerable to expansion, much of the process involves picking among threats to deflect, accepting those on which there is consensus, and taking a chance (risk) on others. At the same time, capability is also variable, in that additional resources can be allocated to efforts like military forces to reduce or expand what is left at risk. This is not a straightforward process, since there are always multiple claimants to scarce resources. The process is tilted toward inflated risk because of human imagination, but the result is an ongoing tension between those who emphasize threat and those who prefer to regulate resources that can produce capability. That competition is at the heart of the policy and strategy process.

Policy Options

When a national security crisis arises and there is disagreement or confusion about how to respond to it, a frequent charge leveled at decision-makers is that the United States does not have a "strategy" to deal with the problem at hand. It is a criticism that often has some merit, but it often arises from a cursory understanding both of what a strategy is and how it translates into actions when problems arise. Because of this difficulty and the complex circumstances and steps surrounding how strategy is crafted and applied, it is useful to organize thinking about it using the same kind of conceptual progression introduced in the last section.

$$\text{Strategy} \longrightarrow \text{Levels of Strategy} \longrightarrow$$
$$\text{Policy} \longrightarrow \text{Issues and Competitors}$$

Strategy

The term strategy has a simple origin and meaning, although it has been appropriated by so many different entities and areas that some of that meaning has become diluted, as has some of its focus. The term was originally military, but it has been expanded to include virtually any area that requires some forethought and application. In its most fundamental sense, strategy is *a plan of action to organize efforts to achieve objectives.* In simple terms relating to national security concerns, strategy is the way the country organizes to deal with the threats that are presented to it.

This simplicity of definition is somewhat misleading, because it can suggest a kind of orderliness and consensus that often does not exist. Strategy derives from an assessment of the national security environment to which plans must be applied. This is straightforward and not overly controversial when there is consensus on two elements: what the threat is, and basically what must be done to cope with it. During the Cold War, for instance, the threat was clearly the expansion of Soviet (and Chinese) communism, and there was virtually unanimous agreement on the need to frustrate that expansion and somehow to defeat communism. The result was the strategy of containment, which served as the bedrock of national security strategy and policy until the demise of the Soviet

Union in 1991. Hardly anyone questioned the existence or essential wisdom of the construct, and one hardly ever heard the accusation that the United States did not have a national security strategy then.

This consensus dissolved when the threat fell apart with the dissolution of the communist threat. Containment prevailed, but its success left a conceptual void. Since 1991, there has not been a conceptual threat of the magnitude of communism. International terrorism has been the substitute. While there is broad agreement that terrorism is the major operational threat facing the United States, that consensus does not extend to how dire the threat is and especially how to manage or defeat it. Strategic development thrives on order and agreement, and these have been missing. The charge that the country lacks a strategy to deal with terrorist-related problems is really an assertion that there is disagreement on the nature and resolution of the terrorism problem that frustrates strategic development. This problem is explored in more depth in chapter 2.

Levels of Strategy

Strategy development and implementation is a *multi-level process* that moves from the broadest and most general level to greater levels of specificity and detail. Ideally, the process is deductive and thus logical, but that is not always the case in a complex and often confounding international environment, and because of the inability or unwillingness of strategists to follow a clear path to the strategy's objective of providing a plan of action to secure the country's interests.

The strategy process begins with an assessment of the country's most important interests and, of most pertinence to the strategy process, those environmental forces that seek to interfere with achieving those goals. Grand strategy is the most general, sweeping statement of that assessment, identifying those impediments to national safety that are most important and threatening and suggesting general guidelines for neutralizing those threats. In the Cold War, the general threat was the expansion of Soviet communism, and the strategy of containment was a politico-military response the objectives of which were to halt the political expansion of communist states and the frustration of their military expansion. The containment line around other, more specific implementing strategies (e.g., the size and configuration of American and allied military forces) followed from this general guidance. The process then moves into more specific planning (strategic) actions by constituent parts of the national security apparatus, down to campaign and battlefield tactics.

Part of the current national security problem is that the principles lack such clarity, making the fashioning of plans for implementation more ambiguous than in a condition of compelling threat. Terrorism suppression may have supplanted communism as an organizing objective of the strategist, but it is not as clearly defined as communism and thus does not provide the same directive quality to the strategist. The terrorist threat is important and dangerous, but it is not clearly as dire as was the Cold War threat. At the same time, it is not clear how to combat terrorism: it is not unambiguously a military threat for which conventional military solutions flow as strategic planning becomes more specific, and there is no consensus about the best method of reducing its influence. The general statement of terrorist suppression may represent as close to a grand strategic organizing principle as is available, but it does not provide a clear operational direction. This is frustrating for all concerned in the process: it is, after all, difficult to plan a journey when one is not certain where one is going or how to get there. These conditions make the framing of policy a more difficult and contentious task.

There are other sources that ensure the strategy process is not a seamless, analytically deductive exercise. Most of these are human. For one thing, the fact that strategy cascades downward as its mandates are made operational means many different people from different, and in some cases competing or even antagonistic, perspectives become involved. All these groups may not agree with whatever strategy is being implemented or with one another, and the result is to diffuse and dilute some of the conceptual "purity" of the original formulation. No strategic statement is so unambiguous that parts or all of it are not subject to interpretation and the opinions of people in the process. Much national security policy is made and implemented by the military, which suggests a certain orderliness and discipline in formulating and especially executing orders, but the process is by no means perfect.

Once again, the process of moving through the strategy process can be easier or more difficult depending on the degree of unanimity and clarity around the strategy. The menace of Soviet military power (and especially a Soviet nuclear arsenal clearly capable of destroying the United States) tended to create unanimity about the gravity of the threat and led to acceptance of implementing strategies designed to flesh it out. That clarity and direction is absent today, where there is not the same kind of unanimity surrounding the nature and gravity of the threat and thus what plans of action are appropriate to deal with it. With a maximum threat, strategy-making and implementation is easier and more straightforward than in a more ambiguous environment.

Policy

These problems extend to the level of policy, where they are often most visible. Strategy and policy perform the same purposes in the realms in which they are applied, and the *Oxford Dictionary* goes so far as to designate the two terms as synonyms. Like strategy, policy is "a course or principle of action adopted or proposed by government" or some other source. What differentiates the term in application from strategy is the context in which it is used. Most variations of strategy arise from military considerations and applications, the context in which the term is used here. Policy, on the other hand, can consist of actions in a wide range of contexts, but is used most often in the political realm where the major actions taken involve the allocation of societal resources—generally monetary— to social and political problems that require the expenditure of societal resources to implement.

The policy function can (and does) involve questioning strategic dictates and demands, but its function within the strategy process is to provide the resources necessary to carry out national security strategy. Its impact may be to expand strategic horizons with abundant resources, to reinforce the strategic preferences presented to it by providing requested support, or to constrict strategic plans by providing less support than requested. In a perfectly deductively organized policy process, the policy process would simply provide the wherewithal to allow the implantation of strategy. That is, however, seldom the case.

The policy level reflects, and to some extent even magnifies, the source of dissension found throughout the process. In a situation where there is unanimity about the threat and the priority of countering it, the problem is not acute, but that is not obviously the case in the contemporary environment, where there is abundant disagreement on just about everything. Dissent is more obvious at the policy level than at other levels because of the very public nature of politics: it is, after all, the people's elected representatives who are spending taxpayers' money, and since there is rarely universal agreement on how those dollars should be spent, there is questioning of the allocation of funding for national security, as there is for all government activities.

Issues and Competitors

The final link in the strategy process is issues and competitors. Making and implementing strategy is a multiple-player, interactive process, usually among countries that disagree on interests at play in a situation and who aspire to mutually exclusive outcomes. The degree to which the process is adversarial and the extent of policy options that may be considered will vary depending on how deeply and profoundly held the differences are, but it can never be assumed that there is some point of stasis where both or all sides agree on the parameters and details of a strategic path. Strategy, in other words, is a constantly changing entity and can only be understood as an ongoing process, not a journey with a concrete, predetermined destination.

These dynamics extend to the domestic side of strategy-making. Different political elements, for instance, have contrasting views on the heart of grand strategy, and thus implementing strategies. These preferences cascade through the process affecting, for instance, predilections toward a more militantly military as opposed to diplomatic approach to reconciling differences with other countries. Although national security occupies an elevated position in the hierarchy of national values, it is also not above the fray of domestic politics, whether it be matters of how much federal money is allocated to implementing strategic policies or even in whose congressional constituency a defense contract is let. The net result is that the strategy process is inevitably "messier" than an abstract, sanitized depiction might suggest.

Consequences: What to Do?

The purpose of this chapter has not been to provide vantage points or solutions to any of the numerous national security problems the country confronts. Rather, it has been to introduce ways to grasp national security questions and, in the process, to provide a useful framework within which to organize thinking about those problems. It has proceeded from two basic vantage points that are applied in the case studies that follow. One of these has been labeled *perspectives on the problem*, and it refers both to the substantive nature of the problem, the positions that both or all sides take on it, how important the issue may be, and to what lengths the United States may be willing to pursue different means to affect outcomes it prefers. The context within which this occurs is one of disagreement both among American analysts and between the United States and those with whom it competes.

The second vantage point refers to the *processes* by which the country decides, if it can, on its basic national security strategy and how that determination translates into more specific actions and policies it may take. This is a hypothetically deductive process that is, in application, more complex and "messier" than any depiction may make it appear. There is generally no good answer to the question "what is the strategy here?"

This chapter and what follows do not propose to "tell" or lead the reader to *what* to think about the national security cases included in subsequent chapters or about what to conclude about future problems that will inevitably arise in national affairs. Rather, it has the more modest intention of trying to help the reader learn *how* to organize thinking about national security matters. Hopefully, the result will be a reader who feels and is better equipped to confront thinking about matters of the country's safety in the world.

Study/Discussion Questions

1. Why do people have difficulty reaching judgments about national security subjects? Do you personally experience any of this reluctance?

2. What is national security? What are the component factors in determining national security? Define each concept and how they are related to one another.

3. What is intersubjectivity? How does its absence affect the different factors in national security determination from interests to risk?

4. What is strategy? At what levels does it operate, and what complicates its translation into policy?

5. Take any current national security situation and apply the security/strategy nexus to it. Are the outcomes it produces for you different for you than if you did not use the criteria?

Bibliography

Art, Robert A., and Kenneth B. Waltz (eds.). *The Uses of Force: Military Power and International Politics.* Seventh Ed. Lanham, MD: Rowman & Littlefield, 2009.

Berkowitz, Bruce. *The New Face of War: How War Will Be Fought in the Twenty-First Century.* New York: Free Press, 2003.

Builder, Carl. *The Masks of War: American Military Styles in Strategy and Analysis.* Santa Monica, CA: RAND Corporation, 1989.

Drew, Dennis M., and Donald M. Snow. *Making Twenty-First-Century Strategy: An Introduction to Modern National Security Processes and Problems.* Montgomery, AL: Air University Press, 2006.

Fromkin, David. *The Independence of Nations.* New York: Praeger Special Studies, 1981.

Gaddis, John Lewis. *Strategies of Containment: A Critical Appraisal of American National Security Policy during the Cold War.* Revised and Expanded Ed. New York: Oxford University Press, 2005.

Liddell Hart, B. H. *Strategy.* New York: Meridian Press, 1991.

Lissner, Rebecca Friedman. "The National Security Strategy Is Not a Strategy: Trump's Incoherence Is a Reminder of Why a New Approach Is Needed." *Foreign Affairs Snapshot* (online), December 19, 2017.

Morgenthau, Hans J. *Power Among Nations.* Seventh Ed. Revised by Kenneth W. Thompson and W. David Clinton. New York: McGraw-Hill Educational, 2005.

Nuechterlein, Donald E. *America Recommitted: United States National Interests in a Restructured World.* Lexington: University of Kentucky Press, 1991.

Schelling, Thomas G. *Arms and Influence.* New Haven, CT: Yale University Press, 1966.

Snow, Donald M. *Cases in International Relations.* Seventh Ed. Lanham, MD: Rowman & Littlefield, 2018.

———. *National Security.* Sixth Ed. New York and London: Routledge, 2017.

———. *Thinking about National Security: Strategy, Policy, and Issues.* New York and London: Routledge, 2016.

Stares, Paul B. *Preventive Engagement: How America Can Avoid War, Stay Strong, and Keep the Peace.* New York: Columbia University Press, 2018.

Summers, Harry G, Jr. *On Strategy: A Critical Analysis of the Vietnam War.* Novato, CA: Presidio Press, 1982.

Thucydides. *The History of the Peloponnesian Wars.* New York: Penguin Books, 1954.

Waltz, Kenneth. *Man, the State, and War: A Theoretical Analysis.* New York: Columbia University Press, 1959.

———. *Realism and International Politics.* New York: Routledge, 2006.

I

STRATEGIC DYNAMICS

Military matters are not the totality of national security concern, but they remain the central problem for most national security strategists. Military security was the dominant theme of twentieth-century national security. The focus was on the thermonuclear confrontation between the United States and the Soviet Union, the ultimately existential extension of twentieth-century warfare. The devastation nuclear weapons could produce rendered such wars obsolete, but the weapons remain.

The emphasis in military security has shifted in this century. Geographically, it has moved to the developing world. It is a different kind of military phenomenon. Most of its causes are either internal within emerging states or in evangelical appeals based in one or a few states. It is smaller in extent, because the participants lack the means or motives to act outside their borders. When outsiders like the United States involve themselves in these wars, they face new and often confusing military situations for which historical experience is an imperfect guide.

The six chapters in this part reflect three points of emphasis about the changed environment. The first two chapters examine the dominant forms of twenty-first-century violence. Chapter 2 focuses on asymmetrical war, an ancient way of fighting that has been updated and applied in much of the developing world. Chapter 3 looks at terrorism, also a historic approach to fighting that is, in many senses, a form of asymmetrical warfare but that poses a direct threat to the United States and other developed countries (as well as developing states).

The second emphasis is on the revival of interest in and the salience of the nuclear problem. After the Cold War ended, attention turned away from "nukes," but it has been revived in recent years with the efforts of some developing states to join the nuclear "club." This changed focus requires a renewed understanding and adaptation of old concepts to new times. Chapter 4 looks at the revival of concern about the basic concepts and dynamics of nuclear deterrence and particularly on how to ensure the inhibitions on thinking about nuclear weapons use can be reinforced. Chapter 5 examines attempts to avoid the spread of nuclear weapons to non-possessing states, including the anomalies and difficulties of gaining acquiescence to attempts to prevent or limit proliferation.

The last two chapters in the part exemplify the dynamics addressed in the first four chapters. Both are developing world situations with a nuclear component and conflict between the United States and others. Chapter 6 analyzes the rocky nuclear relationship with North Korea, and chapter 7 focuses on the relationship between the United States and Iran. Both have been prominent contemporary problems for the United States.

2

Asymmetrical Warfare
The New American Way of War?

The evolution of how war is physically fought is one of the most profound but least well examined aspects of contemporary national security calculation. Until the end of the Cold War, global violent conflict had basically operated from the premises and principles, organization, and manpower and physical configurations of European-style warfare as it had evolved since the end of the Thirty Years War (1616–1648) or even before. War was characterized by the clash of large, nationally defined armed forces attempting to defeat one another either by effectively destroying the other's forces in battle or convincing the opponent of the futility of continuing the effort—overcoming "hostile will and ability," in classic formulations. These conflicts were often fought between coalitions of states and generally ended with a negotiated peace that concluded the state of war. The armed clashes between these forces were generally massive, their conduct extremely bloody, and their goriness expanded with the application of new discoveries to weapons use (see the Brodies, *From Crossbow to H-Bomb*). The penultimate example was World War II, when an estimated forty million combatants and an equal number of noncombatants were believed to have perished.

There has not been such a "conventional" war on a mass scale since World War II ended. The Cold War was a "cold" (i.e., non-shooting) continuation of that kind of competition, as both major sides organized and prepared for a conflict that would probably have vastly exceeded the second world conflict of the twentieth century in carnage. Somewhat ironically, a major reason the Cold War did not turn "hot" was the major post–World War II weapons innovation in each country's arsenals: nuclear weapons and delivery systems. These weapons were so destructive that they produced what I have called a "necessary peace" wherein war was avoided because of mutual fear of the outcome, rather than because of any affinity between the potential combatants (see chapter 4 for a discussion). Combined with reduced rivalry and hatred among possible major combatants since the Cold War ended, the result has been to render conventional, or symmetrical, war obsolete.

European-style warfare dominated the pattern of violence for three centuries or more, but it was not the only model of warfare available. The other form, which had developed largely in the Far East, was what is now called asymmetrical warfare, a term coined in a *World Politics* article by Andrew Mack in 1975 to explain, among other things, the reason the United States did not prevail in Vietnam. If Western-style warfare was premised on the massive smashing together of opposing armed forces, the asymmetrical tradition was less direct and was designed to give a chance of success to weaker forces by altering patterns in ways that gave lesser (by conventional standards) forces a chance to prevail. This tradition is often dated to the legendary (and he may literally have been a legend rather than a single person) Chinese strategist Sun Tzu, and it became popularized in the twentieth century in the thoughts of Chinese communist leader Mao Zedong and his Vietnamese counterpart Vo Nguyen Giap. The United States first encountered an opponent practicing a variant of the asymmetrical approach in Vietnam, and it was not decisively successful in the endeavor. It has not directly confronted anything but asymmetrical opponents since.

The rise to prominence of asymmetrical warfare in the pantheon of global violence is so strategically important as to make it the lead-in chapter in this book. First, it affects how war is fought, including the means used. European-style, symmetrical warfare is now largely obsolete, and so are most of the means used to fight in that manner. The old forces and force configurations associated with European-style war may be less relevant than they were before, but this realization has hardly been acknowledged by the military community, a problem discussed in chapter 13. Second, asymmetrical warfare is a strategic approach used by weaker forces confronting firepower-superior opponents, a situation most prevalent in the developing world. Indeed, most national interest–involved situations for which American force might be employed are in what I have called developing world internal conflicts (DWICs), and in these places, it is not always clear American interests are sufficient to warrant direct American involvement (see *Cases in International Relations,* Seventh Edition). Third, it is also unclear that the United States has an effective plan or doctrine to fight and prevail in these kinds of wars (see *The Case Against Military Intervention*).

Asymmetrical warfare thus challenges conventional strategic calculation in fundamental ways. Conventional warfare strategies including the development and patterns of employing armed forces are challenged. The settings in which forces might be introduced require a rethinking of the level of interests that must be activated to use force. The possibility that any application of American force will be quixotic and ultimately unsuccessful affects whether a positive force decision is rational. All these effects make understanding the "beast" symmetrical warfare represents crucial to contemporary American national security.

Perspectives on the Problem

The United States has had an episodic experience with what is now called asymmetrical warfare. During the American Revolution, some groups active in the Continental cause were practitioners of asymmetrical techniques, notably people like Ethan Allen and the Green Mountain Boys in Vermont and Francis (the "Swamp Fox") Marion in South Carolina, and their efforts frustrated the British to the point that one British general once referred to their methods as the "dirty little war of terror and murder." The United States has more often confronted asymmetrical opponents, from the Plains and Southwest Indians at the turn of the twentieth century, to the insurgency in the Philippines, to isolated resistance in World War II in the Pacific. Vietnam was the first major encounter opposing asymmetrical opponents, and the American military experience has been almost exclusively against asymmetrical foes since.

Understanding asymmetrical warfare as a strategic problem is at least a two-step process. The first step is defining what it is and how it works. The second step is an examination of why it has been such a successful means for encountering and prevailing in the contemporary environment. Both steps are necessary before one can weigh options for dealing with the national security consequences of opposing an asymmetrical warrior.

Definition and Dynamics

The key to understanding the phenomenon captured in the concept of asymmetrical warfare is the contrast between symmetry and its opposite, asymmetry. In more general terms, symmetry refers to the relationship between parts of a whole body: something is said to be symmetrical if it can be divided into two parts and those two mirror one another. Asymmetry refers to the conditions where the two sides are different from one another and do not reflect one another.

This distinction can be applied to warfare. Conventional, European-style warfare is said to be symmetrical because the opposing sides are similar, virtual reflections of one another. In practice, this means the two sides are similarly organized and equipped, with similar forms of command hierarchies, similar strategic and tactical ideas, and fighting for similar purposes and outcomes. They follow the same rules of fighting and engagement (similar rules of war), and their similarity even extends to things like wearing similar uniforms, having roughly the same internal command structures and ranks, and the like. The typical goals of symmetrical forces are to engage one another in combat or maneuver and, as the outcome of combat or its threat, either to defeat the opponent by destroying its forces or military cohesion or by convincing the opponent that continued resistance is futile. Wars fought using this model typically have defined beginning and end points—a declaration of hostilities or military invasion, and a negotiated or imposed settlement to end the fighting and to restore peace.

Asymmetrical warfare lacks these characteristics. Using the definition adopted for *The Case Against Military Intervention*, asymmetrical warfare refers to "the situation where one party fights in one manner, while the other party does not fight in that same manner, adopting different methods and usually ignoring the rules of engagement (ROEs) that opponent prefers." In most cases in the contemporary world, that means that one side fights in a conventional, European style and the other side fights differently, throwing aside conventional distinctions, rules, and the like, and proceeding in a different manner. The asymmetrical warrior is the fighter who defies whatever convention is generally accepted in warfare. Conventional, or symmetrical, warfare is associated with European-style fighting not because it is inherently virtuous or somehow "better" than asymmetrical alternatives, but because it has been the major form that evolved during the period of European dominance of international violent relations.

The first thing to note about asymmetrical warfare is that it is not a military strategy but rather a methodology. It begins from the first premise that a group has decided that the only way to accomplish its goals (which may mean avoiding being conquered or annihilated by an enemy or overthrowing a government with which it disagrees) is through the application of military violence. If it analyzes its circumstances and determines that it is too militarily disadvantaged to pursue its goals by fighting its opponent on that adversary's terms (using the other side's "conventional" rules of engagement (ROEs)), then it may decide to abandon those rules and fight another way. It may decide to go asymmetrical, in other words. The methodological underpinning of this determination is that resistance must be undertaken in a different manner than by conventional ways of fighting to have a chance of succeeding.

This determination tells the asymmetrical warrior *that* he must adopt a different approach to violent conflict, but not *what* that approach should be at the strategic or tactical levels. Asymmetry is the approach of the weak facing a stronger opponent. In the contemporary world, this means that those who choose asymmetry have determined that they do not have any realistic chance of prevailing in a contest with the conventional, firepower-heavy, probably technologically superior opponents they face. If they stand and fight that opponent on its terms they will, very simply, lose. In most contemporary situations, this calculation is framed in terms of internal struggle among factions within a country, and the price of unsuccessful prosecution of the cause means physical death. This situation is especially stark when the other side is either armed by or has the physical assistance of a major outside power's armed forces.

These distinctions help explain why some groups choose asymmetrical approaches to the conflicts they initiate or in which they find themselves thrust. It is an ancient instinct that has been contemplated since the first group found themselves threatened physically by a visibly larger and stronger enemy. The first question that someone in this circumstance faces is how to turn the tables and somehow to neutralize the military advantages that the other side possesses: how to avoid defeat. The second question is how the asymmetrical warrior can turn the situation to its advantage, either defeating or adequately discouraging the opponent so that it quits the field and allows the weaker side to achieve its own goals.

Why Asymmetric Approaches Work

Almost all the time, forces adopting the asymmetrical methodology start from a disadvantage that often borders on desperation, even virtual hopelessness in strictly military terms. Adopting an asymmetrical strategy is rarely a first choice, because the dictates for the success are difficult to achieve given the likely balance of forces with which the budding asymmetric warrior is faced. Although there are as many asymmetrical strategies and tactical approaches as there are movements that adopt them, they all share two related problems at the outset: they are far weaker in lethal capability—size of forces and firepower, as the most obvious indicators—than their opponents; and they have little if any reasonable prospect of vanquishing the opponent by force of arms.

These realities create for the asymmetrical warrior a different set of criteria for achieving whatever political goal they seek. For symmetrical warriors, the goal is to defeat the enemy as preface for imposing their will upon the vanquished foe. The conventional military force, in other words, *wins by winning*, which means it is not successful until it has defeated the opponent on whatever field of combat their war defines. The asymmetrical warrior, on the other hand, has little illusion about this outcome: the opponent is too strong and the asymmetrical warrior too weak ever to seek or achieve conventional military victory. The goal of the asymmetrical warrior is thus to survive and gradually move the military situation to the point that the opponent comes to believe it also cannot prevail and that continuing the effort makes no sense. For the asymmetrical force, the key dictate is patience and survival, which allows it gradually but inexorably to outlast the enemy: the asymmetrical force seeks to *win by not losing*, a decidedly different goal than its antagonist. The key strategic goal is perseverance and patience greater than that of the opponent.

Asymmetrical strategies deriving from this fundamental characteristic do not always succeed, but they do often enough to encourage weaker combatants to consider the approach. More to the point, asymmetrical approaches have been particularly effective when confronting an opponent such as the United States, which has arguably not developed an effective counter-strategy for defeating forces adopting it. Asymmetry creates military conditions that can frustrate the strongest of opponents, including the United States. For this reason, it is important to understand why asymmetric approaches in fact do prevail. Since the asymmetrical warrior cannot overcome the opponent by the conventional application of force to defeat that foe, what can he do?

The most basic purpose of an asymmetric warrior is to turn the psychological balance of the contest to his or her favor. A battle of attrition aimed at the physical defeat of a superior force will generally not work due to the imbalance of forces available. As a result, fighting toe-to-toe is a recipe for disaster. The conventional foe cannot be driven from the field; rather, that opponent must be convinced to leave on its own. The opponent must be convinced that its continued attempt to subdue the asymmetrical warrior is futile and is more expensive than it is worth: the effort is simply not worth it.

There are two key dynamics that apply to achieving this outcome. The first is *cost-tolerance*, a term Dennis Drew and I elaborated in *From Lexington to Baghdad and Beyond*. The idea of cost-tolerance is straightforward. The pursuit of any military end creates costs for both sides in terms of physical exertion, cost, and most importantly, human suffering. These costs may be tolerable and bearable if one is moving toward a desired conclusion. In this case, the costs are tolerable and the sacrifices and suffering they entail is bearable, and the level of sacrifice does not exceed the sacrifice one is willing to bear.

The unconventional warrior knows its prospects for conventional success are sufficiently dismal that it no longer makes sense in cost-benefit terms to pursue

defending homeland row will to
right is greater

that goal. The key element instead is to maximize the pain that is inflicted on the conventional warrior to the point that its losses and suffering are so great and the benefits of continuing so meager that continuing to pursue them is no longer worth the effort. This means conducting both physical and psychological actions against both the opponent's forces and, where the opponent is a Western democracy, convincing the public to withdraw support from the effort. The purpose is not to "defeat" militarily an opponent that is too powerful to beat. Rather, it is to convince that opponent to quit. The desired outcome is not victory in the conventional sense. It is convincing the opponent that continued prosecution of hostilities no longer makes sense and should be abandoned. The asymmetrical warrior succeeds not by defeating the enemy (win by winning); he wins when the opponent's cost-tolerance is exceeded (the calculation that the costs are greater than the possible gains) and the conventional warrior leaves. The asymmetrical warrior has thus won by not losing.

The second concept is *importance of the outcomes to the participants.* A major characteristic of situations in which asymmetrical warfare occurs is the physical imbalance of forces between the contestants, and this disparity is particularly pronounced when the symmetrical opponent is aided by an outside party like the United States and its overwhelming conventional force superiority. This, of course, is the configuration of asymmetrical warfare that most affects U.S. national security calculation and thus is the focus here.

The secret to a successful asymmetrical strategy is protraction of the conflict. A powerful conventional foe cannot be defeated; instead, that foe must be *out-lasted.* The key element is patience. This principle leads to the influence of dedication to the competition: how important is the outcome to each side? Protraction means forcing the superior force to endure more suffering and frustration than makes sense for it to absorb. This is partially accomplished by creating suffering and pain for the superior force: terrorist-like actions that kill enemy combatants not with the goal of defeat so much as raising questions about whether the effort is worth it. It is also accomplished by demonstrating to the opponent and its support base that it is not winning and *cannot* prevail.

Implementing an asymmetrical strategy thus requires time and long-term commitment. Particularly when the situation is internal within developing states (the setting in which most asymmetrical campaigns occur), the outcome of the conflict is more important to the asymmetrical warriors than those it opposes, and this is particularly true of outside intervening powers like the United States. Put simply, who prevails is likely to be considerably more important to the indigenous base of the asymmetrical warriors than is the commitment of those they oppose. For the indigenous forces, the outcome is of the highest priority—often literally a matter of life and death—and their cost-tolerance is going to be very high and very difficult to overcome. For the superior symmetrical opponent, interests are more limited and less important. Their cost-tolerance, in other words, is more shallow and easier to overcome, because quitting does not have the same potential consequences that it has for the asymmetrical warriors. This imbalance of importance of the outcome is the nub of the problem the United States confronts in asymmetrical warfare situations.

Policy Options

Although the importance of asymmetrical warfare is not often portrayed in this manner, it is a central element in applying solutions to politico-military situations around the globe in which the United States might be tempted to involve itself with military force and in its ability to pursue national interest in the developing world. This is true because the overwhelming bulk of unstable situations in which the U.S. military force is used are in the developing world (the DWICs), where American interests are not demonstrably vital, where it has not been terribly successful, and where its cost-tolerance is suspect.

Conceptual Mismatches

There are two separate conceptual mismatches that individually and in tandem help define the problem confronting opponents fighting asymmetrically pose for the United States. The first is the *interest-threat mismatch*. The heart of this paradox is the disconnection between the hierarchy of interests the country has in different places in the world and threats to those interests. During most of the twentieth century, the two conditions were aligned: the places where the United States had the most vital interests (notably in Europe) were also the places where the greatest threats existed. The Soviet menace of Western Europe during the Cold War is the exemplar. The Soviets posed a direct existential threat both to the American homeland and to its European allies, and the vitality of those interests dictated where American national security efforts had to be directed.

The situation is not so clear or deductive anymore. The world remains an unstable place where threats to American interests abound, but the places which are threatened are not clearly where important, and especially vital, American interests are engaged. This presents a conundrum if one believes, as most policymakers do, that American military force should be reserved for application in places of the greatest importance to the United States. In the contemporary environment, those interests are hardly threatened (e.g., Western Europe), whereas the threats that do exist are in places where the United States does not possess adequately important interests to justify the use of force. International terrorism seems to be an exception: terrorists clearly imperil basic, vital interests of both the country and its friends, but the exception proves the rule because of the second mismatch.

Compounding the misalignment between threats and interests is a second problem, the *threat-force mismatch*. Conceptually, the problems are similar. In this second case, the mismatch is between the threats that do exist and the available kinds of forces to apply to ameliorating or neutralizing them. Despite the efforts by Gen. David Petraeus and others to develop a workable counterinsurgency doctrine (asymmetrical warfare is often associated with developing world insurgent warfare), the United States has yet to fashion a successful method of defeating movements employing variants of asymmetrical warfare under the rubric of counterinsurgency (or COIN, in military-speak). In confrontations from Vietnam to Iraq and Afghanistan, the United States has faced the kinds of dynamics already described, and although it has not been vanquished in any military sense, neither has it prevailed over asymmetrical opponents. The results have been protracted involvement in seemingly endless and indeterminate interventions (see the examination of Afghanistan in chapter 9) or withdrawal when cost-tolerance was exceeded (Vietnam). Both mismatches are also discussed in chapter 14.

This situation is exacerbated because of the flexibility of asymmetrical approaches to war. As noted, there is no set asymmetrical "playbook" that can be studied and against which it is possible to prepare for the future. As a methodology, asymmetrical warfare provides broad principles around which strategy and tactics can be articulated and applied, such as the mobile-guerrilla strategy devised by Mao Zedong in China or the people's war approach of General Giap of North Vietnam. The heart of asymmetry, however, is adaptation of methods to individual circumstances, not the imposition of a set of doctrinal dictates on a situation.

The result is that no two asymmetrical wars are identical. Rather, asymmetrical warriors use the past experiences of others who have faced similar problems selectively: adopting those techniques that have succeeded in past situations they think are analogous to their own situations and rejecting elements of other strategies they deem inappropriate. This complicates planning to counter the problem, because the opponent does not know exactly what the problem that must be overcome is and thus has difficulty honing planning contingencies to deal with them. These difficulties compound those raised by the two mismatches.

The Asymmetrical Warfare–Terrorism Nexus

Distinguishing what is or is not an example of asymmetrical warfare is complicated by three additional problems. One is that it is a style of warfare that has had many different names across time. In addition to its contemporary designation, it has also been known as people's war, partisan war, insurgent warfare, low-intensity war (LIC), and guerrilla war, to cite four examples. Wars fought using each of these names vary in the details of their conduct, but share the common methodology of asymmetry. Second, people's views of this style vary depending on the specific situation in which they are applied. The French partisan efforts against the Nazi occupation are very popular and approvingly received; Vietnamese General Giap's people's war against the United States was not. Third, the asymmetrical philosophy can intermingle in application with other forms of violent resistance. Terrorism is the prime example.

Terrorism is conceptually a form of asymmetrical warfare. Its goal is to achieve political ends it cannot achieve against a militarily superior enemy, and its primary mission is to attack the cost-tolerance of its target population so that they conclude acceding to terrorist demands is less painful than the anxiety of potential or actual terrorist violence against them. Most terrorist movements are weaker than the kinds of active military actions associated with asymmetrical warfare, but virtually all asymmetrical warriors (as well as many more conventional warriors) employ terrorist tactics as part of their conduct of hostilities. Terrorists are asymmetrical warriors, and asymmetrical warriors employ terrorism. This connection is further explored in chapter 3.

What this depiction suggests is that it is not easy to develop clear, overarching policies and strategies toward instances of asymmetrical warfare in the world. Policy, in the sense of ways the United States should respond to different situations in which asymmetrical approaches are present, is complicated by levels of U.S. interest involvement that often do not rise to the level of vitality, the historic key for committing American forces. Strategies are similarly complicated both because every asymmetrical situation is to some extent unique (no two asymmetrical wars are the same), and because of the absence of a strategy that has been demonstrated to be effective in defeating the basic approach. These difficulties, of course, are exactly the intents of the asymmetrical warrior, and they make policy and strategy much more difficult to devise and apply.

Consequences: What to Do?

Violent conflicts in the developing world (DWICs) are the dominant form of violence in the international system, and as such, they are the major military contingency with which the American national security community must grapple. Nuclear weapons still exist and the avoidance of nuclear war remains an existential priority, and special attention has been devoted to the asymmetrical threat of terrorism, but the generic problem of asymmetrical warfare looms over strategy. As experience beginning with Vietnam has shown, the United States has no "magic bullet" that ensures it can defeat asymmetrical opponents whose actions adversely affect American interests. How should the country confront this problem?

One can argue the concern is exaggerated. Asymmetrical wars break out in far distant locations where clear American interests are not clearly engaged and where outcomes do not threaten core interests or values. The United States (like everyone else) has no strategic/tactical package that can defeat these movements, but it has been able to contain them in enough places and to prevent their success and thus their appeal to others facing similar challenges. The America First / neo-isolationist advocacy that has gained some traction in the Trump presidency downplays this form of conflict, implicitly arguing the best policy for the United States is to ignore situations where an encounter with an intractable opponent is likely to be inconclusive. If one cannot win the "game" but the outcome is not all that important, why play?

The other side of this argument is that the failure or inability to deal decisively with this problem weakens the United States with other parts of the world, notably developing world countries with some fear or grievance with the United States. Nuclear proliferation, the subject of chapter 5, provides an analogy. A major reason some countries desire nuclear weapons is because they believe their possession insulates them from hostile military actions. North Korea (see chapter 6) is a prime example. The inability of the United States to defeat asymmetrical challenges in developing-world countries may provide an analogous dynamic.

One reason, for instance, that the United States never seriously considered a personal military role in Syria (see chapter 10) has been the belief that doing so would result in a long, frustrating, and inconclusive outcome. That, of course, is exactly the kind of situation associated with asymmetrical warfare. Is the kind of inhibition associated with non-intrusion in Syria a good or bad thing?

If one assumes that it is inadvisable simply to ignore or categorically avoid with major American forces situations where an asymmetrical foe will be encountered (a debatable proposition), what strategic choices does the United States have? The preference one supports says something about the degree of activism and forceful leadership that one prefers for the United States in the international environment. In some ways, it is a question of leadership or isolation; in others, it could be considered a matter of the level of enlightenment and realism about the American role in the world.

Four alternatives, from least to most activist, can be raised. They are important to consider if one believes that the dominant form of violent challenges in the world to which the United States might have to respond come from asymmetrical opponents in the developing world. If asymmetrical challenges to an American-preferred status quo are vital to American interests and leadership, the question and its answer are important. Currently, asymmetrical warfare planning and preparation is not central in American national security planning or force structure. Moving asymmetrical war to a central role in American security would have major implications for strategy and many of the political concerns contained in the chapters of Part III.

The first policy alternative is to avoid the problem to the greatest extent possible: not making the asymmetrical warfare a central concern for strategy or force development. The rationale for this position, elaborated in *The Case Against Military Intervention*, is that it would keep the country aloof from these situations, and this would be a virtue since they are almost exclusively conflicts and involvements where American interests are not adequate to justify military intervention, where the United States cannot prevail, and where abstention is the most realistic course. By this reasoning, staying out of Syria is the useful precedent.

The second possibility is to develop a limited capacity for involvement, which is effectively current policy. Under this orientation, the United States would be willing to support the efforts of others through technological means (e.g., drone aircraft for reconnaissance), supplying arms and other assistance to those resisting the asymmetrical warriors, and even modest insertions of specialized American personnel such as Special Operations forces (SOFs) for training resisters and limited combat. This is essentially the role the United States played in the defeat of the Islamic State (IS), which was a quasi-asymmetrical opponent (see *Cases in International Relations*, Seventh Edition, for an explanation), and is playing a role in parts of Africa (see chapter 13).

A third possibility is to enhance the mission, training, and force composition of the military to take on a larger role through force enhancement and technological reorientation. This effort is also part of American strategy: Special Operations Command and its place in the military hierarchy have indeed been enhanced and the number of Special Forces has been expanded. At the same time, technological innovations like the development of drones for reconnaissance and attack missions (see chapter 17) have also been emphasized. The problem of this solution currently is reluctance within the military to embrace this role at the expense of traditional budgetary and strategic considerations.

Finally, there could be a major reorientation of American strategy and forces that moves response to asymmetrical threats to the position of the central role in defense efforts. If it is true that twentieth-century conventional warfare is indeed obsolete, then central planning and force orientation to deal with that contingency is an albatross that could be partially lifted. This would be a radical reorientation that would be resisted vigorously by the existing military, who would feel threatened by it and who would insist that any reorientation be *added* to the existing structure, a costly possibility (see chapter 14).

The problem of asymmetrical warfare is difficult and has ripple effects on a great deal of the national security enterprise. How it is approached clearly has implications in several areas that have been identified and will be elaborated upon in subsequent chapters. Realizing your view may be tentative and subject to revision, what do you think the United States should do about the problem of asymmetrical warfare?

Study/Discussion Questions

1. Contrast symmetrical and asymmetrical warfare structurally and historically. Why is symmetrical/conventional warfare sometimes referred to as "obsolete" in contemporary terms?

2. Why is understanding asymmetrical warfare important in national security strategy terms? Discuss in military and political terms of American interests and patterns of international violence.

3. How does asymmetrical warfare work? Why is it a methodology and not a strategy? Why and under what circumstances does it succeed? Include a discussion of cost-tolerance in your answer.

4. What conceptual mismatches make dealing with asymmetrical threats difficult? How are asymmetrical warfare and terrorism related? Explain.

5. What approaches can the United States take in dealing with the problem of asymmetrical warfare? Describe and evaluate each in terms of their effectiveness and desirability. Which do you favor? Why?

Bibliography

Bacevich, Andrew C. (ed.). *The Short American Century: A Postmortem*. Cambridge, MA: Harvard University Press, 2012.

Barnett, Roger W. *Asymmetrical Warfare: Today's Challenge to U.S. Military Power*. Washington, DC: Potomac Books, 2013.

Berkowitz, Bruce. *The New Face of War: How War Will Be Fought in the 21st Century*. New York: Free Press, 2003.

Brodie, Bernard, and Fawn Brodie. *From Crossbow to H-Bomb: The Evolution of Weapons and Tactics of Warfare*. Bloomington: Indiana University Press, 1973.

Brzezinski, Zbigniew. *Strategic Vision: America and the Crisis of Global Power.* New York: Basic Books, 2012.

Clark, Wesley. *Winning Modern Wars: Iraq, Terrorism, and the American Empire.* New York: PublicAffairs, 2003.

Giap, Vo Nguyen. *People's War, People's Army.* New York: Praeger, 1962.

Haass, Richard N. *Wars of Necessity, Wars of Choice: A Memoir of Two Iraq Wars.* New York: Simon and Schuster, 2009.

Kaurin, Pauline M. *The Warrior, Military Ethics, and Contemporary Warfare: Achilles Goes Asymmetrical.* New York and London: Routledge, 2016.

Mack, Andrew J. "Why Big Nations Lose Small Wars." *World Politics* 27 (2) (April 1975), 175–200.

Mao Zedong. *The Collected Works of Mao Zedong.* Vols. 1–4. Beijing, China: Foreign Languages Press, 1967.

———. *Mao Tse-Tung on Guerrilla Warfare.* Translated by Samuel B. Griffith. New York: Praeger, 1961.

O'Hanlon, Michael. *The Wounded Giant: America's Armed Forces in an Age of Austerity.* New York: Penguin Books, 2011.

Snow, Donald M. *The Case Against Military Intervention: Why We Do It and Why It Fails.* New York and London: Routledge, 2016.

———. *Cases in International Relations.* Seventh Ed. Lanham, MD: Rowman & Littlefield, 2018.

———. *Distant Thunder: Patterns of Conflict in the Developing World.* Second Ed. Armonk, NY: M. E. Sharpe, 1997.

———. *The Necessary Peace: Nuclear Weapons and Superpower Relations.* Lexington, MA: Lexington Books, 1986.

———. *Thinking About National Security: Strategy, Policy, and Issues.* New York and London: Routledge, 2016.

———. *UnCivil Wars: International Security and the New Internal Conflicts.* Boulder, CO: Lynne Rienner, 1996.

Snow, Donald M., and Dennis M. Drew. *From Lexington to Baghdad and Beyond: War and Politics in the American Experience.* Third Ed. Armonk, NY: M. E. Sharpe, 2010.

Sun Tzu. *The Art of War.* Translated by Samuel B. Griffith. Oxford, UK: Oxford University Press, 1963.

United States Army and United States Marine Corps. *Counterinsurgency Field Manual: Army Field Manual 3-24, Marine Warfighting Publication 33.5.* Chicago: University of Chicago Press, 2006.

3

The Evolving Face of Terror
The Dilemmas of Terrorism Strategy

Terrorism has become the signature national security problem of this century. It burst onto the American consciousness on September 11, 2001, with the largest terrorist attack in American history against the World Trade Center in New York and the Pentagon in Washington, DC. It was an event that shocked and frightened American citizens and quickly caused a continuing rage that President George W. Bush typified as the "war on terror" from the rubble in Lower Manhattan. The concern underlying that emotion continues and has spread to other parts of the developed world (especially Western Europe) and locales in the developing world, including the Middle East that has been the seedbed of this wave of terror. The effort to defeat, control, or eradicate the problem is now almost two decades old as a major, prominent national priority, and a solution remains elusive. Developing and implementing an effective terrorism strategy has yet to occur.

Given the national attention the fight against terrorism has received, this may seem an inexplicable failure, but it really dates back at least two millennia. Most historians of terrorism agree that the first instances of what is now called terrorism occurred in biblical times, specifically in terms of Jewish resistance to the Roman occupation that reached a climax with the mass suicide at Masada. Terror has ebbed and flowed as an international phenomenon ever since, but it has never disappeared and has never been "destroyed" altogether. Various terrorist groups have arisen, been dispatched and disappeared, but it has never been eliminated as a problem or potential problem. Terrorism, in other words, has endured, even if individuals practicing it and the causes they served have not. It is a distinction worth remembering.

Modern terrorism conducted for explicitly political purposes is normally associated with the so-called Reign of Terror during the evolution of the French Revolution, a campaign generally credited to the political activist Robespierre who, ironically, employed terrorist violence to promote political democracy and the suppression of its opponents. During the nineteenth and the first half of the twentieth century, terror was mostly associated with anarchist violence and state applications in places like Nazi Germany and the Soviet Union. It was mostly isolated to parts of the developing world during the Cold War, and only arose as a major force after the end of the communist-anticommunist competition.

Although periods of active terrorism have often had a religious overtone or core (the Inquisition, for instance), its emergence in the current century as Islamic religious terror is a relatively new phenomenon, and one that continues to bedevil those who oppose it. The Middle East incubation of modern terror is not unique by any means and is related to the major spate of instability and violence that plagues the area, but isolating the physical sources and religious inspiration that gives rise to terrorism remains a major source of concern.

Because the United States and Americans are major stated targets of terrorist actions, they have become the major post–Cold War national security focus of strategists. Between the end of World War II and the collapse of Soviet communism in 1991, preventing and if necessary fighting a war to avoid the imposition of communist rule in North America and deterring a cataclysmic nuclear war had been the clear foci of strategists and had produced the clearly articulated, highly supported strategy of containment. After communism imploded, there was little left to contain, and the strategy lacked its past relevance. During the 1990s, thinkers struggled to redefine and adapt the strategy to a new and less threatening environment without great success. When Al Qaeda–controlled aircraft slammed into Manhattan and Washington, DC, a worthy successor strategic threat presented itself to the strategic community. The problem of terrorism strategy has engaged national security planning ever since. It is difficult to argue it has yet devised a satisfactory strategic response.

Perspectives on the Problem

The first problem of devising a successor to containment that can deal with terrorism is that it poses numerous kinds of threat. The Cold War threat was *existential*, deflecting the possibility of a Soviet military action that could destroy the United States and its allies. The threat was recognized as dire, encompassing, and requiring concerted effort and national and personal sacrifice. Fortunately for strategists, it was largely conventional in military terms, an extension of the dynamics that were applied in World War II. It was also considered perpetual for a long time, with a consensus that it could only end with war.

The terrorist threat is different. It is serious, as the 9/11 attacks demonstrated, but it is hardly existential: the terrorists cannot literally destroy the United States unless they gain weapons of mass destruction in very large numbers. The Soviet military machine was a concrete menace that could be measured to calibrate appropriate responses flowing from the strategy of containment that could be applied to the national interest of ensuring American national security. By comparison, the terrorist problem is much more diffused and ethereal, a shifting challenge posed by a host of dangerous but not existential menaces. This does not make the terrorist challenge any less important, but it does mean it poses a problem for which the structure and assumptions of the Cold War paradigm do not provide a precise analogy.

It has been a principal challenge for the national security to produce a new grand strategy and set of implementing strategies to replace the Cold War construct and to provide guidance for dealing with the unique challenges of terrorism. The efforts to accomplish this goal have, to this point, been arguably unsuccessful in articulating the parameters and nature of the threat as preface to formulating a strategy. The quest is one for which the framework suggested in chapter 1 may be of some instructive value. Formulating a useful perspective on terrorism strategy begins by defining the term and exploring the parts of the terrorism problem at which efforts might most usefully be directed.

Defining Terrorism

In the wake of 9/11, terrorism not only entered the popular lexicon, it became ubiquitous to describe virtually all nefarious, violent behavior. The U.S. government emotionally declared "war" on terror (something known as the global war on terror or GWOT) and reorganized itself to meet the challenge through the creation of the Department of Homeland Security (DHS).

There has, of course, not been a successful foreign terrorist attack against American soil since 2001, and the activity that has occurred has tended to be the violence of lone wolves, usually with unclear motives and goals, even if they are sometimes "inspired" by the philosophies of members of foreign-based radical groups. Smaller acts of terror by arguably deranged individuals have become the norm against Americans, and more organized terror has moved overseas, from spectacular but limited instances in Europe to more concerted attacks in parts of Africa and the Middle East. Just as the rise and fall of larger terrorist organizations like Al Qaeda (partially thanks to the assassination of its founder and leader Osama bin Laden) and the Islamic State (which has shrunk to the point its territorial base has evaporated) has changed the shape of the threat, so too has the basis for dealing with it changed as well.

Part of the difficulty of an expansive designation of organized violence involves how to determine what is and is not terrorism, a matter of definition. Definitions of terrorism abound in the literature, a sample of which is listed in the bibliography at the end of the chapter. All share three elements: the nature of terrorist acts, the objects of those attacks, and the reasons for them. The characterization of terrorist acts tends to emphasize their illegality. The implication is that dealing with terrorism has a criminal, and thus policing, element. Depictions of objectives tend to focus on why particular sites were chosen, adding a motivational and even psychological element. Purposes tend to focus on underlying reasons beyond individual sociopathic motives to include the underlying political demands that characterize organized terrorist movements. Some sources, including the U.S. government, include an exclusion of government from the possible perpetrators, a position I reject: terror is terror, regardless of who commits it (an exclusion with which the reader may disagree).

Some definition of terrorism is necessary both so that the observer can determine whether actions and events are instances of terrorism or something else and to guide those dealing with its counteraction. I have adopted the following definition of terrorism: *"the commission of atrocious acts against a target population normally to gain compliance with some demands the terrorists insist upon."* (For a discussion, see Snow, *Cases in International Relations,* Seventh Edition or earlier editions.)

Applying this definition excludes some acts often described as terrorism from the phenomenon. Many of the individual acts of so-called "lone wolves" who commit terroristic attacks cannot be attributed to any motive beyond themselves and are more properly thought of as acts of revenge (the 2017 attack on a social service department in San Bernardino, California, for instance) or even pure criminality or psychological imbalance (e.g., the mass murders in Las Vegas in late 2017). These acts, which garner many media and political headlines, are important and merit serious attention, but combining them with the acts and motives of politically oriented groups like Al Qaeda or the Islamic State enters distortion into devising methods and capabilities surrounding a national terrorism strategy. Both are important, but they are apples and oranges and should be considered as such. The actions of deranged loners "inspired" by internet entreaties by evangels representing terrorist organizations like the late Anwar al-Awlaki are a confounding element in a clean distinction.

Terrorism Objectives

Before one can begin to devise a way to deal with the terrorism problem, one must first specify what aspect of terrorism one is talking about, which of those aspects is most crucial to the continuation of terror, and which aspect can most successfully be "attacked." Even if one can eliminate the random criminal/ psychological actions of lone wolves, there are three candidates. Each poses a different problem and a different strategic approach to counter. Any attempt to formulate a coherent terrorism strategy must have elements that deal with each object that includes different approaches and personnel.

The first object of terrorism strategy is *terrorism* itself, the philosophy and belief that the kinds of actions associated with terrorism offer a way to accomplish political ends that some aggrieved group holds and wants its opponents to accept. Obviously, campaigns of terror are extreme, dangerous to perpetrator and target alike, and will infuriate that target. As a result, the recourse to terrorism tends to be undertaken only by the most desperate groups who, generally, espouse ends the majority opposes and cannot be brought to support. The only way the terrorist can succeed is to convince the target that bowing to the terrorist demands is less painful than continued resistance and thus continued victimhood, a process Drew and I have described as overcoming "cost tolerance."

Forcing acceptance of their views on a resistant opponent is the heart of the philosophy of terrorism. It is an approach, and not a set of procedures or a blueprint for action, and it is normally only attractive to the severely disadvantaged minority in places it is tried. Because it represents an approach that tends to appeal only to minorities, it tends to fail in the broad sense of achieving the goals for which it is adopted. It does, however, provide a way to gain publicity that may frighten the target population, and it often has enough tactical success (i.e., successful terrorist attacks) to offer some hope to its proponents.

Despite limited success, terrorism has been enduring. Groups have chosen it as their method of gaining goals despite its strategic failures (i.e., achieving its grand goals), and the current spate of religious terrorism suggests that its attraction to the desperate is likely to continue. If one decides to adopt the eradication of terrorism as the strategic goal of antiterrorist activities, one of the major conceptual conundrums to be overcome is devising an approach that can succeed when the efforts of others have failed. A world in which terrorism was universally rejected to accomplish goals would be a far happier place, but no one has yet figured out how to get there.

The second, and most visible object of strategy is *terrorists* themselves. It is, after all, individual terrorists, acting either alone, within organizations, or from the inspiration of terrorist leaders or groups that commit the atrocities that kill or maim people and that are a virtually ubiquitous part of contemporary attention. In Europe and elsewhere outside North America, it is terrorists acting under the direct auspices of groups like Al Qaeda and its affiliates like AQAP (Al Qaeda on the Arabian Peninsula), IS, or Boko Haram who carry out terrorist acts and whose suppression is the direct objective of terrorist suppression efforts. In the United States, terrorists since 9/11 have been lone wolves who carry out actions for mysterious reasons and who usually die in the process.

Terrorism efforts have tended to be concentrated on terrorists. They are, of course, the most concrete and visible manifestation of terrorist activities, and capturing or killing them exacts revenge that can partially mitigate the impact of the destruction and suffering that terrorists inflict on society. Implicitly, most of the terrorism suppression actions have understandably been concentrated on eliminating people who are terrorists. It is an approach that has had success in the past. There is a saying that "terrorist organizations come and go, but terrorism persists." This truism reflects that some of the time, terrorist suppression efforts succeed, and the terrorists either are eliminated or fade away. Unfortunately, eliminating existing terrorists has not solved the problem of terrorism per se.

In the current environment, there are two major impediments to a strategy based in eliminating terrorists. The first problem is access to the enemy. Unlike traditional military opponents, terrorists (IS was a partial exception that proves the rule) do not organize in standard military formations and present themselves for organized battle in places and by means that traditional opponents employ. Instead, they disperse and hide in remote and inaccessible sanctuaries in which they are hard to locate and target except by unconventional methods like the controversial use of drones (see chapter 17). These terrorists also employ unconventional, asymmetrical means of fighting like that demonstrated in the attack on U.S. Special Forces in Niger in October 2017 (see chapter 13). Lone wolves are typically self-imbedded in target societies and only become visible and targetable if someone turns them in (which rarely happens in advance) or after they have committed a terrorist act. The other problem is that there are conditions in almost all developing countries and the ghettoes of Western cities where conditions for young people—especially males—are sufficiently hopeless and intolerable that they provide a fruitful and seemingly inexhaustible supply of new terrorist recruits. These are the terrorist "swamps" that repeated advocacies argue need "draining," generally with no accompanying strategy for achieving that result.

The third, and in some ways most difficult, visible object is *terrorist ideas*— the expressions of radical, especially *Salafist* minority interpretations of Islam that are contained in the Koran but are not part of the belief systems of most Muslims, and have been the motivating ideological sources for movements like IS. The problem of trying to undercut these kinds of appeals is that members of the non-radical Muslim community who oppose radical ideas themselves become targets of the extremists, and this danger has affected the ability to enlist spirited opposition from the more orthodox Muslim community. Extremist appeals resonate particularly with young and impressionable young men and women, who form the recruitment base for terrorist activism.

A Complex Cauldron of Factors

This list of objects of terrorism strategy is unconventional in standard discussions of terrorism and what to do about it in at least two ways. The first is that it does not place premier emphasis on terrorism as a military contest—a "war." The basis of the war analogy that emerged in the smoldering ruins of 2001 was understandable in the wake of the attacks and the post–Cold War strategic environment of which militarization in strategic response had been the not inappropriate norm. The effect, however, has been to channel thought and advocacy inside the intellectual framework to the idea of a military problem with a primarily military solution. The second source of unconventionality is the iteration of other parts of the problem that are fundamentally non-military in nature.

Finding ways to undermine the attraction of terrorism and to counteract the recourse to terrorist ideologies has a military component, but it requires intellectual changes in the potential or actual terrorist opponent. The questions that must be confronted deal with different dynamics, such as how potential terrorists can be convinced that the methodology is not appropriate for them or that it cannot help them accomplish their goals. Those who are vulnerable to terrorist appeals must be convinced that their ideas are wrong or unattainable through terrorist violence and that there are more appropriate ways to accomplish what they seek to accomplish. These are primarily mental, intellectual constructs, and they must be folded into the witches' brew in the cauldron of terrorism suppression.

Policy Options

When one looks at the extraordinarily diverse and difficult list of concerns with which terrorism strategy must contend, two basic questions arise. The first question is what should be done, and it is largely a matter of the end state that is desired. Should the objective be the eradication of terrorism or its control? At the visceral level, a world in which terrorism was not practiced by anybody against anyone would certainly seem desirable, but is it possible to achieve that end? Desirability collides with feasibility and, as already suggested, the historical record does not offer clear evidence that a strategy of eradication works. In more literary terms, is a strategy of eradication quixotic? Moreover, is it a more realistic goal depending on the terrorism object at which it is aimed?

The second question, which derives from the first, is who should conduct and lead the effort? Is the military and its approach to strategic problems the best agency to lead policy, or does the complexity of the terrorism problem suggest that other institutional and perspectival agencies would be more appropriate? Aspects of the terrorism problem—dealing with active terrorist groups, for instance—may suggest a military emphasis, but they may also lead to the conclusion that a law enforcement or intelligence perspective is most sensible. Dealing with the counteraction of terrorist ideas or discrediting adherence to terrorism may require a different perspective altogether.

During the 2004 presidential election campaign, the parameters of the strategic debate were laid out for public attention in the second televised debate between incumbent president George W. Bush and his Democratic challenger John Kerry. The candidates were asked what they believed the purpose of the "war on terror" should be. The challenger said he believed the objective should be to treat terrorism essentially the way one deals with persistent societal violations like gambling and prostitution and to try to contain or limit it. His reasoning was that, as a practical matter, it is impossible to eliminate terrorism, a position reinforced by historical experience. Thus, the most realistic policy the country could follow was to limit the damage it could do. The president forthrightly declared the purpose should be to destroy terrorism altogether—to eliminate it. The president's response was far more popular with the audience, capturing the public fervor unleashed by the 9/11 attacks three years earlier. Senator Kerry's answer was arguably more realistic.

Eradication or Containment?

What strategy best protects the United States and American citizens from the ravages of terrorist violence? A strategy that is aimed at and that could successfully eliminate terror would be the optimal solution, but is it possible to achieve? Moreover, what would have to occur for this goal to be reached? Would all three of the objects of terrorist suppression have to be achieved? How? The elimination of terrorism as a blueprint for action requires demonstrating that it is so irrational to pursue it that anyone looking at terror would conclude it makes no sense to try it. That is hardly the case in the contemporary world. A strategy aimed at eliminating terrorists requires not only killing or capturing all practitioners and convincing the captives of the error of their ways. It probably also requires draining the "swamps" of misery that promote terrorist recruitment. Both goals are difficult, expensive, and uncertain of success. Discrediting the ideas that motivate terrorists in individual situations is theoretically possible, but unless some method is devised that eliminates all the reasons for which terrorism occurs, the ultimate goal of ending terrorism is a very tall order.

This leads to the second possibility, which is that the goal of eradication cannot be achieved. If it is the case that one cannot rid the world of this evil, what then? It is demonstrably true that terrorism has not been so systematically discredited that no one chooses it: there is still a willing pool of people who become terrorists, and there seems to be no shortage of reasons for people to conclude that acting as terrorists is societally acceptable. It is an unsatisfying question to raise, but if strategy is going to be relevant to the problem, it is one that must form a parameter for strategy.

This leads to the question of who should take the lead in formulating and enforcing terrorist strategy. The origin of the strategy concept is military, and the military is clearly relevant to a suppression/elimination strategy, certainly at the level of containing terrorists. But there is clearly more to dealing with terrorism than that. The model partially applied to the development of the DHS forms a good example of the jurisdictions and responsibilities that go into the major element of a likely strategy aimed at containing terrorists.

The basic model consists of three major activities involving three major lead agencies in three different environments. The first venue is the international environment, any place outside the territorial United States where terrorist activity aimed at Americans may be devised. There are two responsibilities involved: intelligence gathering aimed at identifying terrorist opponents and learning their plans, and taking proactive or retributory actions against those individuals and groups. The lead agencies are the intelligence community (notably the CIA) and the U.S. military, both of which perform the assigned tasks. The second venue is the U.S. border, where officials attempt to prevent potential terrorists (many identified by the CIA or others) from penetrating American soil. This is largely the responsibility of border authorities. The third venue is American territory, where U.S. law enforcement authorities surveil potential terrorists and arrest those plotting or committing acts of terror. The FBI is the lead agency in this task.

This "simple" listing suggests three different lead agencies performing separate kinds of tasks as a minimal part of strategy: intelligence and suppression, border filtering, and policing. Given the jealousies of individual parts of government, finding a strategy that is attractive and responsive to each is not easy. It is a "simple" list in the sense that it is also incomplete. At a minimum, it does not account for cyber activity (see chapter 16) that allows terrorists in remote locations to influence events globally. All this complicates the question of what can be done about the terrorism problem.

Consequences: What to Do?

Dealing with terrorism is a complex, difficult, and frustrating problem. The complexity is both intellectual and operational: it is not clear what approach or organizing concept can be most effective as the basic tenet of terrorism strategy, nor is it obvious who should carry out any strategy and how they should go about it. Were the problem not this way, there would probably be a coherent terrorism strategy in place. It is not clear that such a strategy exists currently.

Goals of Strategy

The quest for a strategy begins with the question of what its goal should be, and this raises a policy/strategy conundrum. A strategy of eradicating terrorism is morally and politically appealing, and policies that would implement such a goal have overwhelming popular support. The question is whether such a strategy can reach its goals, and that leads to an assessment of what objects such a strategy should aim to overcome. Should it try to eliminate the current terrorist threat, which means defeating the current array of terrorist organizations to the point they wither away? Does it include satisfying the demands of terrorists or at least undercutting their appeal? If so, will such an approach have any effect on future recourses to terrorism? Does that matter?

The conundrum, of course, is that the most exacting requisites are relaxed if the goal of strategy is not to eliminate terrorism altogether, but rather to contain it at some "acceptable" level, conceding that it is utopian to believe it can be eliminated as a future prospect altogether. The advantage of such a premise is that it is far more likely to succeed than a strategy of eliminating terrorism. The difficulty is that such a goal is less politically and morally lofty and unlikely to accomplish what all feel is desirable, which is the removal of the terrorist menace altogether. How acceptable or unacceptable a strategy of terrorism management can be depends on how much it proposes to reduce the ongoing mayhem to Americans and others. It is an approach akin to creating expectations about crime: nobody thinks crime can be eliminated altogether, but a strategy and policy that makes people feel safe from the effects of crime is probably acceptable to them.

A more limited goal of terrorism containment has the added advantage of concentrating on the most tangible and targetable symbols of terrorism. The heart of a strategy that seeks to contain terrorism can incorporate the elimination of individual terrorist groups and the threats they pose. The advantage of doing so is that one can measure progress in terms of capturing territory where groups are located (e.g., evicting IS from the "caliphate" in Iraq and Syria) and body counts of terrorists and their leaders who are eliminated. A campaign that seeks attrition as a major goal and form of measuring success further draws the subject back more closely to traditional national security parameters and conceptual frameworks. The closer it comes to wiping out a specific terrorist threat, the more satisfying and "victorious" it seems. It also implicitly admits that the outcomes of modern warfare are rarely decisive in the traditional sense of an opponent admitting defeat and quitting the field (a problem addressed in chapter 2).

A containment strategy cannot, however, entirely avoid collateral concerns not always part of national security strategy formulation and execution. For any strategy to be even arguably successful, it must also deal with the problem of the appeal of specific terrorist organizations to vulnerable potential recruits. It is often argued by national security experts that the United States (or anyone else) cannot "kill themselves out" of the terrorist threat. What this means is that the reduction of the problem entails both reducing the current array of terrorists but also eliminating the conditions that facilitate the decision by others to become terrorists. This is the problem of "draining the swamp," and it must include a comprehensive approach to the places and conditions from which terrorist recruits arise.

There are, of course, two separate terrorist objects with which strategy must deal. The first is foreign terrorists operating out of the Middle East against American and other targets. They pose a threat to the United States but more often to allies and friends in Europe and elsewhere (most recently in Africa). The current strategic response, which has been at least partially successful, has admixed the employment of American Special Forces in parts of Africa (see chapter 13) and drone attacks against terrorist concentrations (see chapter 17).

The other, and in some ways more bedeviling, problem is that presented by lone wolves operating in the United States. Some of the mayhem that is ascribed to these attacks is probably incorrect; the phenomenon combines actions by electronically recruited converts and criminals and mental health cases. The problems associated with controlling these kinds of threats, however, is entirely different than that associated with "regular" terrorists operating from overseas. It also points to the fact that terrorism strategy must be based on different opponents acting in very different settings that must be confronted in very different ways by different kinds of personnel.

Whatever strategic course one selects is thus necessarily multifaceted and requires the input and expertise of people and institutions outside the conventional strategy process. A strategy that emphasizes the current terrorist problem most obviously concentrates on terrorists as the major object. It is necessarily a two-pronged strategy with different actors and instruments carrying out policy. The overseas operation against the organized threat is clearly military in focus, with the immediate goals of killing as many terrorists (especially leaders) as possible, denying them physical sanctuary in the countries where they seek and claim refuge, and aiming to disrupt operations, including the recruitment of additional jihadis (warriors).

This emphasis is intuitively appealing, but it also contains complicating pitfalls. Its attractions are largely political: it appears, for instance, proactive and robust and against an intransigent, clearly evil opponent rather than appearing weak, reactive, and even pusillanimous (as some critics allege). It is a strategic goal more closely aligned to traditional national security activities, since it emphasizes military action and thus reinforces the "war" image.

It also has noticeable drawbacks. The first and most obvious is whether it will work. Terrorists practice a form of asymmetrical warfare (chapter 2) that emphasizes not losing over traditional victory: their goal is institutional survival, and they are skilled at it. Second, many of the terrorist organizations are housed in remote, forbidding landscapes, where there may not be a functioning government to aid efforts (e.g., Yemen) or where governments are reluctant to cooperate with antiterrorists who violate their sovereign territory to attack the terrorists (e.g., Pakistan and parts of Afghanistan). The recourse to less invasive attacks by weapons like drones does not ameliorate this problem.

Third, there is the prospect that actions may be counterproductive. As noted in chapter 17, drone attacks from the sky against terrorist-housing villages may enrage the residents and make them ready recruits for the terrorists. As the old Pashtun saying goes, "Kill one enemy, make ten more." At the same time, a strategy of attrition is only effective if it interrupts the recruitment process for replacement terrorists, which is a question of swamp draining that military approaches do not even address.

This example is presented because it suggests how difficult devising a terrorist strategy is in practice. What has been presented is not comprehensive, because it does not even speak to the question of domestic lone wolf terrorists: how they are recruited through cyberspace, how they can be identified within society and suppressed before they act, and what government efforts can accomplish this task. Moreover, a comprehensive strategy must also address the other objects of strategy. It must discredit the reasons people become terrorists (terrorism ideas), because they form at least part of the basis for recruitment. Ultimately, some strategy must be devised that demonstrates conclusively and unambiguously that terrorism never makes sense to realize one's goals. That is the end goal of terrorism strategy.

This leaves the question of what terrorism strategy should be. The preceding discussion has sought to demonstrate it is not an easy question to answer. Political calls that "we need a strategy" or that we should "make war" on terrorism are not very helpful guides, but what should be the basis for forming policy? What do you think?

Study/Discussion Questions

1. Compare the problem of national security strategy during the Cold War and since 9/11. How are they similar and different? Can one be used as a model for the other?

2. Define terrorism. What are its major components? Based on the definition, what are the major aspects of the terrorism problem? Elaborate.

3. What concerns does terrorism strategy have to deal with? What should be the goal of terrorism strategy?

4. What are the consequences of the choices of analogy about terrorism for terrorism strategy in terms of eradication or control of the problem? Elaborate.

5. What do you think the objectives and consequent strategic approaches of terrorism suppression should be? Why?

Bibliography

Combs, Cynthia C. *Terrorism in the Twenty-First Century*. Eighth Ed. New York: Routledge, 2017.

Cronin, Audrey Kurth. *How Terrorism Ends: Understanding the Decline and Demise of Terrorism Campaigns*. Princeton, NJ: Princeton University Press, 2011.

———. "Sources of Contemporary Terrorism." In *Attacking Terrorism: Elements of a Grand Strategy*, edited by Audrey Kurth Cronin and James M. Ludes, 19–45. Washington, DC: Georgetown University Press, 2004.

Etchevarria III, Antulio J. *Strategy: A Very Short Introduction*. Oxford, UK: Oxford University Press, 2017.

Freedman, Lawrence. *Strategy: A History*. Reprint Ed. Oxford, UK: Oxford University Press, 2015.

Hoffman, Bruce. *Inside Terrorism*. Third Ed. New York: Columbia University Press, 2017.

Jacob, Edwin Daniel (ed.). *Rethinking Strategy in the Twenty-First Century: A Reader.* London: Palgrave Macmillan, 2016.

Jenkins, Brian. "International Terrorism." In *The Use of Force: Military Power and International Politics,* edited by Robert J. Art and Kenneth N. Waltz, 77–84. Lanham, MD: Rowman & Littlefield, 2004.

Laqueur, Walter. *A History of Terrorism.* New York: Routledge, 2001.

————. *No End to War: Terrorism in the Twenty-First Century.* London: Bloomsbury Academic, 2004.

Law, Randal D. *Terrorism: A History.* Second Ed. Boston: Polity Press, 2016.

Martin, Gus. *Understanding Terrorism: Challenges, Perspectives, and Issues.* Fifth Ed. Thousand Oaks, CA: Sage, 2015.

Monaco, Lisa. "Preventing the Next Attack: A Strategy for the War on Terrorism." *Foreign Affairs* 96 (6) (November/December 2017), 23–29.

Nacos, Brigette. *Terrorism and Counterterrorism.* Fifth Ed. New York: Routledge, 2016.

Snow, Donald M. *Cases in International Relations: Principles and Applications.* Seventh Ed. Lanham, MD: Rowman & Littlefield, 2018.

Snow, Donald M., and Dennis M. Drew. *From Lexington to Desert Storm and Beyond: War and Politics in the American Experience.* Third Ed. Armonk, NY: M. E. Sharpe, 2010.

Stern, Jessica. *Terrorism in the Name of God: Why Religious Militants Kill.* New York: ECCO, 2003.

Stern, Jessica, and I. M. Berger. *ISIS: The State of Terror.* New York: ECCO, 2015.

Weinberg, Leonard, and Susanne Martin. *The Role of Terrorism in Twenty-First Century Warfare.* New Directions in Terrorism Policy. Manchester, UK: Manchester University Press, 2016.

White, Jonathan R. *Terrorism and Homeland Security.* Ninth Ed. East Windsor, CT: Wadsworth, 2016.

Wood, Graeme. "What ISIS Really Wants." *Atlantic* 321 (2) (March 2015), 78–90.

4

Nuclear Deterrence Redux

The New Shadow of the Mushroom-Shaped Cloud

When the Cold War ended in 1991, the direst element of the threat underlying the U.S.-USSR confrontation—the fear of a global nuclear war that could metaphorically reduce the world to a black, irradiated cinder—appeared to disappear with it. Nuclear weapons, delivery systems, and their deployment in huge superpower arsenals had been the most visible and frightening challenge to national security and had spawned elaborate "theories" of nuclear deterrence between the two "scorpions in a bottle" (see the title of chapter 6 in this book). At the heart of the strategic imperative for the United States' survival was avoiding nuclear war, and the "shadow of the mushroom-shaped cloud" hung over mankind on a slender thread like the Sword of Damocles.

The threat seemed to disappear with the end of the Cold War, but it appears to be back, if in a somewhat different form. The old Cold War rivals still retain very large and destructive arsenals that are smaller than before, but much of the ideological rationale for employing them has disappeared. The threat of *massive* nuclear war has diminished considerably, but that does not mean the danger posed by nuclear weapons has ceased. Instead, it has changed. The largest nuclear powers have accepted deterrence as the operating principle for regulating their conflictual behavior. It is new nuclear powers that may not have embraced these concepts, which are different from the presumptions underlying traditional deterrence. The question is how and why.

In the contemporary international system, the heart of the nuclear shadow has moved from what used to be called *vertical nuclear proliferation* (increases in the size of the arsenals possessed by nuclear weapons states) to *horizontal nuclear proliferation* (the spread of nuclear weapons to states that previously have not possessed them). These have always been separate concerns and have been treated as such. What causes countries to decide to try to become nuclear powers is different than what motivates an already nuclear-armed state to expand its arsenal to greater potency and is underlaid by different calculations and motives. The two kinds of acts are qualitatively different, and efforts to shape and contain either decision by outsiders must be different as well. Dealing with each problem is an exercise in deterrence: keeping someone from doing something one does not want them to do. In the nuclear context, the use of nuclear weapons in war is the event to be deterred. Horizontal proliferation control—or acquisition deterrence—seeks to avoid nuclear use by keeping states from getting nuclear weapons. Vertical proliferation—or employment deterrence—is largely concerned with keeping nuclear powers from using the weapons they have.

The new shape of the mushroom-shaped cloud has changed. It no longer concentrates so much on the largest countries and weapons capabilities that threaten mankind in the way the Cold War confrontation did. Rather, it is directed at the problem posed by smaller states, mostly in the developing world, that may choose to gain nuclear weapons capability, why they choose to try to do so, what can and cannot be done to dissuade new countries from exercising the nuclear "option," and what new and dangerous challenges these prospects pose for the international system. Both forms of nuclear dynamic were matters of concern during the latter twentieth century, but vertical proliferation overshadowed weapons spread to other states. In the new world of deterrence, those priorities have reversed: horizontal proliferation, its dynamics, and their implications form the new heart of nuclear thinking. One underlying imperative transcends time: the purpose is to make sure that the system's perfect post-1945 record of avoiding nuclear war remains intact.

Perspectives on the Problem

The nuclear age was officially christened in the New Mexico desert at White Sands on July 16, 1945, when the United States successfully exploded the first nuclear device. Only weeks later, atomic bombs were dropped on the Japanese cities of Hiroshima and Nagasaki on August 6 and 9, 1945, to convince the Japanese government of the futility of further resistance and thus to obviate the need for a bloody American invasion of the Japanese home islands to end World War II. The nuclear "genie" was officially out of the bottle. Nuclear weapons moved to the center of national security concerns and national strategy formulation.

The awesome destructive impact of the new form of weaponry was immediate. In 1946, two books, one famous and the other not so famous, were published that largely defined how the world, and especially Americans, have viewed nuclear weapons ever since. The famous book was Bernard Brodie's *The Absolute Weapon*. Its title gave away its thesis. Brodie argued that these new weapons were so destructive that they must never be used. He echoed sentiments expressed by Gen. Leslie Groves, the military commander of the Manhattan Project (the code name for the American weapons research program), that after the White Sands demonstration, the principal job of the military must be to prevent war from occurring. The emphasis of nuclear thinking on deterrence (avoiding war) has its origins in this reasoning. The other book, *There Will Be No Time* by William Liscum Borden, argued that no matter how horrible they might be, nuclear weapons are, after all, weapons, that weapons are almost always used at some time, and thus the effort must be both to prepare for that exigency and to find ways to limit the carnage. So far, Brodie has been right, but both strains remain part of the strategic debate. The worry is that Borden may have been correct in the longer term.

Much subsequent strategic development about nuclear war flows from these two positions. The overarching principle that defines this debate is the enormous uncertainty about the ability of two nuclear powers using those weapons against one another to limit the destruction. Brodie thought they could not, making war avoidance the only value. Borden felt use was inevitable and that devising means to limit the war was the supreme value. We still do not know who was correct in his assessment. Most of us do not want to find out.

Understanding nuclear weapons and their role in global affairs begins with two dimensions of nuclear dynamics that define the balance and thinking about the utility of the weapons. The first dimension is physical and threat-driven—the deadly characteristics of the weaponry and the means for delivering nuclear weapons. Collectively, these two aspects of nuclear capability define the physical problem they pose. The second dimension is conceptual and strategic, and it refers to the determination of the usability of the weapons in war, a debate that hinges critically on the debate initiated by Brodie and Borden in 1946. The heart of the conceptual debate is the issue of nuclear deterrence. The second dimension is more concerned with convincing nuclear states they cannot profit from using the weapons.

The Physical Dimension

The physical problem posed by nuclear weapons is defined in two basic ways. The first is the kind, quality, and quantity of nuclear devices that a state possesses. Nuclear weapons (bombs or explosives) are the product of one of two physical reactions, both of which begin with the breaking apart (fission) of isotopes of unstable elements of uranium, a process that releases enormous energy that forms the basis of the nuclear explosion and its deadly effects in terms of heat, fire, blast overpressure (wind), and both immediate and residual radiation.

These explosions come in two forms. The first is a fission bomb, which involves the splitting apart of unstable isotopes. This is the physical reaction of the first nuclear weapons, such as the device exploded at White Sands and the bombs used against Hiroshima and Nagasaki. The deadly yields of these "atomic" bombs, as they are colloquially known, is normally measured in *kilotons*, the equivalent of exploding thousands of tons of TNT, and they are generally considered "dirty" bombs, because a large part of their physical effect is to create residual radiation that lasts for long periods and causes lingering radiation death. The second form is the fission-fusion bomb, also known as the hydrogen or thermonuclear bomb. It begins with a fission reaction, which creates sufficient heat to trigger the fusing together of deuterium and tritium particles to create a qualitatively larger effect. The explosive power of thermonuclear weapons is generally measured in *megatons*, the equivalent of exploding *millions* of tons of TNT. In the contemporary context, the DPRK (North Korea) has progressed from the possession of atomic to hydrogen bomb capability.

The progression from fission to fission-fusion possession changes nuclear calculations in two ways. One is obviously destructive: hydrogen bombs are qualitatively and quantitatively more destructive than atomic bombs, and this alters the calculation of using them. Whereas it is possible (if possibly fanciful) to calculate surviving a war in which atomic bombs were employed, that calculation evaporates when thinking of a thermonuclear war. Second, the physics of thermonuclear warheads is such that hydrogen bombs can be made lighter and more compact than fission bombs—including compact weapons that can be placed atop ballistic missiles.

The second characteristic of nuclear weapons is how they are sent to target. The 1945 bombs were delivered by conventional aircraft, but airplanes can be intercepted and destroyed before they reach target, thereby making them potentially vulnerable. Modern, advanced delivery is by ballistic missiles, rockets carrying the weapons at speeds where they are extremely difficult to intercept. The ultimate forms are land-based intercontinental or submarine-launched ballistic missiles (ICBMs and SLBMs). These largely negate any possibility of being intercepted if launched in large (or possibly small) numbers: a ballistic missile will almost certainly penetrate attempts to intercept it and will complete its deadly mission. Furtive efforts have been ongoing for over a half-century to develop effective antiballistic missiles (ABMs), but they have not been proven to be effective except against very small missile attacks. The DPRK began to test long-range ballistic missiles wedded apparently to thermonuclear warheads in 2017. It was a game changer.

The Conceptual Dimension

The next step is strategic. Before thermonuclear weapons on ballistic missiles entered the calculus, it was possible (if possibly wrong) to calculate surviving a war in which nuclear weapons were employed. These two "innovations," however, obviated that calculation, because they radically reduced or eliminated the ability to calculate avoiding the cataclysmic consequences of a nuclear exchange. With this radical change, the cardinal reality of the thermonuclear age became the conviction that the only way to avoid being destroyed by nuclear weapons was to ensure there was never a nuclear war. The key concept of the nuclear age became deterrence: the creation of military constructs and capabilities to avoid war. It is a concept grounded in regulating the relations among nuclear powers. It is different from ideas about how to avoid states gaining nuclear weapons in the first place (proliferation).

The world nuclear balance has evolved within the deterrence framework. It is a two-step proposition regarding who does and does not have nuclear weapons. The first step is the effort to enforce horizontal proliferation by dissuading non-weapons states from attaining the capability, as discussed in the next chapter. The results have enjoyed mixed success. Some states have not agreed to restrictions and have gained nuclear capability; others have joined non-proliferation regimes and not exercised the option. Preventing the spread of nuclear weapons has only been partially successful. The second part of the effort has been *employment deterrence*, efforts to dissuade countries who gain the capability from using it against others.

As of 2018, there are eight open members of the nuclear club. They are (with the year of their first nuclear weapons test in parentheses): the United States (1945), the Soviet Union/Russia (1949), the United Kingdom (1952), France (1960), China (1964), India (1974), Pakistan (1998), and North Korea (2006). Israel also has a nuclear arsenal, the existence of which it neither confirms nor denies. South Africa developed and deployed nuclear weapons but disassembled its arsenal during the transition to black majority rule. It is the only state publicly to have "denuclearized" voluntarily. No other state that has gained nuclear weapons has been forced to or has voluntarily done so, despite international efforts (notably surrounding Soviet and Chinese deployment of the weapons). The United States and Russia/Soviet Union have always had the largest arsenals, although current weapons balances are far below Cold War levels. The total warheads possessed by each country is in the seven thousand range (exact numbers are closely guarded state secrets). Other than China, all other possessors have inventories numbered in the low hundreds.

The conceptual challenge is keeping possessors from using their weapons in anger: deterrence. It is an uncertain task, and one with occasionally bizarre constructions. The uncertainty arises from a paradox. The key concept in nuclear weapons dynamics is what would start a nuclear war (the so-called nuclear "threshold," the point at which a situation escalates to nuclear weapons use). No one knows where this is, because it has never been observed: there has never been nuclear weapons use when both or all parties possessed the weapons. The paradox is that no one wants to find out where the threshold is, because the only way to observe it is to cross it. As a result, the nuclear deterrence exercise is an effort absolutely dedicated to avoiding knowledge about its most fundamental dynamic.

This frames the nuclear dynamic. In the 1970s Soviet-American competition, it became enshrined in the concept of "assured destruction." The deterrence of weapons being used against you was based in the promise that if someone attacked and destroyed you, you would maintain the capacity (known as "second strike capability") to retaliate and destroy the initial attacker. Deterrence arose from the realization that launching an initial attack was a delayed method of committing suicide. Thus, peace was based in the idea of threatening self-destructive genocide against an attacker, an idea bizarre enough that an opponent added the word "mutual" to assured destruction to create the acronym MAD. The dynamic apparently worked and, as I argued in *The Necessary Peace,* probably contributed to the end of the Cold War, since both sides came to realize that they could not survive, much less prevail, in a war between them.

Some of these dynamics seem to have gotten lost in contemporary debates about nuclear weapons, and notably the problem that the failure of acquisition deterrence toward the DPRK has created a situation of confrontation that deterrence thinking sought to avoid at all costs. Instead of trying "to live in the logic of the insane" (a section head in *The Shadow of the Mushroom Shaped Cloud*), contemporary considerations seem to proceed as if there was not almost three-quarters of a century of developed thought on the subject. Why?

Policy Options

Nuclear dynamics and the policies and strategies surrounding them have clearly changed. The central feature of international conflict in the world no longer centers on the threat of a massive nuclear holocaust in which the United States and the Soviet Union/Russia hurl tens of thousands of thermonuclear warheads at one another in a civilization-ending cataclysm of fiery violence. The major nuclear powers still maintain nuclear arsenals that could bring civilization to the brink of oblivion, but there are few plausible scenarios for how or why they would. At the nuclear level, that danger has been superseded by less deadly but possibly more likely wars, since the consequences are less severe. In this atmosphere, understanding and knowledge of the dynamics of traditional nuclear deterrence seem to have eroded in political dialogue and even military calculation. But should that erosion be reversed in the face of smaller but still very real nuclear threats?

The heart of the new nuclear deterrence calculus is the tension between acquisition and employment deterrence. Both problems currently are centered on the confrontation between the DPRK and the United States over North Korea's burgeoning weapons program, but the outcome will influence the shape of nuclear power politics in the future as well. Both these problems were part of the traditional deterrence equation, but the solutions that were developed in that context have changed.

One aspect of this challenge is the intermixing of the two problems by the principal parties. Although North Korea has an ongoing nuclear program, the United States has treated the confrontation as an acquisition deterrence, proliferation problem, insisting that the DPRK cease development and abandon their program as a precondition for progress toward reconciliation. Such an approach has *never* worked: no state that has developed and fielded nuclear capability has been coerced into reversing that decision. In fact, avoiding coercion by the United States is, for some developing-world countries, a major reason for developing the capability in the first place: the Saddam Effect.

The other way to approach the DPRK program is as an employment deterrence problem: how to persuade a country that has nuclear weapons not to use them. The rationale for this approach has always been based in the uncertainty of any conflict in which two nuclear-armed opponents fight. It is arguable that nuclear weapons are the reason for this: countries are too frightened of the uncertain dynamics if "the balloon goes up" (Cold War–speak for the beginning of a nuclear exchange) to let their disagreements get out of hand for fear of the worst. This has been the rationale for maintaining arsenals in the past. Has anything really changed?

In the ongoing U.S.-DPRK confrontation, the two sides have argued opposite positions on the nature of the problem. The United States implicitly framed the North Korean nuclear weapons as a proliferation problem by insisting that the only acceptable outcome for the Americans is a "rollback" of the DPRK effort to the pre-2006 condition before the North tested and subsequently fielded its first nuclear devices. This position has precedent but has never succeeded. In the 1960s, for instance, then secretary of state Dean Rusk railed about the perils of a Chinese population of over a billion people, each armed with a nuclear weapon, and Mao Zedong tantalizingly suggested China was the only country that could survive a nuclear war because of the size of its population, both clearly provocative arguments. If there is a difference this time, it is the mountingly shrill condemnation coming from the United States, capped by Trump's threat at the United Nations on September 19, 2017, that DPRK refusal to dismantle its nuclear program could mean the United States "will have no choice than to totally destroy North Korea" and that Kim Jong Un was on a suicidal path with his program, a suggestion the North Korean dismissed by calling Trump a "dotard" (an elderly person with diminished mental capacity). This bombastic rhetoric has continued, particularly since Trump and Kim began negotiations toward DPRK "denuclearization" at the Shanghai summit in June 2018.

Redefining Deterrence Strategy

The North Korean position is that its efforts fall within the spirit of deterrence. It is an important international position and especially for future nuclear aspirants, since their success or failure will embolden or discourage others. It has emphasized that its intent is to create a capability that can reach American soil, which is the emotional heart of American objections to the program but congruent with the traditional structure of nuclear deterrence postures and threats. On September 16, 2017, Kim explained the North Korean goal in conventional deterrence terms: "Our final goal," he said, "is to establish the equilibrium of real force with the United States and make the U.S. rulers dare not talk about military action." In simple language, the DPRK has felt it needs adequate force of its own to deter the United States. That perceived need may seem incongruous to Americans, but it has traction in parts of the developing world.

If there is a bright side to this confrontation, it is that both sides have taken such strong, emotional public positions that there is a good deal of room to negotiate de-escalation simply by ratcheting back the rhetoric. To Cold Warriors who crafted the structure of twentieth-century deterrence, the loud, vitriolic, and confrontational rhetoric from both sides violates deterrence "rules" to defuse conflicts and move away from the nuclear "brink." Had this situation arisen forty years ago, deflating the rhetoric would have been the first order of business. Both sides have seemed to recognize this dynamic and have dialed back their confrontational rhetoric.

The world's first nuclear war would be an unprecedented and unpredictable physical and geopolitical event with global ramifications, and its avoidance is clearly the most important strategy goal, followed closely by attempting to erect physical and conceptual barriers to a repeat of the process. How the ongoing conflict is resolved will also have important ramifications for global relations—and especially the American role in the world—going forward. The Americans set themselves up rhetorically so that the failure to disarm North Korea is an inevitable, self-inflicted geopolitical defeat that will somehow have to be reconciled. Even if the DPRK program is constrained, which is unlikely, the North Koreans have been able to claim they faced down the Americans on equal terms under any circumstances. This has clearly been a Kim regime goal and could be an encouragement for others who want to gain nuclear weapons status to reduce American influence over them. The result can hardly reinforce proliferation efforts, and it will almost certainly strengthen the arguments of those who want to gain the weapons.

Iran, the subject of chapter 7, is a special case in point. After much cajoling and castigation, the Iranians negotiated an agreement under which they renounced becoming a nuclear power in multilateral negotiations. Despite partisan criticisms in the United States, they have basically lived up to their obligations, and their reward has been renunciation by the Americans and Trump's unilateral withdrawal from the arrangement. The North Koreans, who rejected similar overtures, are now apparently succeeding in going toe-to-toe with the Americans. Some Iranians have obviously experienced buyer's remorse at the choice they made.

There is, of course, a danger in reemphasizing nuclear deterrence with the DPRK or Iran as participants. The danger is that the de facto recognition of new developing-world members of the nuclear club makes prohibitions on and discouragement of weapons spread to less stable parts of the world more intellectually difficult to justify because that spread has been normalized by the Iranian and North Korean precedents. In the 1950s and 1960s, there were "horror scenarios" of a world of twenty to thirty nuclear powers, all with the ability to push the nuclear "button" and throw the world into potential nuclear holocaust. Those predictions have proven to have been overblown so far, but that could change. Does deterrence work when volatile neighboring enemies have nuclear weapons? It has so far between India and Pakistan, but does it elsewhere? No one knows, and like the nuclear threshold, most of us do not want to find out.

That said, the avoidance of nuclear war arguably remains the paramount military imperative in the world. Stating that proposition a third of a century ago was mundane, because it was so widely accepted. Those in leadership positions have apparently lost some of their overarching fear of acting in ways that might conceivably lead to nuclear exchange. Deterrence took the "military option" effectively off the table in relation to nuclear weapons states, but the "shock and awe" of massive, including thermonuclear, options has led leaders to threaten one another and to escalate their threats as if the shadow of the mushroom-shaped cloud no longer hangs over them. It does.

Consequences: What to Do?

What should the United States do in these circumstances? There are at least three broad options raised by the U.S.-DPRK experience that could apply more broadly to the future. The first is to continue confrontation, including its centerpiece of insisting that North Korea abandon its nuclear program. The second is an attempt to lower the temperature of the conflict by engaging China and others, through a vehicle like the six-power talks, to negotiate an arrangement between the DPRK and others that could cause the North Koreans to cap their program or even modestly to reduce it. The third is a more comprehensive negotiation centered on the United States and the DPRK to reach an agreement that has some prospect of forming a long-term, if cool, relationship between the two. Each has applications for other situations that may arise, as suggested in chapter 5.

The current debate has been prejudiced by the surrounding partisan rhetoric. Within the current U.S. administration, there is at least a rhetorical preference for tough-sounding military solution options, including the imputation that possibilities featuring diplomatic efforts are somehow effete, and that pursuing them shows American weakness in the world. Diplomacy, on the other hand, would clearly be aimed at lowering the confrontational nature of the crisis and, in the process, lessening the likelihood of accidentally slipping into war. The idea that doing so takes the military option "off the table" is largely specious. The United States does not need to keep reminding the world it could incinerate the DPRK; that is a fact (admittedly grisly and genocidal), and it remains under any circumstances. The same applies to Iran and other possible possessors in the future.

Framing the debate in terms of military threats may seem proactive, but it is also the riskiest strategy. Its proponents maintain that it is the only "manly" approach that Kim Jong Un and his rogue regime will understand, but it also is the option most likely to lead to the purposeful or accidental escalation of the situation to violence, with incalculable potential to ravage the region and possibly beyond. Could, for instance, China sit idly by as the Americans "totally destroy" a country on its border?

The other options emphasize politico-diplomatic approaches to reining in the North Koreans. The second position essentially aims at recreating a dialogue for talking with the North Koreans through a vehicle like the six-power talks now that bilateral talks have stalled. There are two obvious objections to this avenue. One is that it has essentially failed in the past. This option was devised when George W. Bush came to office. Bush did not want to deal one-on-one with the North Koreans, feeling one-on-one talks rewarded the DPRK's uncooperative, even intransigent, behavior, thus producing undesirable outcomes. The DPRK nuclear tests followed shortly on the heels of the collapse of these efforts.

The third option is a more comprehensive regional approach that would feature direct one-on-one talks between the Americans and the North Koreans, a resumption of advocacy of the summit option. Efforts to find an avenue for reaching a peace treaty ending the Korean War would provide an opening for such an approach where both sides could claim success (the hallmark of a successful negotiation), and might provide an opportunity for gradual implementation of limits (but not elimination) of DPRK nuclear capabilities. Negotiated limits on the number and range of North Korean missiles in return for guarantees of DPRK security and possible economic incentives like sanctions relaxation, could be included. Other involved states like China could take part in the security guarantees, since maintaining the DPRK as a buffer to South Korea (ROK) is one of their prime goals. A reduced threat to the ROK and Japan could sweeten their approach as well.

The primary barrier to the second and third options is the insistence by the Trump administration on treating the situation as an acquisition deterrence problem. While "denuclearization" remains the non-negotiable goal of the Americans—effectively reducing the conflict to a proliferation problem—this almost certainly will not happen. The DPRK program exists and the relationship between the two antagonists is in fact an employment deterrence problem. American insistence, if anything, makes the United States the principal party to be deterred. If the United States continues to frame solutions that feature the problem as possibly amenable to a "military solution," it is not at all clear who is deterring whom.

In the early summer of 1914, the storm clouds that would burst and result in the largest and deadliest war to that point in history were gathering in terms of a series of diplomatic, geopolitical maneuvers. Each of the individual machinations was arguably innocuous and none individually could justify the accumulation that is much clearer with the 20/20 clarity of hindsight. At that time, no one acted decisively to interrupt the cycle because they did not believe the accumulation could lead to a conflict they believed to be impossible and the prospects of which they did not fear. They were, of course, wrong in the deadliest sort of way. Nuclear deterrence, as it developed during the second half of the twentieth century, was designed to act as an intellectual, geopolitical governor on that sort of behavior, and its existence and the absence of nuclear war coincided in a much more heavily armed nuclear atmosphere than today.

The dynamic then was that the parties did not fear the prospects of war more than they cherished the geopolitical gains of smaller victories. They remembered later why there had to be deterrence. Have we forgotten? What do we need to do to make sure the shadow of the mushroom-shaped cloud remains a metaphor, not a physical specter to us all? Does the 2017 U.S.-DPRK standoff and possible solutions offer useful guidance? What should we do? What do you think?

Study/Discussion Questions

1. Discuss the evolution and key concepts of nuclear weapons strategy, notably forms of deterrence. How have these ideas been revived in the twenty-first century?

2. Discuss the major physical dimensions of nuclear weapons. What are the major characteristics of these weapons, and how and why are each of them important in understanding nuclear balance and deterrence?

3. How has the problem of avoiding nuclear war been approached historically and in the contemporary context? What are acquisition and employment deterrence, and how do they offer different approaches? Why is the distinction critical in the current nuclear situation? Include in your answer the "denuclearization" approach and the "Saddam Effect" as variables.

4. What are the basic options available for attempting to maintain deterrence in the contemporary context? Discuss the pros and cons of each.

5. Why is the outcome of the U.S.-DPRK confrontation important as a precedent for the future? Why do you think so?

Bibliography

Borden, William Liscum. *There Will Be No Time: The Revolution in Strategy.* New York: Macmillan, 1946.

Bracken, Paul. *The Second Nuclear Age: Strategy, Danger, and the New Power Politics.* New York: Times Books, 2012.

Brodie, Bernard. *The Absolute Weapon: Atomic Power and World Order.* New York: Harcourt Brace, 1946.

———. *Strategy in the Missile Age.* Princeton, NJ: Princeton University Press, 1959.

Cimbala, Stephen J. *Deterrence and Nuclear Proliferation in the Twenty-First Century.* Westport, CT: Praeger, 2000.

Clark, Ronald W. *The Greatest Power on Earth: The International Race for Nuclear Supremacy from Earliest Theory to Three-Mile Island.* New York: Harper and Row, 1980.

Delpech, Therese. *Nuclear Deterrence in the 21st Century: Lessons from the Cold War for a New Era of Strategic Piracy.* Santa Monica, CA: RAND, 2012.

Guertner, Gary L., and Donald M. Snow. *The Last Frontier: An Analysis of the Strategic Defense Initiative.* Lexington, MA: Lexington Books, 1986.

Kim, Sung Chull, and Michael D. Cohen (eds.). *North Korea and Nuclear Weapons: Entering the New Age of Deterrence.* Washington, DC: Georgetown University Press, 2017.

Larsen, Jeffrey, and Karry M. Kartchner. *On Limited Nuclear War in the 21st Century.* Palo Alto, CA: Stanford Security Studies, 2014.

Lowther, Adam B. (ed.). *Rising Powers, Rogue Regimes, and Terrorism in the 21st Century.* London: Palgrave Macmillan, 2012.

Moon, Katharine H. S. "Caught in the Middle: The North Korean Threat Is Ultimately South Korea's Problem." *Foreign Affairs Snapshot* (online), September 1, 2017.

O'Neil, Andrew. *Asia, the United States, and Extended Nuclear Deterrence: Atomic Umbrellas in the 21st Century.* New York: Routledge, 2013.

Roehrig, Terence. *Japan, South Korea, and the United States Nuclear Umbrella After the Cold War.* Contemporary Asia in the World. New York: Columbia University Press, 2017.

Sagan, Scott D. "The Korean Missile Crisis: Why Deterrence Is Still the Best Option." *Foreign Affairs Essay* (online), September 10, 2017.

Snow, Donald M. *National Security.* Sixth Ed. New York: Routledge, 2017.

———. *The Necessary Peace: Nuclear Weapons and Superpower Relations.* Lexington, MA: Lexington Books, 1987.

———. *Nuclear Strategy in a Dynamic World: Policy for the 1980s.* Tuscaloosa: University of Alabama Press, 1980.

———. *The Shadow of the Mushroom-Shaped Cloud.* Columbus, OH: Consortium for International Studies Education, 1978.

5

Dealing with Nuclear Proliferation
The NPT and BMD Approaches

As introduced in chapter 4, one way to avoid nuclear war is to ensure that countries that do not currently have nuclear weapons do not get them. In terms already raised, an important cornerstone of nuclear dynamics is acquisition deterrence, and its principal method is non-proliferation, or more specifically the avoidance of horizontal nuclear proliferation.

Non-proliferation has always been a preferred approach of countries that already have nuclear weapons when dealing with countries that do not. The effort to keep additional countries from acquiring weapons of mass destruction has centered on arms control agreements to convince potential proliferators to negotiate away their right to gain nuclear weapons capability (acquisition deterrence). The Non-Proliferation Treaty (NPT) of 1968 was the culminating prime example of this form of deterrence, and it remains in effect. Employment deterrence efforts have sought to convince those countries that had the arsenals not to use them or that their use would fail to produce desired outcomes. Efforts to devise successful ballistic missile defenses (BMD) are the prime example.

Both forms of initiative are Cold War constructs with their roots in the Soviet-American nuclear confrontation. It has been a truism of the nuclear age that countries acquiring nuclear weapons believe their own acquisition is acceptable, but that the efforts of other states should be discouraged because of the allegedly nefarious intents and destabilizing effects that additional "fingers on the nuclear button" produce. Attempts to control who has nuclear weapons culminating in the NPT go back to the 1950s, when the nuclear "club" consisted only of the United States, the Soviet Union, and Great Britain, and the further weapons spread was a matter of conjecture. Similarly, theoretical BMD efforts predate the development of missile delivery systems to carry nuclear bombs to targets. The concentration of early efforts was on the deterrence of nuclear exchange between the two major nuclear powers. Only as additional states have acquired arsenals that could conceivably endanger a nuclear weapons state—notably the United States—has BMD become a nuclear proliferation issue.

Both proliferation control and missile defenses were major components of the Cold War era that waned with the end of that conflict. None of the major nuclear powers dismantled their arsenals (they did reduce their size) after the Cold War ended, but the reasonable prospect that anyone would use nuclear weapons in anger faded as a central national security concern in a less confrontational environment. Concern over nuclear politics remained publicly dormant for over a decade. The activation of nuclear weapons interest and programs in a series of developing-world countries has returned nuclear weapons to the international agenda with North Korea and Iran as the flash points. The problem of nuclear weapons has not gone away. It has just resurfaced in a modified form.

The effort to inhibit nuclear weapons spread to non-possessing states is sometimes emotional to the point of being hysterical, and it has been applied against potential proliferators using both positive rewards for abstinence and negative sanctions when proliferators ignore international attempts to inhibit their actions. Ultimately, there is no legal or other inhibition suggesting that states cannot pursue the option or that they should somehow be treated as criminals or rogues by other states if they choose to pursue the nuclear option. There is a moral argument to be made for the proposition that a world of less—preferably zero—nuclear weapons states would be a safer and better place for humankind. When this case is made by nuclear weapons possessors (which it often is) against aspirants, the advocacy is arguably not only condescending, but hypocritical as well.

The dynamics of missile defenses are different. The pursuit of physical defenses against nuclear attack, of course, depends on the technological and scientific base of the country undertaking it. It is a dynamic that generally applies between nuclear possessors rather than in didactic interactions between possessors and non-possessors. The attraction of defenses is to lessen the awful effect of nuclear attack, preferably to zero (it is arguable that anything short of perfection in the performance of defenses is unacceptable, given the destructive capabilities of the weapons). The problem has been the technical inability to devise and produce a defensive system capable of effectiveness against any but the smallest attacks.

The North Korean nuclear breakout that accelerated during 2017 has brought these two concerns together with some urgency in the American national security debate. The North Koreans are the only signatory to the NPT that has ever signed and then removed itself from the agreement—an action that is permitted under the terms of the treaty. With the rise to power of a member of the third generation of the Kim family in 2011, Kim Jong Un, the pace and intensity of that effort has accelerated dramatically, with North Korea demonstrating advanced warhead capabilities, the development of workable missile systems, and the projected marriage of the two capabilities, an event that would conceivably permit the Democratic People's Republic of Korea (DPRK) to attack the United States with missile-launched nuclear weapons.

The North Korean breakout has added a concept to the nuclear arms control agenda—*denuclearization*. Acquisition deterrence failed in the DPRK case, and proponents of the NPT (notably the United States) have tried to recoup the situation by convincing the North Koreans to abandon their program—to denuclearize themselves. It is virtually certain to fail. As noted, the only state to abandon an arsenal was South Africa for special reasons. Precedent works against the effort. Moreover, the DPRK arsenal is fundamental to their national security goal of deterring the United States and is too important to negotiate away.

Perspectives on the Problem

As the preceding discussion should indicate, the two problems and approaches emphasized in this chapter are conceptually disparate in content and purpose. They currently congeal in the matter of deterring the DPRK, but they have precedential importance as well. In addition to trying to put a lid on the North Koreans, the outcome of current efforts may have important impacts on the future of nuclear weapons possession generally. A major candidate for weapons spread, at least as actively portrayed in some American circles, is Iran, a country which has the physical capability for a nuclear breakout but has indicated it does not plan to develop the capability. Despite formal conclusion of a treaty where it denounces the nuclear option (and which the United States has denounced), it faces hostility and suspicion within elements of the U.S. community about its intentions. There is also a deep suspicion among some other developing countries that the most effective way to avoid undesired American interference in its internal politics is to gain nuclear weapons and thus to *deter the United States.* There is, for instance, agreement among many that had Iraq and Libya not abandoned nuclear developmental programs, their governments would not have been overthrown and that their leaders, Libya's Muammar Gaddafi and Iraq's Saddam Hussein, might still be alive and in power.

Nuclear Proliferation and the NPT

Nuclear weapons possession is a decidedly mixed virtue. They were born out of a scientifically based competition among physicists in the period between the world wars (see Clark, *The Greatest Power on Earth*). No one knew with certainty what the outcome of that research would be, but the pursuit continued in countries on both sides of the war, based either in the desire to gain a decisive advantage that would win the war (especially by the German Nazis) or to avoid the other side gaining that advantage (principally the United States). The American Manhattan Project that ultimately succeeded in producing the first workable weapon was heavily influenced by correspondence between Albert Einstein and President Franklin Roosevelt suggesting the catastrophe that would ensue should Germany be the first to weaponize nuclear physics—a status it came dangerously close to achieving.

The United States exploded the first weapon at White Sands, New Mexico, on July 16, 1945, and then used the explosives against the Japanese cities of Hiroshima and Nagasaki on August 6 and 9 of that year. Once the nuclear "genie" was out of the bottle, it was just a matter of time until the capability was obtained by other states. Proliferation was virtually inevitable.

The dynamics of nuclear weapons possession and possible utilization are complex and largely beyond the present concern with proliferation. Two concerns must be addressed, however. The first is why countries desire to obtain nuclear capability; the motivations vary. The second is the question of how the international system has attempted to retard or stop the spread of nuclear weapons, an effort that has been concentrated on obtaining international agreements prohibiting proliferation.

Why Pursue the Nuclear Option? States decide either to pursue nuclear weapons possession or not for several reasons that can be related to one another. Two were present in the World War II rationales of the major powers in that war. Additional reasons have emerged in the contemporary environment and help provide the incentives for possible future proliferators. Five will be mentioned.

The first two reasons come from the formative period in the 1930s and 1940s. One is that possession of nuclear weapons would provide decisive military advantage for the possessor. The destructive power of nuclear weapons is so enormous that the threat, or even worse, the actuality of even a few weapons being used against an opponent would be so disastrous that an opponent would surrender rather than suffer them. If it did not, even the selective use of the weapons against an enemy could bring it to its knees and force its capitulation. This was, of course, the rationale and purpose of American use of nuclear weapons against Japan, and it succeeded in that purpose. The lesson may, however, be idiosyncratic, since the American use occurred when only it had the weapons and the Japanese could not threaten retaliation following an attack (the heart of deterrence).

Fear of the possibility of suffering a nuclear attack provides the basis for the second rationale, which is that one gains power and advantage over an opponent if one has the weapons and the opponent does not. Whether the possession of the capability has operational significance in an environment in which multiple states have nuclear weapons and where their use, especially against a defenseless enemy who could not retaliate in kind, would be universally condemned and sanctioned mitigates this advantage. One of the continuing anomalies about nuclear weapons is whether, in a world of several nuclear powers, their actual use—as opposed to the threat of that use—has operational significance.

Despite questions about whether nuclear weapons use has meaningful benefits, the third reason for possessing them is the prestige that potential proliferators believe comes with being a nuclear power. This attraction is a holdover from the Cold War. The term *superpower* was informally bestowed on the United States and the Soviet Union because of their possession of huge nuclear arsenals, and the term was used to denote the most powerful and consequential countries in the world. No other state approximated the arsenal size or lethality of the superpowers, but the designation reverberated downward to other states: having nuclear weapons makes countries more important than not having them.

The fourth reason for having nuclear weapons is their coercive value, mostly against adversaries who lack them. The dynamics of coercion may be difficult to demonstrate because of systemic aversion to the use of nuclear weapons. Additionally, despite the absence of any history of the results of usage, possessing the weapons may influence a country's enemies, especially in highly volatile, high-stakes situations. The prototype is the coercive application of Israel's nuclear arsenal. Israel neither admits (nor denies) having a nuclear arsenal nor what its size might be, but Israel's adversaries believe that arsenal is adequate to destroy their Middle East adversaries if they threatened Israel's existence. It is probably not coincidental that direct threats against Israel have virtually disappeared since 1973, when the Israelis allegedly armed their nuclear arsenal during threatening days of the Yom Kippur War. The situation may also help explain the intensity of their opposing weapons spread to a regional adversary—Iran (see chapter 8).

Finally, nuclear weapons may be useful as deterrents against nuclear attack. This is the historic rationale for the Cold War, but it has been extended to other states since. Westerners (especially Americans) have some difficulty accepting the notion that they need deterring, but the extension has primarily been adopted by states who feel threatened by American domination (including military) and who feel that American intrusion and coercion can best be avoided if one has nuclear weapons. This general point has already been raised, but it is worth reiterating. Many in the developing world look at the Gaddafi and Saddam Hussein precedents and believe the only sure way to avoid a similar coercive future fate at U.S. hands is by arming themselves with nuclear weapons. This motivation may help explain the North Korean case as noted.

The NPT Response. The desire to limit the spread of nuclear weapons is virtually as old as the weapons themselves. It has been a unique enterprise, filled with contradictions and arguable hypocrisies that have made its history one of mixed success. In the 1960s, there were ominous fears that the number of states who would exercise the nuclear option would rise to twenty to thirty members, and that amount of proliferation has not occurred—at least for now. At the same time, there has been slow but steady expansion in the number of states who have felt the need to contemplate acquiring nuclear weapons.

The original nuclear weapons states have led the non-proliferation movement. Their major tool for doing so has been multilateral diplomacy aimed at getting non-weapons states not to exercise the option that the original proliferators were the first to take. The United States, the Soviet Union, and Great Britain have provided this leadership. It began with the 1963 Nuclear Test Ban Treaty, which outlawed atmospheric testing of weapons and was gradually extended to prohibit testing nuclear devices everywhere but underground. The public premise of these efforts was to keep states from fouling the ecosystem with radioactive fallout from the explosions. The underlying proliferation emphasis was to slow or prevent proliferation.

The effort culminated in the 1967 negotiation of the Treaty on the Proliferation of Nuclear Weapons (NPT), which went into effect in 1968 and remains the centerpiece of formal non-proliferation efforts. The three states that led the test ban negotiations were the major sponsors of the NPT. The agreement they reached creates a series of differential and arguably asymmetrical obligations for the states who sign it.

The NPT creates two distinct categories of members, countries that already possessed nuclear weapons at the time it was negotiated and states that did not. Each class incurs different obligations. Nuclear possessors agree on several restrictions of their behavior. The most important obligations are not to assist those who do not have the weapons to get them (Articles 1 and 4 are devoted to this self-abnegation). Since the purpose of the treaty is to avoid others getting nuclear weapons, this restriction is arguably not a sacrifice. In addition, Article 6 of the treaty obligates the possessors to avoid vertical proliferation (adding to their arsenal sizes) and to move toward nuclear disarmament. During the Cold

War, none of the possessors acted visibly to disarm, leading some non-members (notably India) to believe that the nuclear states were interested solely in freezing their own advantages. If they do not disarm, they are essentially being asked to do nothing.

The non-weapons states incur the real sacrifices. Non-possessing states agree not to solicit help from possessors in developing nuclear programs (Article 2) or to divert peaceful nuclear programs to weapons status (Article 4). The development and continuation of peaceful nuclear power programs is permitted, as is outside help from possessors to non-weapons states in promoting peaceful use of the atom (Article 5). This distinction is easier to make in theory than in application, since it permits nuclear states to engage in ambiguous assistance that could have both military and civilian applications (the case of Iran in chapter 7 is a prominent example). The treaty provides for signatory states to withdraw from the agreement by filing a letter of intention three months in advance of exercising that option (Article 10). Only North Korea has done so.

Experience has shown that there are three kinds of non-possessing countries with different views of the NPT and their relation to it. The first are states that have concluded they do not want to develop the weapons because of special circumstances (e.g., Sweden during the Cold War, since doing so would have aggravated relations with the Soviets and might have had repercussions for neighboring Finland) or because they had concluded doing so did not serve their interests (e.g., Switzerland, which has remained a neutral noncombatant country for over five hundred years). The second category are states that lack the technical ability, expertise, or access to materials to develop the weapons (e.g., most African states other than South Africa). For both these categories, signing the NPT and accepting its restrictions entails no significant costs.

The third category—states that do not have weapons but are unwilling to forgo their future development—is the most problematical. For these states, agreeing to NPT strictures affects them negatively by restricting their options. Their alternative is not to sign, which the most prominent of them (like India, Pakistan, and Israel) have exercised. As a practical matter, the aim is influencing these states, trying to avoid other states from joining the DPRK and withdrawing, and promoting dismantling of existing arsenals.

Has NPT succeeded? The answer is mixed. It has not kept the original, large possessors from maintaining their arsenals, although they all have reduced their size since the end of the Cold War. The number of nuclear states has not increased dramatically, but it has not remained static. The goal of nuclear disarmament remains a distant dream. As a result, managing the problem caused by nuclear weapons includes a hedge to convince potential nuclear aggressors that their efforts would be futile.

The Ballistic Missile Defense Option

On January 16, 2018, the potential reality of nuclear war and its awful consequences was demonstrated graphically to the citizens of Honolulu, Hawaii, when the Hawaiian civil defense system issued a warning that nuclear-tipped missiles were headed toward the fiftieth state. The result was mass panic throughout the city, complete with citizens (including many students from the University of Hawaii) fleeing on foot, hoping somehow to avoid the effects of the detonation. A particularly poignant scene captured by television was of a man lowering his young daughter through a manhole into the sewer system hoping that being underground would somehow shield her from the deadly effects.

The alarm, of course, was false, the result of an employee hitting the wrong button on a computer console, and the warning was cancelled thirty-eight minutes after being issued. The event was, however, the first time since the Cold War that such a prospect had seemed imminent, a stark warning for generations that believed they had evaded the horror of nuclear war. Among the strongest reactions was what could be done to avoid the anticipated catastrophe should deterrence fail. In the case of an attack on Hawaii, the answer was very little if anything. The simple fact was that almost three-quarters of a century after the first nuclear explosion and a half-century after nuclear weapons were placed on ballistic missiles, there is no effective defense against them beyond persuading others not to launch an attack (deterrence).

This situation is unsatisfactory to nearly everyone, resulting in a universal desire somehow to rectify the vulnerability that exists. The problem comes from both aspects of modern nuclear weapons: the bombs themselves and how they are delivered to targets. The bombs are a problem because of the awesome destruction and lingering effects (radiation) associated with their detonation. Ballistic delivery created what has remained the nearly impossible task of intercepting and destroying those bombs before they can be delivered to target—ballistic missile defense (BMD).

The Problem and Barriers

The task of BMD is formidable to the point that it has not been successfully accomplished despite years of concerted effort from the scientific and engineering communities. As noted earlier, theoretical speculation on how to negate offensive nuclear-bearing ballistic missiles predated parallel activity on offensive missiles, and the theoretical difficulties were largely overcome before the first offensive missiles were tested. The devil in the details has been how to translate theory into practice. It has not been satisfactorily overcome: had the Honolulu alarm not been false and had the attack contained multiple offensive warheads, there was very little that could have been done to mitigate the disaster.

An authorized U.S. Government 2016 publication on the history and evolution of missile defense uses a popular analogy to depict the problem in its title: "hitting a bullet with a bullet." The depiction is not precise (a missile defender might not literally have to "hit" an incoming missile to disable it) but is an evocative analogy. Ballistic missiles are essentially bullet-like projectiles that travel at incredible speeds of up to fifteen thousand miles an hour, making the task at hand very exacting and difficult.

The history of the effort has been tortured. The original concept was to develop antiballistic missiles (ABMs) to perform the task by essentially being the bullets that destroyed the other bullets. The Americans and the Soviets signed a treaty in 1972 to allow the construction of two ABM systems in each country. The action was controversial because it was not clear how effective the systems might be, which in turn caused critics to say their existence might lull the two sides into what would be a false security undercutting deterrence, making the effort disreputable among some nuclear analysts. During the 1980s, President Reagan proposed a much more complex, comprehensive scheme, the Strategic Defense Initiative or SDI, to provide a "geodesic dome" over U.S. territory against attack. The proposal was widely ridiculed as impossibly complex and disappeared when Reagan left office (see Guertner and Snow). Since then, efforts have been more limited and subdued, currently centering on the Terminal High Altitude Area Defense (THAAD) system, a "light" ABM system designed to protect against small launches.

Why this convolution? The major basis is scientific skepticism about achieving the mission. For a BMD system to be very helpful, it would have to work essentially perfectly (destroying all incoming missiles) the first time it was employed and in the absence of any ability to conduct realistic prior tests of its workability. The problem is less intense against a "light" attack (a few missiles), but the classic response to ABM systems has been to overwhelm them with more offensive weapons than they can possibly accommodate, something that can easily be done to a light system. Moreover, faith in a BMD system that did not work perfectly would be the ultimate cruelty and delusion. If states used nuclear weapons because they felt they could defend themselves and the defenses proved ineffective, the result would be disastrous. The fact that a defense might be an illusion cannot be discounted in advance.

Policy Options

Proliferation control and missile defenses are subsets of the broader problem of nuclear war avoidance. Stopping and rolling back the number of nuclear weapons states is a priority, because the fewer states that have nuclear weapons, the fewer can use them against others. Conversely, as additional states gain the weapons, they multiply the prospect of nuclear usage by some unknown factor. Should new nuclear states escalate their differences to the point of nuclear exchange, what happens next? To cite an oft-speculated late 1990s scenario, were India and Pakistan to engage in a conflict that escalated to nuclear exchange, would the war remain contained on the Indian subcontinent, or would it inexorably spread to other parts of the world? No one knows. No one *wants* to know.

Missile defenses allegedly serve as a hedge and a reinforcer of deterrence. They are a hedge in the sense that they might absorb part—hopefully all—of an attack, allow the attacked state to survive, and leave the attacker vulnerable to a deadly retaliation, all employment deterrents. They reinforce deterrence if they can be made effective enough that they could absorb nuclear attacks so totally that they would render nuclear weapons "impotent and obsolete," Ronald Reagan's dream for the SDI.

The purpose of nuclear planning remains the avoidance of nuclear war: deterrence. After the end of the Cold War, this purpose faded from public scrutiny, but the North Korean breakout and the possibility of other proliferators has renewed that concern and interest. In these circumstances, what can be done to make anti-proliferation and BMD efforts contribute to the overall goal of deterrence?

Each area could contribute to the effort, but would the prospects of success justify the expenditure of time and effort in the face of other national security demands for resources and energy? The answers are different depending on whether proliferation suppression or missile defense is the subject of examination.

Proliferation control has received the greatest attention recently because of the North Korean effort and the possibility Iran might renounce its agreement not to build nuclear weapons, an intent Iran vehemently denies. The question is what can be done to reinforce non-proliferation by potential nuclear possessors and possibly to reverse the actions of states like the DPRK that have crossed the nuclear weapons threshold.

Is the NPT an effective tool in preventing nuclear weapons spread? One can argue both ways. Positively, almost all countries are parties to the agreement and have, in the process, renounced their intention and right to build the weapons. One can argue, of course, that the treaty itself may have had little to do with this self-denial. Renouncing or defying NPT restrictions labels a country an international outlier, but if a country like India, Pakistan, or Israel decides its vital national security requires that it possess the arms, that resulting stigma does not override the perception of national need.

This creates a conundrum. Non-proliferation agreements reinforce the predilections of those with no interest in getting nuclear weapons, but may have little effect on those who may want to exercise the option. The solution to this dilemma is to convince those who may make or have made a positive weapons decision that they do not need to do so, in which case they can join the agreement and "denuclearize," in current parlance. At that point, however, it is arguable they have nothing to gain from joining NPT, since it does not protect them from anything.

A parallel form of reasoning surrounds the advocacy of missile defenses. The desire to protect one's country from a nuclear attack is clearly understandable and justifiable. Indeed, it can be argued that it would be irresponsible not to try, since the protection of the population from death and destruction is the most vital national interest. The problem, of course, is that nobody has successfully designed and built a BMD system that meets the very stringent requirement such a system has. Systems like THAAD may be able to destroy a very small launch against a state, but it could easily be overwhelmed by a large (or heavy) launch by a power with a large arsenal. Given the destructive capacities of a nuclear attack, the system would have to work almost perfectly the first time it was ever tried without an unambiguously realistic test in advance (how does a country simulate an attack by hundreds or thousands of weapons against it?).

The result is a dilemma not unlike that surrounding the NPT. No one can deny that the instinct to protect the population is a valid undertaking, but can it succeed? The United States has been actively invested in the attempt for well over a half-century and has not succeeded in any definitive way. The problem has been that hard to overcome. But what if it appears to succeed? Would possession of a BMD system make its possessor more assertive, even aggressive in its relations with others? Potential nuclear opponents of the United States appear to fear it would, and they have consistently tried to undercut the American program. What if they are correct, but that the belief in the system's effectiveness turns out to be a chimera?

Consequences: What to Do?

It has been the evolving dynamic of nuclear weapons since the United States and the former Soviet Union began to field large and growing arsenals of nuclear explosives on ballistic missiles against which there was (and is) no effective defense. The only way for humankind to avoid extinction in a radioactive nuclear holocaust has been to avoid such an event in the first place: deterrence. Anti-proliferation efforts like NPT have sought to contain the expansion of the problem, and missile defenses have sought to ameliorate its consequences, both with debatable effectiveness. Deterrence remains the only clear way to avoid Armageddon.

Is there an alternative? Theoretically, the safest world would be one in which nuclear weapons no longer exist. Nuclear disarmament has been advocated since the nuclear arms race blossomed, and Soviet and American leaders since Dwight Eisenhower and Nikita Khrushchev have declared that a nuclear war would be unacceptable. At Reykjavik, Iceland, in 1984, Soviet leader Mikhail Gorbachev and American president Ronald Reagan agreed in principle on nuclear disarmament in a private meeting, only to be intercepted and dissuaded by their aides (see Oberdorfer).

Disarmament also has its potential pitfalls. Nuclear weapons have been invented, and the knowledge of how to build them cannot be destroyed. In a disarmed world, the clandestine development of even a few nuclear arms could provide the cheater with much more leverage than a few weapons now give possessors. At the same time, the knowledge that conventional conflicts between nuclear powers could escalate has almost certainly limited recourse to violence in other forms. Would nuclear disarmament simply make the world safer for other forms of violence?

Avoiding nuclear war is arguably the highest national security priority of the United States and every other country in the world. The question of avoiding such a war, deterrence, has returned to center stage internationally due to the contemporary actions of the DPRK and possibly by other states. How does one reduce the resulting nuclear anxiety that panicked the citizens of Honolulu and the rest of us by extension? This chapter has presented two forms that disarmament reinforcement is currently proposed to take. Are either of them effective? Should U.S. strategy and policy implementing the strategic goal of nuclear war avoidance emphasize one or the other, or is neither avenue productive? If not, what are the alternatives to standing, however briefly, in the shadow of the mushroom-shaped cloud? What do you think?

Study/Discussion Questions

1. What is the rationale for non-proliferation efforts? What states have promoted it most strongly? Why?
2. What is the NPT? What kinds of differential obligations does it create for parties to it? What kinds of states have embraced or rejected it? Has it been successful?
3. What is ballistic missile defense? How is it supposed to work? What have been the major problems and barriers associated with achieving an effective BMD system?

4. What options are available through proliferation control and BMD to reinforce nuclear deterrence in the contemporary system? How does each contribute to the goal?
5. How are proliferation control and BMD related? Can they be combined in a deterrence strategy to deal with threats like those posed by states like North Korea? Does advocacy of disarmament play a role? What do you think the United States should do to enhance the stability of deterrence?

Bibliography

Bracken, Paul. *The Second Nuclear Age: Strategy, Danger, and the New Power Politics.* New York: St. Martin's Griffin, 2013.

Campbell, Kurt M., Robert J. Einhorn, and Michael B. Reiss (eds.). *The Nuclear Tipping Point: Why States Reconsider Their Nuclear Options.* Washington, DC: Brookings Institution, 2004.

Carter, Ashton, and Daniel N. Schwartz. *Ballistic Missile Defense.* Washington, DC: Brookings Institution, 1984.

Clark, Ronald W. *The Greatest Power on Earth: The International Race for Nuclear Supremacy from Earliest Theory to Three Mile Island.* New York: Harper and Row, 1980.

Debs, Alexandre, and Nunno P. Mentiero. *Nuclear Politics: The Strategic Case of Proliferation.* Cambridge Studies in International Relations. Cambridge, UK: Cambridge University Press, 2017.

Fry, Michael P., and N. Patrick Keatinge. *Nuclear Non-Proliferation and the Non-Proliferation Treaty.* London: Springer, 2011.

Guertner, Gary L., and Donald M. Snow. *The Last Frontier: An Analysis of the Strategic Defense Initiative.* Lexington, MA: Lexington Books, 1986.

Joyner, Daniel H. *Interpreting the Nuclear Non-Proliferation Treaty.* Oxford, UK: Oxford University Press, 2011.

Lieber, Kier A., and David G. Press. "The Rise of U.S. Nuclear Superiority." *Foreign Affairs* 85 (2) (March/April 2006), 42–54.

Oberdorfer, Don. *The Turn: From Cold War to a New Era: The United States and the Soviet Union, 1983–1990.* New York: Poseidon Press, 1991.

O'Reilly, Kelly P. *Nuclear Weapons and the Psychology of Political Leadership: Beliefs, Motivations, and Perceptions.* New York and London: Routledge, 2016.

Perkowich, George. "The End of the Proliferation Regime." *Current History* 105 (694) (November 2006), 355–62.

Ratcliff, Jonathan E. B. *Nuclear Proliferation: Overview, History, and Reference Guide.* New York: CreateSpace Independent Publishing, 2016.

Sagan, Scott D., and Kenneth N. Waltz. *The Spread of Nuclear Weapons: An Enduring Debate*. New York: W. W. Norton, 2012.

Snow, Donald M. *Nuclear Strategy in a Dynamic World: Policy for the 1980s*. Tuscaloosa: University of Alabama Press, 1981.

Sokolski, Henry (ed.). *Reviewing the Nuclear Non-Proliferation Treaty (NPT)*. Washington, DC and Carlisle, PA: U.S. Department of Defense and Strategic Studies Institute, 2012.

United Nations Office for Disarmament Affairs. *Treaty on the Non-Proliferation of Nuclear Weapons (NPT)*. New York: United Nations, 2018.

United States Department of State, Bureau of Arms Control. *Treaty between the United States of America and the Union of Soviet Socialist Republics on the Limitation of Anti-Ballistic Missile Systems*. Washington, DC: U.S. Department of State, May 26, 1972.

United States Government and U.S. Military. *Hitting a Bullet with a Bullet: A History of Ballistic Missile Defense (BMD)*. Washington, DC: Progressive Management, 2016.

6

Two Scorpions in a Bottle
Managing the DPRK Nuclear Threat

In a 1953 *Foreign Affairs* article, J. Robert Oppenheimer, the controversial theoretical physicist often referred to as the "father of the atomic bomb" said, "We may be likened to two scorpions in a bottle, each capable of killing the other, but only at the risk of its own life." The two scorpions were the United States and the Soviet Union, and the condition about which he worried was the decision by both to develop and field thermonuclear (fusion) warheads to add to arsenals that would be augmented by intercontinental ballistic means of delivery against one another's population. Both sides would soon be able to destroy the other. The only means of avoiding that fate was the knowledge that the initial attacker would be destroyed in retaliation—everyone would lose.

The analogy between that situation and the ongoing, episodic standoff between North Korea and the United States may be overblown, but it represents a real national security problem. The United States could physically destroy the Democratic People's Republic of Korea (DPRK) without suffering a similar fate. If the DPRK nuclear program continues, North Korean missiles might reach American soil, but the result would not approach the mutual devastation of the Cold War scorpions. Asian neighbors might suffer grievously (notably South Korea and Japan), but the United States would survive. Still, the possibility remains that the long nuclear peace since 1945 could be broken.

The crisis that crystalized in 2017–2018 is not entirely new. North Korea has pursued nuclear weapons since the 1950s, when DPRK leader Kim Il Sung authorized the pursuit of nuclear technology because the United States stationed weapons in South Korea aimed at the DPRK. The two countries have been at odds since the Korean War, and similar crises have occurred periodically ever since. The expansion of North Korea's nuclear program has made the debate increasingly shrill and alarmist. The result has not been to clarify the parameters of the debate or to advance solutions that might be mutually acceptable to all concerned. Rather, it has promoted often emotional, simplistic assertions on all sides.

The issue is more complex than a "simple" confrontation between a nuclear-armed DPRK and the potential victims of North Korean weapons use, notably the United States. Other countries directly affected by the DPRK program include the Republic of Korea (ROK or South Korea), Japan, and China. The PRC has served as the primary protector of the DPRK and fears the geopolitical consequences of a DPRK collapse and incorporation into the ROK (the most likely outcome of a collapse of the North Korean regime). The broader

65

international community is also affected because of their general opposition to nuclear proliferation. There is further international concern that the success of the North Koreans in facing down the Americans will reinforce the "Saddam Hussein Effect," thus encouraging more proliferation.

The current crisis is familiar to those who have followed the Korean situation over the years. Crises arise episodically, usually when the United States and South Korea conduct military exercises clearly designed against the DPRK, and the North Koreans respond with threats and bluster that lead to fears of escalation to war in which both sides accuse the other of being the precipitant. After some percolation, both sides back away from the brink and the situation reverts to "normal." Nothing is resolved, and it is not clear either side is serious about taking steps that might lead to some permanent resolution.

The result is a kind of ritual dance that has been played out episodically since the end of the Korean War in 1953. In the past, the consequences have been limited to the immediate Korean Peninsula, because the North Koreans could not carry the battle beyond that venue. The DPRK nuclear program has, however, widened the nature of the game dangerously. Does that possibility make finding a resolution more important than it has been in the past?

Perspectives on the Problem

Several international entities have interests in how the nuclear problem on the Korean Peninsula is resolved. The diversity and dispersion of motives each interested party holds is striking, making it difficult to reach common grounds for discussion and resolution. Five countries have prominent, important interests in this problem.

DPRK (North Korea)

The heart of the dispute, of course, is the North Korean weapons program, an initiative now in its third decade but which has accelerated greatly since Kim Jong Un came to power in 2011. The program has been pursued aggressively despite opposition from the international community, but the regime has remained determined to establish the DPRK as a full-scale nuclear power, and it has succeeded. For a country that is as marginal and poor as North Korea, their obsession may seem irrational given the quality of life in the country, yet the Kim regime has succeeded in making the DPRK a real nuclear power and has, in Sagan's view, transformed its geopolitical status. As he puts it, "North Korea no long poses a nonproliferation problem. It poses a deterrence problem."

Understanding why the DPRK is obsessed with nuclear prowess requires placing the country in perspective. North Korea is an artificial state that resulted from the 1945 expulsion of Japan from the peninsula and the establishment of what were supposed to be temporary occupation zones in 1945. Before the 1905 Japanese occupation, there was always one Korea; since 1945 there have been two. North Korea got the short end of the stick in this division—it was smaller, poorer, and had only the Soviet Union to aid in its development (not a Soviet specialty). The North invaded the South in 1950, and after the Korean War ended in 1953, the United States aggressively rebuilt and developed the ROK, while the DPRK languished as an extremely poor, backward totalitarian state. Over time the contrast has only become more dramatic: according to *2016 CIA World Factbook* figures, the population of South Korea is roughly double that of the North (forty-nine to twenty-five million); the GDP for the ROK is $1.67 trillion (thirteenth in the world); for the DPRK, GDP is $40 billion (106th in the world). The DPRK is a desperately poor country with a cruelly repressive regime that has always thrived on isolation and is loved by essentially no one outside its borders. The closest thing to an international friend it possesses is China, but that relationship (see below) is mostly instrumental for the Chinese. Reunification is a dream of many Koreans; the DPRK realizes that should that come, it would disappear the same way East Germany vanished in 1991.

North Korea is also geopolitically disadvantaged. It sits in the middle of a region of some of the most powerful, prosperous states in the world (the ROK, Japan, and China) with the United States lurking in the background as the primary outside power. Without nuclear weapons, the DPRK would make no impact on the international politics of East Asia.

The United States is near the top of the DPRK's list of enemies, with past experiences that are relevant to the current confrontation, notably its nuclear dimension. During the Korean War, for instance, some Americans hinted an interest in "salting" the DPRK-Chinese boundary with cobalt so that any troops entering the DPRK would be irradiated and killed. After the war ended with an armistice that has never been elevated to a peace agreement (the United States and the DPRK remain technically at war), the United States stationed nuclear weapons in the ROK as a threat against a renewed DPRK invasion until 1991. The nuclearization of the peninsula by the United States provided the conceptual seed for Kim Il Sung, the original North Korean leader, to begin thinking about his country as a nuclear power. In the contemporary condition, an added incentive for a nuclear capability is the existence of a large ROK military force, notably a reserve capability of 4.5 million.

Finally, there is a domestic political element for the North Korean regime. The DPRK is a truly wretched place where life is hard for the population, and anything that can divert the populace from its misery and increase their national pride is useful to the regime. Confrontation with the world's most powerful country inflates the pride of the citizenry while simultaneously justifying the continuing deprivation caused by pouring scarce resources that could be used to alleviate human suffering into nuclear weapons.

The result is that North Korea is a paranoid hermit, but one whose paranoia is not entirely unsurprising or unwarranted and which must somehow be dealt with to end the ongoing crisis. Put simply, without its nuclear weapons, the DPRK is a very remote, largely insignificant place surrounded by enemies. Nuclear weapons are its sole claim to international status that the Pyongyang regime has on which to hang its hat, and the heralding and saber rattling of its leadership is, in important ways, their way to achieve international notice. How much attention would the world pay to Kim Jong Un without his missile tests?

Abandoning the nuclear weapons program without some substituting basis of international recognition is a very difficult "sell" for the North Korean regime.

These perceptions create a unique DPRK strategic culture that was articulated over a half century ago by Kim Il Sung but which is hardly ever mentioned in official American discussions of the North Koreans. On April 14, 1965, Kim gave a speech ("On Socialist Construction in the Democratic People's Republic of Korea") in which he spelled out three fundamental principles of North Korean ideology under the principle of *Juche*, a concept normally translated as self-reliance. The principles are political independence, economic self-sustenance, and self-reliance in defense. All are designed to protect North Korean isolation and aloofness from the rest of the world. They remain the backbone of the DPRK's worldview—including the reinforcement of self-protection by possessing nuclear weapons. A policy designed to change North Korean behavior must start from determining how to moderate the juche principle of self-defense autonomy. It also creates an ideological foundation and continuity in DPRK policy that is at odds with the depiction of the current leadership as irrational "madmen." As Kang put it recently, "Kim Jung Un is no buffoon."

The United States

The connection between the United States and the DPRK derives from the Korean War, where the United States fought and basically twice defeated the DPRK (see Brodie or Snow and Drew for an explanation). Fighting ended with a ceasefire in 1953, and ever since the two countries have glowered at one another across the heavily militarized frontier at the 38th Parallel dividing the Koreas at Panmunjom, with no positive movement toward a permanent agreement ending hostilities. In 1976, they came close to war when two American soldiers were killed over the cutting down of two trees along the frontier.

American interests center not so much on dealings with North Korea as they do on the mischief the DPRK can create in the region, and more recently with the United States itself. The United States opposes the wretched DPRK human rights record and particularly the practice of imprisoning American visitors, but these are not the central concerns. The major U.S. interest is the stability and prosperity of the ROK, which is directly imperiled by enormous DPRK artillery capability aimed directly across the border, and especially at the roughly ten million residents of Seoul and the approximately twenty million more South Koreans within DPRK range. The United States would like to see a restoration of the peninsula to its historic condition as a single state, but it feels it must not endanger the ROK.

DPRK nuclear warheads and ballistic missile delivery systems create direct and personal American interest in North Korea. From the vantage point of Kim Jong Un, the program has been a significant success even if the DPRK never fires a weapon in anger at anyone (an act that would almost certainly result in its utter decimation). International approbation is a form of recognition, and unless sanctioning produces results that significantly hurt the elite (as opposed to the citizenry at large), they are probably tolerable. Threatening the United States puts the North Koreans more centrally in the spotlight—where they desperately crave to be—without necessarily imperiling them more than they were before.

The result is a dilemma for the United States. Matching the fiery rhetoric from Pyongyang frightens Americans with no visible effect on Pyongyang beyond more vituperative rhetoric. The two scorpions are in effect yelling at one another in the bottle; why is not clear. American insistence that the North Koreans denuclearize before an agreement is reached has never succeeded in the past and almost certainly will not now. This partially reflects a difference in what the two sides mean by denuclearization: the U.S. version is North Korea must dismantle its entire arsenal and program; the DPRK retorts that it means the United States must remove its military presence (including nuclear-capable forces) from the peninsula. It is a significant divide.

People's Republic of China

Chinese motives are geopolitical, tying the DPRK to overall Chinese aspirations in East Asia. The United States believes that China is the only country with sufficient leverage and influence to cause the North Koreans to back down from the nuclear confrontation, and that it is in their inherent interest to do so. The Chinese, however, see the outcome as a cornerstone of American acceptance of their dominant regional position, which requires American military withdrawal from the ROK. DPRK nuclear weapons are a bargaining chip in their strategy.

The relationship between China and the DPRK is complex and ambivalent. The Chinese have no love for or affinity with the DPRK regime, despite the fact both are nominally communist. The DPRK communist experiment has been such a dismal failure and the North Koreans' human rights record so appalling that the Beijing regime does not nurture close ties with it and regularly participates in largely rhetorical condemnations. At the same time, China is the only country with sizable economic relations with the DPRK, and PRC "volunteers" did aid the North Koreans in their war against the United States in the 1950s. The PRC would prefer a qualitatively different DPRK neighbor than they have, but they want there to be a DPRK.

The key to the DPRK-PRC relationship is their common boundary. The frontier between the two, largely defined by the Yalu River, is 885 miles, by far the DPRK's longest (its other boundaries are a roughly ten-mile frontier with Russia and roughly 149 miles with the ROK). The Chinese frontier was a critical part of the Korean War (the United States went to great efforts to try to keep Chinese forces from coming across it to join the fight), and literally millions of North Koreans daily cross the bridges over the Yalu River to work in PRC factories at very low wages.

For China, the border's security is the precondition for more active, effective Chinese efforts to bring pressure on the North Koreans. The PRC might not like the DPRK partner it has, but it is absolutely committed to the existence of a DPRK between themselves and South Korea. This insistence flows from a root national security interest of China: the avoidance of a hostile power on its border, a principle common to all states. This concern extends to Korean reunification.

China will entertain a unified Korea (which almost certainly would be dominated by the non-Communist ROK) if the Seoul regime is no longer propped up by an American military presence (see chapter 12 for a fuller discussion).

This dynamic affects the Chinese in the current crisis. They fear the collapse of the DPRK if juche-based self-defense causes a violent confrontation, because any climactic outcome would likely lead to ROK-dominated reunification. The effect could be an ROK on their border that was an effective Trojan horse for the United States. In addition, such a calamity would also likely result in the flight of millions of North Koreans across the frontier into China for economic reasons, creating a massive, unwelcome refugee problem.

Republic of Korea

South Korea is the most directly and intimately affected of all the states dealing with the DPRK nuclear program and has thus been the most active advocate of negotiations and a peaceful settlement. Moon states the matter succinctly and directly. "For South Korea, it [DPRK nuclear weapons] is an existential threat." In addition to the American presence, the major reason the North Koreans have historically felt the need for a robust military capability is to avoid domination militarily and economically by the South and ultimately being absorbed into a peninsula-wide Republic of Korea.

The peninsula has been one of the tensest, most militarized parts of the globe since 1953. Both sides mass huge military capabilities along the 38th Parallel that separates them, with the ROK side including twenty-eight thousand Americans as a "trip wire" in the event of a DPRK invasion south. The American presence irks the DPRK and symbolizes continued American antagonism against which they must defend as part of juche.

The ROK is a major party to the nuclear standoff in two ways. First, the issue of reunification is the major political stumbling block in peninsular politics. If (or when) Korea returns to its historic status as a single state, there will no longer be any basis for deep-seated antagonism between entities on the peninsula. Any solution that assuages Chinese concerns about the consequences of possible reunification must include assurances that the ROK will not create a hostile frontier with the PRC.

Second and more importantly in the current crisis, war on the peninsula would largely decimate both countries. It has long been at the heart of DPRK threats that should war occur, its fury would be first directed against the twenty-five million South Koreans within easy artillery range of DPRK weapons, an attack with unfathomable consequences for the South Koreans. War avoidance is thus a primary goal of the ROK, but it is at least partially subverted by the well-understood undercurrent of South Korea's desire to unite the peninsula as part of a democratic ROK.

Japan

The position of Japan on the nuclear threat in the area resembles that of the ROK. Japan is a close neighbor of the two peninsular states. At its closest point, it is only about two hundred miles from the main Japanese island of Honshu to part of the ROK. Japan and the DPRK are farther apart across the Sea of Japan, but all of Japan is vulnerable to a possible missile attack by the North Koreans. In the event of war, Japan could easily become the victim of North Korean attacks aimed either at Japanese capabilities and facilities or at the American military presence in Japan.

The Japanese situation is also different in other ways. For one thing, there is an element of strain and antagonism between Japan and Korea (notably the DPRK) that goes back to the forty-year occupation of the peninsula by Japan as part of the settlement of the Russo-Japanese War in 1905. That occupation was particularly brutal and left a strong residue of anti-Japanese sentiment that has dissipated more in the ROK than in the DPRK. Second, there is an obvious strong anti–nuclear weapons sentiment in Japan that is the direct legacy of World War II in the Pacific. One possible Japanese response to the DPRK nuclear program would be to develop and field its own nuclear forces, which they could physically do in a relatively short period of time. There is a large and understandable residual aversion to the weapons within the population. Japan is philosophically more committed to denuclearization than any other country in the East Asian region.

Policy Options

The DPRK nuclear problem poses a major strategic challenge for the United States introduced in chapter 3. American strategy based in acquisition deterrence is arguably irrelevant given their arsenal, their apparent commitment to maintain it, and the apparent lack of enthusiasm among others like China for trying to dismantle, as opposed to containing, it. The strategic problem is now employment deterrence, and it affects all parties.

Accepting that change is prefatory to choosing a policy option to pursue. What should the United States seek out of the resolution of the nuclear standoff on the peninsula? Is the U.S. insistence on nuclear disarmament by the North Koreans realistic, and if so, how does it deal with the DPRK ideology of juche? Does the United States simply attempt to impose, or force, the DPRK to abandon its program, and if it does, how is the DPRK to maintain its insistence on a self-reliant national security policy? Should the United States work harder to gain Chinese assistance in affecting an outcome, and what price is it willing to pay for that help? That price almost certainly includes a guarantee that the outcome will not include a potentially hostile Korea on its border. How does that assurance occur?

Approaches to the Problem

There are three main ways that the United States and those who support it can pursue this problem, each with different emphases and likely outcomes. One is *engagement,* an active attempt to initiate and participate in direct negotiations with the DPRK that began in 2018. The key "weapon" in such an approach should be the use of formal, quiet diplomacy. The second is the use of additional *sanctions* against the DPRK regime, using economic deprivations as a primary tool to force regime compliance. This is the heart of the 2017 UN sanctions resolution. The third is the use of *military options*. This is the most potentially destructive possibility. Each option deserves some consideration.

Adopting a strategic approach depends on the kind of problem that exists and how to accommodate it. The dominant view has been that the United States should aim its policy at reversing the DPRK program and returning North Korea to non-nuclear status, treating the situation as a reinstated acquisition deterrence exercise. The problem is that DPRK proliferation is a done deal: North Korea is a nuclear power, and no nuclear power has been forced to abandon an operational capability. Is the real problem how to influence how that program progresses, as the Chinese have suggested, or trying to find a compromise that might allow the North Koreans to take down their program while maintaining a sense of juche-based security for themselves? Indeed, is there any real alternative to such an approach?

Engagement must begin with a frank dialogue about the most basic concerns of all parties and a willingness to find ways to accommodate those concerns. In this case, the heart of disagreement is whether the DPRK should continue to develop its nuclear arsenal, freeze or reduce what it currently possesses, or disarm. Given their dire assessment of the threat they face, the North Koreans find disarmament unacceptable and view freezing with suspicion.

Is a negotiated settlement based in DPRK denuclearization possible? Given the centrality of the juche principle of self-reliance on defense and the apparent belief that nuclear deterrence is the only way to guarantee its security without outside help, getting the DPRK to abandon or scale back its nuclear forces in effect requires them to abandon the critical element of their secure national existence. The North Koreans know that no country that has fielded nuclear weapons has ever been attacked, which is clearly their national security goal. They do not view those events as unrelated. From their perspective, American demands that they denuclearize are very suspicious and potentially dangerous to them.

Influencing the DPRK

There are only two ways to convince the North Koreans to moderate their current position. One is to convince them they do not have to rely entirely on themselves for their safety. Is it possible, for instance, to imagine negotiating a regional agreement where the participating members form a mutual defense arrangement to defend one another, including the DPRK? China would have to be the military pivot of such an arrangement, and their agreement to bear such a burden would almost certainly have to include an agreement to maintain an independent DPRK that would not be reunited with the ROK. The South Koreans would be the key factor in such an agreement. To assuage the DPRK, the United States probably would not play a central security role and probably would have to sweeten the deal by loosening sanctions and even aiding DPRK economic development, another North Korean regime goal. It might also include an initiative to enter negotiations for a formal peace treaty ending the Korean War (also a DPRK priority), and even to remove the American military presence from the ROK.

The second and third options have been matters of public advocacy, especially in the United States. Severe economic sanctions against the regime have been in place for some time, but their effectiveness has been limited by two factors. The first is the juche principle of economic self-sustenance, which means there is comparatively little that can be added to a sanctions list that will greatly affect the North Koreans. Deprivation, moreover, has been a way of life in the DPRK, and the regime is reasonably inured to additional suffering of the population. Second, most of what little economic commerce the DPRK has is with China (about 73 percent of imports and 67 percent of exports). China broadly supports sanctions, but their enthusiasm is diluted by the fear of the consequences of DPRK collapse (reunification and a flood of refugees across the border). It is unclear that sanctions will be decisive in gaining DPRK support for ending the continuing crisis.

The threat of military action has, of course, been a staple of North Korean national security self-reliance for decades, but until recently, that threat was principally limited to mayhem against the ROK or Japan; attacking either one would have resulted in military counteraction that would clearly have left the DPRK the loser. The current crisis expands the threat both to the nuclear level and to additional targets, including American territories. The possession of an arsenal of thirty to sixty nuclear warheads (the generally accepted estimates) means the DPRK could wreak catastrophic destruction on the ROK and Japan before its destruction in retaliation, and missile delivery puts U.S. targets under the gun. The question is (and always has been) the circumstances in which the DPRK would *use*, as opposed to threatening to use, those weapons, which is an employment deterrence question. Starting a war may make no sense, but *possessing* a nuclear force may be entirely rational: it provides the DPRK a much more prominent place in the international system, and it reinforces national security self-reliance by raising the costs of attacking the country. This latter point is critical: any proposed solution that does not contain an ironclad affirmation of the juche principle is simply not going to be accepted by the North Koreans.

The final "option" is to do essentially nothing to move the situation to a more permanent, stable base. That has been the de facto choice in the past. Harsh rhetoric and blustery threats in both directions have been followed by retreating from the brink and resuming the status quo on both the peninsula and in U.S.-DPRK relations. That basic scenario essentially played out again in 2018, with the exceptions that the two national leaders were prominent figures and the South Koreans played a crucial mediating role. The approach has worked until now, but the margin for error is much smaller now with the possibility that a shooting conflict could escalate to nuclear exchange. Is that tolerable?

Consequences: What to Do?

What can alleviate this long-festering situation? There are two general approaches that can be taken to try to reach some closure, or at least accommodation, on the division: punitive or reconciliatory. The major punitive approaches have been toughened economic sanctions and the threat or possible employment of military force to compel DPRK compliance with international preferences. Both threats have been at the heart of most American discussions on the subject at various points in the dispute since 1953, and they are the most prominently advocated "solutions" today. Both tell the North Koreans to buckle under to outsider demands, in effect abandoning traditional DPRK policy based in juche. Unsurprisingly, the North Koreans show no enthusiasm for either and have resisted them. If that remains true, the dogged pursuit of either will likely fail. As Delury puts it, "Neither option would end well."

The other approach is reconciliatory, attempting to fashion an outcome where all sides feel their situation is enhanced by any agreement reached. The Japanese and South Koreans, for instance, need to believe they are no longer under the risk of aggression by the North Koreans, the Chinese must be assured that any outcome will not run the risk of placing a hostile country on their border in place of the DPRK, and the United States and the ROK must feel an enhanced security from possible DPRK nuclear provocations. Most pivotally, the DPRK must believe that an outcome enhances the three pillars of juche.

At the heart of any solution that might produce resolution are two basic elements: North Korean belief it is safe enough from outside threats that it can reduce the pace of its military expansion, and Chinese assurance that the outcome will not lead to reunification of the peninsula by the ROK and thus a potentially hostile power on its border. The two conditions are related. If the DPRK feels itself more at ease about its existence, it can lower its rhetoric and act in a less provocative manner that makes others feel less frightened of its nuclear weapons. China can aid in making the necessary assurances of that security if it is reassured that it is not abetting placing an enemy on its doorstep.

The vital first realization in this process is that DPRK behavior likely will not change if it is treated as an irrational rogue, but instead as a state with legitimate interests that begin with its own sense of security in a region where it is a small and, without nuclear weapons, vulnerable and largely inconsequential player. As Delury argues, "If the United States hopes to achieve peace on the Korean Peninsula, it should start finding ways to make Pyongyang feel more secure." At the same time, China is unlikely to become as active a change agent as the United States would like until it feels assured the process will not result in the hostile state on its border, the avoidance of which impelled them into the Korean War. These conditions may be necessary, but they may not be sufficient to produce stability. Even if they are accepted, that also leaves the question of how to reach agreement: through reconciliatory or punitive means.

What should be done? The question goes beyond the U.S.-DPRK confrontation. Internationally, continuation of the North Korean nuclear program weakens nuclear proliferation disincentives, and the apparent ability of North Korean weapons to fend off the demands of the United States, in effect to deter the Americans, may encourage others who fear the United States. The cost to the United States may be a drastically reduced military presence on the peninsula. Should the approach be how to disarm the DPRK or how to incorporate it into the deterrence system which has prevented nuclear weapons use since 1945? The June 12, 2018, meeting between Trump and Kim Jong Un produced a general agreement in principle to denuclearize the Korean situation, but it is by no means clear whether or how that agreement in principle can be translated into a resolution acceptable to both. The two scorpions can still bite one another and preventing that from happening is still an unsolved problem. What do you think should be done?

Study/Discussion Questions

1. Why have the two "scorpions in a bottle" been a national security lightning rod? Why is resolution of their standoff important?

2. The U.S./DPRK confrontation is complicated because of the number of parties involved and their conflicting interests. Who are the parties? What are their interests and how do they conflict?

3. Are the positions of the DPRK and PRC unreasonable from their perspectives? How should the United States deal with them?

4. Assess the U.S. demand for "de-nuclearizing" the Korean peninsula as a strategy. Does it increase U.S. national security?

5. What two approaches for dealing with DPRK nuclear weapons are available to the United States? Discuss each. Which better serves U.S. national security interests? Why?

Bibliography

Allison, Graham. "China vs. America: Managing the Next Clash of Civilizations." *Foreign Affairs* 95 (5) (September/October 2017), 80–89.

Brodie, Bernard. *War and Politics.* New York: Macmillan, 1973.

Central Intelligence Agency. *2016 CIA World Factbook.* Washington, DC: CIA, 2016.

Cha, Victor. *The Impossible State: North Korea, Past and Present.* New York: Ecco, 2013.

Cha, Victor, and David C. Kang. *Nuclear North Korea: A Debate on Engagement Strategies.* New York: Columbia University Press, 2010.

Christensen, Thomas J. *The China Challenge: Shaping the Choices of a Rising Power.* New York: W. W. Norton, 2015.

Delury, John. "Take Preventive War Off the Table: The Risks of Trump's Tough Talk." *Foreign Affairs Snapshot* (online), August 22, 2017.

———. "Trump and North Korea: Reviving the Art of the Deal." *Foreign Affairs* 96 (2) (March/April 2017), 2–7.

Juche: The Banner of Independence. Pyongyang, North Korea: Foreign Language Publishing House, 1977.

Kang, David. "The Wolf of Pyongyang: How Kim Jong Un Resembles a CEO." *Foreign Affairs Snapshot* (online), August 9, 2017.

Kim, Sung Chull, and Michael D. Cohen (eds.). *North Korea and Nuclear Weapons: Entering the New Age of Deterrence.* Washington, DC: Georgetown University Press, 2017.

Lankov, Andrei. "Changing North Korea: An Information Campaign Can Beat the Regime." *Foreign Affairs* 88 (6) (November/December 2009), 95–105.

————. *The Real North Korea: Life and Politics in the Failed Stalinist Utopia*. Oxford, UK: Oxford University Press, 2014.

Moon, Katherine H. S. "Caught in the Middle: The North Korean Threat Is Ultimately Seoul's Problem." *Foreign Affairs Snapshot* (online), September 1, 2017.

Oberdorfer, Don, and Robert Carlin. *The Two Koreas: A Contemporary History.* Third Ed. New York: Basic Books, 2014.

Oppenheimer, J. Robert. "Atomic Weapons and Foreign Policy." *Foreign Affairs* 31 (2) (July 1953), 529.

Pollack, Jonathan D. *No Exit: North Korea, Nuclear Weapons, and International Security.* New York: Routledge, 2011.

Robinson, Michael E. *Korea's Twentieth Century Odyssey.* Honolulu: University of Hawaii Press, 2007.

Sagan, Scott. "The North Korean Missile Test: Why Deterrence Is Still the Best Option." *Foreign Affairs Essay* (online), September 10, 2017.

Snow, Donald M. *Regional Cases in U.S. Foreign Policy.* Second Ed. Lanham, MD: Rowman & Littlefield, 2018, especially chapter 3.

Snow, Donald M., and Dennis M. Drew. *From Lexington to Baghdad and Beyond: War and Politics in the American Experience.* Armonk, NY: M. E. Sharpe, 2010.

Wertz, Daniel, and Chelsea Gannon. *A History of U.S.-DPRK Relations.* Washington, DC: National Committee on North Korea, 2015.

7

The Great Satans

The United States, Iran, and Nuclear Weapons

The United States and Iran have had a tempestuous, schizophrenic relationship since the end of World War II. They first closely encountered one another shortly after the war as both the Soviet Union and the United States attempted to control the oil flow from the Peacock Kingdom. During the quarter-century rule of Shah Reza Pahlavi, the two countries were close allies: American advisors were highly visible architects of the Shah's modernization program, and Iranian students and military were ubiquitous presences at U.S. colleges and military facilities.

It all dissolved in 1979, when the Iranian Revolution forced the Shah from power and into medical exile in the United States and replaced his rule with the Shiite theocracy led by the Ayatollah Ruhollah Khomeini. When the United States refused to deport the Shah (who was in an American hospital dying of cancer) back to Tehran, Iranians stormed the U.S. Embassy grounds in Tehran, seized it, and held the staff hostage for 444 days. Since then, the two countries have viewed themselves as virtually implacable adversaries. Although the term was first coined by the Iranians to refer to the United States, the two countries have viewed one another as "great Satans" ever since.

The enmity between these two states is one of the great anomalies of modern international politics. Since 1979, both the United States and Iran have come to view themselves as implacable enemies for reasons that arose out of the overthrow of the Shah and the hostage taking. There are good reasons these events caused enmity between the two countries, some of which had been festering and growing in the preceding years. The Iranian Revolution that began with demonstrations across Iran in 1978 was quintessentially an anti-Shah outpouring directed at least partly at destroying the growing secularization and modernization of the country, a process in which the United States had been a major architect and symbol. The United States was associated with pro-Shah forces and, after Pahlavi fled the country, he went to New York for medical treatment of the cancer that eventually killed him, under U.S. protection. The Iranian seizure of the embassy in Tehran was, at heart, intended to force the Americans to remand the Shah to the custody of the Revolutionary government, a certain death sentence for the King of Kings. The occupation was excessively long, highly publicized, and humiliating for the United States, and added to the growing enmity between the countries. Both sides contributed to converting an exceedingly close and amicable relationship into one of hatred and rivalry.

It has been forty years since those events, and the adversarial relationship remains. Some level of lingering malice is understandable. Iran, for instance, has been a radical religious dictatorship since 1979, a condition that may be weakening. It has used the United States as a chief whipping boy on which to blame many of its ills, and it does support groups that are acknowledged enemies of the United States and Israel like Hezbollah. Opposition to its old ally has become a bedrock part of U.S. Middle Eastern policy, and anti-Iranian rhetoric from the American political right matches inflammatory rants from Tehran. The two countries, once in deep political embrace, cannot seem to get over calling one another the devil.

The result is an anomaly in major power relations. History and politics culminating in 1979 derailed the most intimate, stable relations between the Americans and the Iranians. The U.S. superpower and the Iranian pivotal state acted in concert to manage the region's one overwhelming asset, petroleum, and the result was a stability that has not been seen since in the area. This stunning reversal raises three questions. Why did it happen? What is the status of the U.S.-Iran relationship and what, if anything, can be done to change it? How might this affect both the Middle East and especially the nuclear proliferation equation?

Perspectives on the Problem

Post–World War II politics has so much to do with the bizarre nature and evolution of U.S.-Iranian relations that one must begin with it to understand the status and prospects of those relations moving forward. The centerpiece of this evolution was U.S. relations with the Shah, which can be divided into three distinct periods, each contributing a different part of the current level of distrust and animosity. The three periods are the rise of the Shah to power in the early 1950s, the reign of the Shah from 1954 to 1979, and the fall of the Shah as the major event of the Iranian Revolution of 1979. Each involves extensive interactions between Iranians and Americans that help define the current animosity both feel toward the other.

The Rise, Fall, and Return of the Shah

Contemporary U.S. relations with the second oldest continuous civilization in the world were born in the aftermath of World War II. During the war, Iran had been a political football between the antagonists—principally Germany and the Soviet Union—over access to and control of Iran's petroleum reserves, the second largest in the world. When the war ended, the Soviets moved into northern Iran to establish puppet regimes that would facilitate their control of Iranian oil. The United States led opposition to these moves and succeeded in causing a Soviet retreat. American motives at the time were largely defined in terms of guaranteed access to oil by American oil companies.

This period brought the United States into intimate relations with Reza Pahlavi, the Shah of Iran who was America's second most important Middle Eastern ally (after Israel) for over a quarter-century. The Shah had succeeded his father (Reza Shah) in 1941 and became the country's ruler after the war.

Due to alleged corruption in the regime, he was removed from office in 1951, and in the country's first and only fully free elections held that year, Mohammad Mosaddegh was chosen overwhelmingly as prime minister. Among his first acts was nationalization of the Iranian oil industry to assure that its profits primarily benefited Iranians.

This act brought the Americans and Iranians into conflict. American oil policy was largely controlled by Western oil companies and their political supporters, most famously the Dulles brothers (see Kinzer, *All the Shah's Men*, for a detailed account). Alleging that the nationalization suggested Mosaddegh was a communist, the Americans and the British launched a clandestine operation against the regime that resulted in a coup that toppled him from power. The coup also returned the Shah to power in 1954.

Removing Mosaddegh had two large consequences on long-term U.S.-Iranian relations. First, pro-democratic forces in Iran blamed the United States for overthrowing Mosaddegh. To this day, whenever the United States chides the Iranians for their failure to move back to democracy, the Iranians remind the Americans who was responsible for overthrowing their only democratically elected government—in effect accusing the United States of hypocrisy. Second, the American role paved the way for a grateful Shah to return to power in Tehran, and the Shah and the United States were politically joined at the hip for the remainder of the Shah's reign. Practically, if one opposed the Shah, one also probably opposed the Americans.

Rule of the Shah (with American Help)

Once he returned to power, the Shah (widely considered a U.S. puppet by Iranians) embarked on an ambitious reform program to transform Iran into a major world power: a return to the glory of the Persian Empire. The chief vehicle for this resurgence was westernization and modernization of the Iranian economy and its military, a program rejected by Mosaddegh earlier. Iran required outside help to accomplish this transformation paid for by its oil revenues. The United States was only too happy to help.

The heart of the program was something called the White Revolution, a series of reforms intended to make Iranian society and its economy thoroughly Western and thus competitive with the Western democracies. This transformation produced a westernized middle class and a technological elite, but it alienated two major segments of the population: the largely rural peasantry that was displaced from its small landholding and forced into squalid urban ghettoes where their lives were generally worse than before, and the power base of the conservative Shiite religious base and its leadership, who watched in horror as Islamic ways were pushed aside by a profligate, authoritarian secular government. The peasant base was progressively alienated, and the religious leadership provided a voice for their discontent that eventually found full expression in the stern visage of Ayatollah Khomeini.

The United States was heavily involved in this transformation. American consultants and technical personnel swarmed across the country to aid in modernization, and Iranian students flooded American universities and colleges and returned home highly Americanized (not necessarily a compliment among Iranians). The American and Iranian militaries cooperated closely under a mutually beneficial bargain. The Americans equipped the Iranians with state of the art systems and assistance, and in return, the Iranians secured the Persian Gulf to make sure the oil flowed unimpeded to Western markets.

Much of this happy relationship was self-delusional. As Tehran and its environs progressively came to resemble the West, the implicit assumption was that the Shah's program was progressing with popular support. The Shah's government, however, was harshly authoritarian and repressive. The symbol of this darker side was SAVAK, the Shah's secret police, who maintained order by repressing (including torturing and killing) dissidents and sending others into exile. It also provided the American CIA with virtually all its data on what was happening in the country, discouraging independent U.S. intelligence collection, and depicted a level of support for the Shah's rule that was simply false. As the 1970s progressed, opposition built that was unrecognized by the Shah's government or its American enthusiasts. As the decade moved toward its conclusion, it erupted like a volcano, burying the hated Shah and the equally hated Americans in its flow.

The Revolution and Its Effects

Very few Americans, including its leaders, saw the Iranian Revolution coming. American officials talked to their Iranian counterparts and read rosy intelligence reports written by SAVAK. They did not recognize the seething resentment of the masses against the Shah's program and their consequent hatred of the Shah and, by extension, his American allies.

What became the revolution began with demonstrations against the Shah in Iranian towns and cities that gradually moved toward Tehran in 1978. The international community, accustomed to the "firm" rule of the regime, waited patiently for the Shah to take decisive action to quell the dissent, but it was not forthcoming. It has been speculated that Pahlavi, who was receiving chemo treatments for the cancer that would kill him, was too debilitated to make decisions, which no one else dared take without his permission. The demonstrations became larger and more frequent and the Shah's power faded. In January 1979 the Shah announced he was leaving the country on vacation. Everyone knew he was really going into exile.

Within days of the Shah's departure, revolutionary succession began. Khomeini returned to Tehran from exile, and the competition over who would rule ensued in the upcoming months. After some infighting and maneuvering among factions, the conservative religious factions succeeded and declared the Islamic Republic of Iran. The transformation of Iran from America's closest regional Islamic ally to its primary adversary had begun. The two major symbolic events of this transformation were the demand by the Iranians for the return of the Shah to Iranian custody for trial for his alleged atrocities over the years and the Iranian seizure and holding hostage of the American embassy in Tehran.

Policy Options

The legacy of American-Iranian interaction between the end of World War II and the Iranian Revolution created a basic toxicity that has dominated relations since. Both sides have contributed to the malaise and have acted, particularly rhetorically, to make matters worse and to virtually assure that animosity does not abate. To most Americans, the vision of Iran is the stern, unforgiving scowl of Khomeini, the proclamation of the United States as the Great Satan, and the forlorn picture of an American hostage in Tehran that opened the nightly news on television throughout the 444 days of the crisis. To many Iranians, the Americans were the vehicle of destruction of their conservative religious society and the sponsors and chief supporters of the hated Shah.

These mutually held images obscure what had been a stabilizing strategic situation for a quarter-century. While the Shah ruled, the Persian Gulf area was politically favorable to American petroleum interests. The Sunni-Shiite divide, with the Saudis leading one faction and the Iranians the other, was simply not a problem when the region's largest, most pivotal state was also its major power. The Arabs of the region did not like the non-Arab Persians, but there was little they could do about it. Middle Eastern conflict was the Arab-Israeli conflict (see chapter 8), not the Persian Gulf and the non-Israeli part of the greater Levant.

Policy options available to the United States regarding Iran must begin with the question of what kind of Middle East best serves American interests. As the Middle Eastern country with the area's largest population at over eighty-one million, Iran cannot be ignored in regional terms. The dual facts that it is also the largest Shiite, non-Arab state (Iranians are ethnically mostly Indo-European Persians) and a major supporter of Shiite causes (e.g., Shiite rebels in Yemen and Palestine) and even terrorist groups like Hezbollah make it the major opponent of Sunni-supported causes which the Saudis generally sponsor unofficially through mechanisms such as private Saudi donations. The result is considerable regional turmoil, a situation that has historically been opposed by the United States as dangerous to Israel.

The three pillars of historic U.S. Middle Eastern policy all touch Iran. The first has always been access to Middle Eastern oil. Iran is the region's second leading producer, although this priority is receding somewhat as the United States moves toward energy independence. The second is the security of Israel, which has changed since the Israeli development of nuclear weapons: no Islamic state has directly challenged Israel since 1973. Iran does assist terrorist groups attacking the Israelis. The third was exclusion of Soviet influence. Recent Russian activism in Syria and dealings with regional powers like Turkey indicate this problem has not gone away entirely.

Contemporary barriers to more normalized relationships between America and Iran can be grouped in four categories. The most dramatic has been nuclear weapons, specifically attempts to avoid Iranian acquisition of the capability. The second is geopolitics, the problem created for the region and beyond of the regional confrontation between the Iranian- and Saudi-led coalitions for sway within the region. The third is the perpetual concern with petroleum, the major source of both wealth and conflict within the region. Fourth is the political evolution of the Iranian Revolutionary system to something with which the United States could feel more comfortable.

Nuclear Weapons and Proliferation

The possibility that Iran might decide to develop nuclear weapons, which they are certainly capable of doing, has been a major international, and especially regional, concern since the Iranian Revolution. The country has a significant cadre of nuclear scientists (many of whom were educated in the United States) and a developed nuclear energy industry that Iran's opponents fear they might decide to "upgrade" to weapons status. Iran is a member of the NPT and has never publicly shown any indication of withdrawal, but unease with the more radical positions of the Iranian Revolutionary government raise doubts about Iran's trustworthiness. Israel, the region's only nuclear power, is particularly concerned about losing its nuclear monopoly and the virtually absolute military hegemony it provides.

Why might Iran "go nuclear"? One major motivation would include the prestige of being a nuclear power and thus the indisputably most powerful state in the region. A second would be deterrence. Like all the other Islamic states of the Middle East, Iran lives under the shadow of the Israeli arsenal and the implied threat it represents to their existence. Iranian nuclear weapons might create a mutual deterrence relationship between the two countries, which Israel opposes on arguably hypocritical grounds.

The great regional and international fear associated with Iranian nuclear weapons development is the danger of making the precarious Middle East situation even more volatile and dangerous than it already is. Iranian nuclear weapons would almost certainly trigger the development of a Sunni bomb by a country like Saudi Arabia, with the already existing Pakistani arsenal and program as a prime candidate for the project. The prospect of Israel, Iran, and Saudi Arabia all having nuclear weapons is frightening in a geopolitical landscape as volatile as the Middle East. Apologists for Iran argue that Israel has already started the problem (which is true), but others argue nuclear weapons in Iranian hands would only make it worse. The special place that protection of Israel has in the United States makes this regional horror scenario an American national security problem as well.

To demonstrate their disinterest in becoming a nuclear power, Iran negotiated a treaty with the world's major powers, the so-called 5+1 group (the five permanent members of the United Nations Security Council plus Germany). They concluded an agreement under which Iran promised not to develop nuclear weapons and to open its nuclear facilities to international inspection without prior notice or constraint. This agreement, known as JCPOA (Joint Comprehensive Plan of Action), was signed on April 2, 2015, in Vienna by the 5+1 powers plus Iran and the European Union with a fifteen-year duration intended to prohibit Iranian nuclear development for at least that long.

Reflecting the malaise of U.S.-Iranian relations, objections to the agreement and calls for the United States to remove itself from it came from the U.S. political right. The opposition argued that Iran cannot be trusted to live up to its obligations under the JCPOA and that it has cheated on inspections requirements. These objections paralleled Israeli concerns and allegedly caused President Trump to remove the United States from the JCPOA on May 8, 2018, an action he could legally take because it was negotiated as an executive agreement rather than a treaty. Had it been a treaty, withdrawal would have required senatorial acquiescence (see Mulligan); Trump's withdrawal did not void the agreement with the other parties but could have negative repercussions for improving U.S.-Iranian relations. The future of the agreement is a matter of debate.

Geopolitics and Oil

The second and third concerns are related. The geopolitical importance of the Middle East, and especially the Persian Gulf area, to the United States has always revolved almost exclusively around access to petroleum from the region. Throughout the reign of the Shah, Iran acted as essentially the American proxy guaranteeing the unfettered flow of oil from the Shiite majority countries at the top of the Persian Gulf (Iran and Iraq) and the Sunni littoral from places like Saudi Arabia and Kuwait. The area was geopolitically important, but it posed no particular national security threat for the United States.

The Iranian Revolution and its aftermath changed that situation dramatically. Among other things, it severed the geopolitical, including military, relationship between the United States and Iran. The Iranian armed forces not only ceased to provide protection for Western oil, they became a threat to that flow. Additionally, the access to Iranian, and Iraqi, oil was denied to the West, making Western consumers more dependent on reserves from the states along the Arabian Peninsula and elsewhere globally. This in turn caused a change in the geopolitical priorities of the Americans. With no "deputy" to enforce secure access to oil, the United States was forced to take up that role personally in the form of a large, continuing naval presence reinforced by ground contingents that remain in place to this day. These military assets were physically based in the Sunni states, who were increasingly at odds with the Iranian Shiites, creating a de facto tilt of American policy from the Shiites of Iran (and Iraq) to the Sunni states, a realignment with no religious base for the United States one way or the other. As the Sunni-Shia rift has widened and intensified, the United States has found itself effectively "pro-Sunni," a position which makes little sense otherwise but is reinforced by the militancy of the Iranian Revolution. Israel has also begun to move toward the Sunni Arabs, a development that will undoubtedly increase pressure from pro-Israeli Americans to avoid contact with Iran. How durable that relationship will prove to be is problematical.

The current Sunni-Shiite confrontation (seen vividly in places like Yemen) is not an American concern, except in two senses. One is Israel: does the outcome affect the viability and security of Israel? Some Sunni states have moderated their opposition to the Israelis presumably to create the appearance of a connection to the Israelis and thus the Americans. The other sense of involvement surrounds access to petroleum. If the United States and its closest allies continue to rely on

Persian Gulf oil, they are dependent on the region and thus retain some stake in regional geopolitics. That dependency is gradually disappearing and in effect freeing the United States of that geopolitical dependency. I have argued (in *The Middle East, Oil, and the U.S. National Security Policy*) that this changing circumstance creates an opportunity for a rethinking of American national security interests in the region, and by extension of U.S.-Iranian relations.

Internal Iranian Politics

Iranian politics are volatile. All three of the political strains that have been forces in Iran since the end of the Second World War are present. The authoritarianism of the Shah is reflected in the harsh, repressive actions of the religious hierarchy that has effectively run the country since 1979. The Shah's repression and terror was motivated by his vision of a return to Persian glory, with the Shah riding astride that engine of renewal. The tyranny of the Shiite clergy is different in its object (some form of religious purity), but not in terms of political means. The heart of the Iranian Revolution has been religious purification and has manifested itself in harsh, puritanical standards and the suppression—including killing—of remaining secular elements from the democratic and secularizing periods. Political democracy is the third element, the legacy of the Mosaddegh era. It has growing support among the young in Iran but has not found the kind of forceful uniting figure to push it into power.

The theocratic and democratizing threads are locked in a competition for control of the political system, and the outcome of that struggle is not yet clear. The structure of that competition pits the head of state, Supreme Leader Ali Khamenei, in competition with the head of government, Hassan Rouhani. Khamenei's official portfolio is limited, but he is recognized as the leading religious figure in the country, which effectively puts him in charge of the revolutionary mechanisms (e.g., the Republican Guard) that enforce the militant Shiism of the revolution, which often includes suppression of secular, and hence democratic, advocates.

The United States would clearly prefer the triumph of democratizing elements but can do relatively little to influence movement toward a democratic system with which it might develop better relations. The United States and the religious right are at basic odds due to American support of the Shah and his assault on religious purity and power. The religious revolutionary sector did, after all, coin the phrase "great Satan" to describe the United States. Because of its complicity in the overthrow of Mosaddegh, there is some reluctance among democratic elements to allow themselves to be associated with the Americans, although many of the changes they favor are compatible with traditional American values. Given this legacy, the most the United States can reasonably do is to cheer very quietly for the democratizing force in the country. Anything more would clearly be counterproductive.

Consequences: What to Do?

The question of what the United States should do in its relations with Iran begins with American strategic interests in that country and region. Because the Middle

East is so divided politically, the American relationship with each of the major players—effectively Iran, Israel, and Saudi Arabia—redounds in its relations with the others and with the kind of Middle East it promotes in the process. Those relations have largely been zero-sum: support for one means opposition to and from the others. This creates the American strategic dilemma, because the historic American national interest has been in promoting regional peace and stability. Until very recently, that preference has been driven by oil; now nuclear weapons have entered the calculus.

The effect is that any U.S. policy discussion about Iran must also account for the impact on the other U.S. partners and regional security. There are two major concerns: relations with Sunni states, including American actions and pronouncements about points where the Sunni and Shiite states come into conflict, and relations with Israel. Current policy tilts heavily toward the Sunni states led by Saudi Arabia and the Netanyahu government of Israel.

The lightning rod in current relations is alleged Iranian nuclear ambitions. The Iranians deny any interest in becoming proliferators and negotiated the 2015 agreement to demonstrate this intent. The American government and Israel believe they are lying. In leaving the JCPOA, the Trump administration cited what it considers loopholes in the agreement, Iranian perfidy, and other objectionable Iranian behavior unrelated to nuclear weapons. Israel simply fears a regional nuclear competitor.

The United States suggested shortly after its withdrawal from JCPOA that it would consider rejoining if the Iranians met several conditions. American secretary of state Michael Pompeo announced these conditions in a May 21, 2018, speech summarized by *Al Jazeera* the next day that listed twelve demands. Only four of these related to Iranian nuclear weapons. The rest dealt with the cessation of Iranian activism elsewhere in the Middle East from Syria to Yemen to Afghanistan and support for terrorist organizations assaulting Israel. All were arguably legitimate concerns, but they had little to do with the JCPOA. Most are more clearly related to Israeli than American interests (unless one considers the two the same).

Do these policies serve American strategic interests in the region? In recent months, there has been a gradual warming of Israeli relations, with one recent *Foreign Affairs Snapshot* article quoting Israel's Lt. Gen. Gadi Eizenkot describing the "moderate" Arab states, notably Saudi Arabia (how the Saudis can be described as "moderate" politically is an interesting question), adding to the implicit union of the United States with the Sunni cause. With American addiction to Saudi oil gradually decreasing, it is hard to see how this "tilt" serves any visible U.S. interest. These same "moderate" Sunni states, after all, helped finance IS through private citizen contributions to the caliphate; there is no public evidence that Iranians did anything like that. The Palestinian question, raised in the next chapter, is also not one where support for the Iranians (who do support Hezbollah) or the Sunnis has appeared to aid the Palestinian cause. These policies arguably do promote Israeli interests, but are American and Israeli national security interests identical?

What would a changed policy toward Iran do to the pursuit of U.S. interests in peace and stability in the region? The heart of any change would have to be aimed at improving, even normalizing, relations between the two countries. The major American concession would be a relaxation of sanctions against Iran that originated in the reaction to the hostage crisis, and which currently limit interaction because of alleged Iranian ties to terrorism and the threat of a nuclear weapons breakout. The sanctions primarily impose American economic, including financial, isolation of Iran from the United States and the entreaty for other countries to follow suit. These restrictions certainly adversely affect life in Iran, creating some incentives to respond favorably to any American attempt to improve relations. During the IS Caliphate crisis, the Iranians in turn offered to assist in dispatching IS, a proposal that was never formally accepted.

The dynamics and substance of improving relations would require a period of adjustment with some uncertain outcomes. From the Iranians, a lowering of inflammatory rhetoric toward the United States and Israel would be a good start, but it is impeded by the cleric-secularist struggle for power. Rouhani would agree to this condition; Khamenei currently would not. From the United States, the possible relaxation of Iranian access to monetary assets still frozen in the United States (some were released as part of the nuclear deal) would provide incentives for the Iranians to cooperate as well.

Why would the United States want to improve these relations? The simple answer is that it would provide an avenue for the United States to take a more neutral stance on the region's volatile geopolitics, and that this ability would promote the peace and stability in the region that has been a historic pillar of U.S. Middle Eastern policy. The process would clearly be opposed by those—notably the Saudis and Israelis—who benefit from American-Iranian antipathy, and they and their supporters would condemn any movement as destabilizing. They might be right, but they might also be self-servingly wrong. During the rule of the Shah, America interacted positively with both sides. The current political or military situation is not analogous, but it is hard to argue the United States' position in the region is better now than it was then.

A more even-handed policy does not have to be isolationist in the America-First sense of U.S. global retreat from world leadership, nor to represent any abdication of other American commitments, such as those with the Israelis. Why the United States should prefer the Arabs over the Persians (which is a basic underlying division in the region), or why the Israelis should be so much more concerned about Iranian-sponsored terrorists than Arab-sponsored terrorists is not clear: Iran, after all, was closer to Israel under the Shah than were the Arabs. The differences between Sunnism and Shiism do not affect Americans in any important way, and anything a less partisan U.S. stance on this divide could contribute could conceivably lower the regional temperature marginally, which might be beneficial.

The issues that a change in U.S.-Iranian relations raise are clearly complex, difficult, unpredictable, and as such, well beyond solution in this brief depiction. Since 1979, fundamental, enduring enmity between the two countries has been the norm, and regional actors and their supporters have feasted on the division for their own ends. American politicians have followed suit, and most of us simply think of the Iranians as the implacable "bad guys" in the region. Is it time to begin to rethink that position? What do you think?

Study/Discussion Questions

1. What is the derivation of the idea of U.S.-Iranian relations as between the "great Satans"? Why is 1979 crucial to this evolution? Why has the gulf between the two countries become anomalous?

2. The period of the Shah's rule is critical in U.S.-Iranian relations. Using the three-fold division in the text, how did it serve to define post-1979 relations? Specifically, how did it contribute to anti-Americanism in Iran?

3. What are basic American interests in the Middle East? Does the enmity between the United States and Iran contribute to securing those interests or does it detract from that goal?

4. Discuss the nuclear weapons component of U.S.-Iran relations. Include the JCPOA and subsequent developments in the process.

5. How do the politics of Middle Eastern oil and internal Iranian political evolution contribute to the state of American-Iranian relations? Discuss.

6. Should the United States consider changing its relations with Iran? Why or why not?

Bibliography

Ananat, Abbas. *Iran: A Modern History.* New Haven, CT: Yale University Press, 2016.

Aslan, Reza. *No God but God: The Origins, Evolution, and Future of Islam.* New York: Random House Trade Paperbacks, 2011.

Axworthy. Michael. *A History of Iran: Empire of the Mind.* New York: Basic Books, 2016.

Bakhtiari, Bahman. "Iran's Conservative Revival." *Current History* 106 (696) (January 2007), 11–16.

Coates-Ulrichsen, Kristian. *The Changing Security Dynamics of the Middle East.* Oxford, UK: Oxford University Press, 2018.

Cooper, Andrew Scott. *The Fall of Heaven: The Pahlavis and the Final Days of Imperial Iran.* New York: Henry Holt, 2016.

Ehteshami, Anoushiravan. "The Middle East's New Power Dynamic." *Current History* 108 (722) (December 2009), 395–401.

Esfandiari, Haleh. "Reform or Revolution? Iran's Path to Democracy." *Foreign Affairs* 97 (1) (January/February 2018), 143–49.

Goldberg, Jeffrey. "How Iran Could Save the Middle East." *Atlantic* 304 (4) (July/ August 2009), 66–68.

Gonzalez, Nathan. *Engaging Iran: The Rise of a Middle East Power and America's Strategic Choice.* Westport, CT: Praeger Security International, 2007.

Housavian, Sayed Shahir Shahidsaless. *Iran and the United States: An Insider's View on the Failed Past and Road to Peace.* London: Bloomsbury Academic, 2014.

Jervis, Robert. "Getting to Yes with Iran: The Challenges of Coercive Diplomacy." *Foreign Affairs* 92 (1) (January/February 2013), 105–15.

Kaplan, Robert D. "Living with a Nuclear Iran." *Atlantic* 306 (2) (September 2010), 70–72.

Khosravi, Shahram. "The Precarious Status of Working-Age Men in Iran." *Current History* 116 (794) (December 2017), 355–59.

Kinzer, Stephen. *All the Shah's Men: An American Coup and the Roots of Middle Eastern Terror.* Second Ed. New York: Wiley, 2008.

————. *Iran, Turkey, and America's Future*. New York: Times Books, 2010.

"Mike Pompeo Speech: What Are the 12 Demands Given to Iran?" *Al Jazeera* (online), May 22, 2018.

Mulligan, Stephen P. *Withdrawal from International Agreements: Legal Framework, the Paris Agreement, and the Iran Nuclear Agreement*. Washington, DC: Congressional Research Service, February 9, 2017.

Parsa, Misagh. *Democracy in Iran: Why It Failed and How It Might Succeed*. Cambridge, MA: Harvard University Press, 2016.

Sick, Gary G. *All Fall Down: America's Tragic Encounter with Iran*. New York: Random House, 1985.

Snow, Donald M. *The Middle East, Oil, and the U.S. National Security Policy: Intractable Problems, Impossible Solutions*. Lanham, MD: Rowman & Littlefield, 2016.

————. "Pivotal States: Confronting and Accommodating Iran." In Donald M. Snow, *Cases in International Relations*, Sixth Ed. New York: Pearson, 2015.

Waltz, Kenneth N. "Why Iran Should Get the Bomb." *Foreign Affairs* 91 (4) (July/August 2012), 2–5.

Wood, Graeme. "Iran: Among the Mullahs." *Atlantic* 305 (1) (January 2010), 15–16.

Yaalon, Moshe, and Leehe Friedman. "Israel and the Arab States: A Historic Opportunity to Normalize Relations." *Foreign Affairs Snapshot* (online), January 26, 2018.

Zaborski, Jason. "Deterring a Nuclear Iran." *Washington Quarterly* 28 (3) (Summer 2005), 153–68.

II

GEOGRAPHIC SPOTLIGHTS

National security policies and strategies are responses to challenges to national interests that the country faces. Most, but not all, of these have a geographic focus, and it is conditions or challenges from different entities, normally other states, that present the challenges with which that policy must deal. The purpose of the six chapters in this part of the text is to examine some prominent examples of places toward which it is necessary to formulate policy.

There are three different foci of the various chapters. Three cases deal with the part of the world that has most engaged the United States, the Middle East. Two chapters address ongoing security challenges posed by American Cold War adversaries, Russia and China. All five of these cases deal with what almost all observers consider vital American interests with at least some traditional military content or potential. The final chapter offers a contrast. It deals with American security policy toward the enormously diverse continent of Africa, which is a place where the United States has traditionally perceived more restrained interests and toward which it arguably has no overarching, coherent national security strategy.

The first three cases deal with long-term American commitments in parts of the Middle East. Since the end of the Cold War, and certainly since the 9/11 terrorist attacks emanating from that region, the Middle East has been the major focus of U.S. national security concern. Chapter 8 looks specifically at the ongoing problem of peace between Israel and the Palestinians. The case emphasizes changes that have occurred in that relationship since the Trump administration came to power. The most important change has involved Jerusalem, to which the United States has moved its embassy (which no other country has done). This decision includes an implicit recognition of Jerusalem as the Israeli capital, which reinforces the emotional difficulty of negotiating peace between the two contestants. Chapter 9 examines American security policy toward Afghanistan, the country where the 9/11 attacks were planned and where its perpetrators were provided sanctuary. The United States has been at war in that country ever since to prevent a recurrence, and lack of progress has made that commitment controversial. The third chapter looks at the Syrian civil war and American (and other) inability to do anything constructive to bring it to an end. The American experience depicted in chapter 10 may be a frustrating model for the effort in Africa described in Chapter 13.

Chapters 11 and 12 look at evolving national security concerns with America's Cold War opponents. Chapter 11 examines evolving U.S.-Russian relations conditioned by increased militancy by the regime of Vladimir Putin to reassert Russian power in a country in demographic decline. It also looks at the issue of Russian meddling in the 2016 American election and Russian aggression in Crimea and Ukraine. Chapter 12 looks at evolving U.S.-Chinese relations since the rise to and consolidation of power by Xi Jinping. Beyond economic relations, it concentrates on differing views of the division of influence in the Asia-Pacific region between the two countries and the delicate problem of Chinese constraint of North Korea and its nuclear weapons.

Chapter 13 offers a sharp contrast with the discrete, defined problems of the other cases. Africa has been at the bottom of the priority list of American national security concern. U.S. interests are least well defined and not as obviously vital in Africa as they are other places. African problems are diverse and often intractable, and it is virtually impossible to form a coherent policy that subsumes them all. The case looks at internal problems in some countries, the intrusion of terrorism into Africa, and the often hideous, even genocidal nature of African internal affairs. It asks the question of whether a comprehensive national security policy toward Africa is possible.

8

The Continuing Middle East Riddle

Jerusalem and the Palestinian State

The longest standing, most difficult Middle Eastern national security problem facing the United States has been the Palestinian quest for a sovereign state on the West Bank of the Jordan River occupied (a term the Israelis dislike) by Israel since 1967. Israel does not publicly rule out the possibility of some form of a Palestinian state, but has consistently taken actions that belie that willingness, notably the continued erection of very permanent-looking settlements on territory that would be part of an Arab Palestine. In addition, the Netanyahu government of Israel attaches conditions to independence negotiations—notably security guarantees for Israel—that the Palestinians systematically reject and that the Israelis know are "game breakers."

The description of this vexing, interminable issue is simple enough. When the state of Israel was declared in 1948 and survived an attack by neighboring Arab states intent on destroying it, one artifact was the physical and political dislodgement of the Arab population that had been residents of what became Israel in the process. Most of the Palestinians, fearing reprisal from the victorious Israelis (who maintain controversially their fear was unwarranted) fled into neighboring jurisdictions, notably Lebanon, Syria, the West Bank of the Jordan River (then part of the Kingdom of Jordan), and the Gaza Strip. These people have not had a sovereign state of their own and join others in a similar situation like the Kurds as a *stateless nation*: a physical nationality that does not have its own sovereign state jurisdiction.

The fate of the Palestinians reflects their expulsion from Israel in 1948, an exodus they refer to simply as *al-Nakbah* (the disaster or catastrophe). It is the nub of the dispute and came to a head in the 1967 "Six Day War," when the Israelis dispatched a coalition of Arab states in their third war (1948, 1956, and 1967) and, in the process, occupied territory belonging to each. This included the Sinai Peninsula and Gaza Strip from Egypt, portions of the Golan Heights from Syria, and the West Bank of the Jordan from the state of Jordan. Egyptian territory was returned to Egypt in 1982 as part of a settlement between Israel and Egypt. The other territories, most prominently the West Bank, remain under Israeli control. Virtually the entire international community condemns this continuing occupation and demands Israeli withdrawal. The Israelis will only agree to discussions about this option on conditions that other states refuse to accept.

The 1967 occupation is the central stumbling block in what has been the major source of regional instability and peace in the area. The status of the West Bank and the plight of the Palestinians are joined. The Palestinians and, at least rhetorically, the other Arab states demand that a state of Palestine be created to end Palestinian statelessness, and the only place on which to create such a state is the West Bank, largely because it was and remains the home of most Palestinians. Almost all world states accept the Palestinian claim and demand that Israel end its physical presence on the West Bank to allow the creation of Palestine. The Israelis, and especially conservative political elements represented in the government of Benjamin Netanyahu, refuse to accede unless their national security interests are guaranteed in any settlement.

The issue is extremely emotional on both sides. Since 1967, the Israeli physical occupation by the Israeli Defense Forces (IDF) and security mechanisms has exercised virtually total control over the area. This control has allowed and facilitated the migration of over two hundred thousand Israeli settlers (mostly immigrants from the Jewish diaspora outside Israel) into very permanent settlements on the West Bank and twenty thousand more to the Syrian Golan Heights, making the Palestinians apparent second-class citizens in the area and making it more difficult to imagine the Israelis will ever negotiate its return to the Palestinians. One result has been violence against Israel by some Palestinians augmented by outsiders, including Islamic terrorists. The result is a volatile, unstable situation that American presidents at least as far back as Jimmy Carter have tried, without success, to mediate, and in the worst of circumstances, could burst into regional violence that is decidedly not in the American national interest.

The major sticking point is the establishment of a Palestinian state on the West Bank. Aspects of disagreement exist about the nature of such a state (would it be a terrorist sovereign launching pad, in the worst Israeli scenario?), what its relationship to Israel would be, and how Israeli concerns about its physical security can be accommodated. All these problems are potentially existential to Israel, and thus highly emotional.

Nowhere is that emotion stronger and more concentrated than over the status of Jerusalem. When the Trump administration declared its intention in December 2017 to move the U.S. Embassy from Tel Aviv to Jerusalem, it intruded into a delicate situation that only became more delicate after the embassy opened in Jerusalem in May 2018. Both the Israelis and the Palestinians claim Jerusalem as their national capital, and neither seems interested in compromising its claim.

Perspectives on the Problem

On January 31, 2018, media reports detailed a jarring statement by Israeli prime minister Benjamin (Bibi) Netanyahu in a joint press conference concluding a state visit by German foreign minister Sigmar Gabriel in Jerusalem. The subject was Israel's preconditions for supporting any kind of independent Palestinian entity on the West Bank, and it reiterated an old Israeli demand that had fallen out of the public discourse during the Obama years. The "first condition" for negotiations, he said, was that they must begin from an understanding that the outcome must include Israeli-controlled security in the resulting territory: Palestine with IDF and Israeli security forces on its territory. Netanyahu would not go so far as to label the resulting entity a sovereign state. "Whether it is defined as a state when we have the military control is another matter," he said. "I'd rather not discuss labels, but substance." The German government, like that of most other countries, has rejected this line of advocacy for years.

The denial of Palestinian sovereignty and the fate of Jerusalem alter the Palestinian debate fundamentally. The fate of Palestine has always been primarily a real estate question: what group of people has the legal and moral strongest claim to sovereign control of the territory. The answer varies depending on confessional preference. The controversy reflects differences between the sides on three fundamental matters, each of which is touched upon in the Netanyahu and Trump statements and actions. These are Israeli security and existence, the "right" of Palestinian Arabs to their own sovereign state, and the symbolic value of Jerusalem. None are trivial matters, and their resolution has proven elusive. Netanyahu and Trump have changed the calculus of outcomes and thus how different resolutions (or lack thereof) affect the interests of the major players, including the United States.

Fundamental Differences

The basic heads of disagreement begin from the dual perspectives of Israeli security and Palestinian sovereign statehood. Each is paramount to the side advocating it, and any resolution that has any chance of mutual acceptance requires one or both sides to take a chance that its interests will not be fundamentally, even fatally, compromised. The concerns are not unreasonable from the perspectives of the parties championing them.

The Israelis view the security issue as existential. Since its inception, Israel has been confronted by a hostile array of Muslim states. Some of these states oppose the existence of the Israeli state; driving the Israelis into the sea was a battle cry of the Arabs in 1948. Because of the Holocaust experience, it is entirely understandable that Israelis would take these kinds of threats very seriously and would act to reduce the likelihood of another attempt at Jewish extermination.

The geopolitical heart of this concern has been the West Bank. Prior to the 1967 war, the Jordanian West Bank bulged into Israel, creating a situation where, at its narrowest point, the distance from the West Bank to the Mediterranean Sea was only ten miles. This was an impossibly narrow distance that the Israelis probably could not defend and, if breached, could cut the Israeli state in two and compromise its viability. Occupying the West Bank removed this obstacle. In addition, Israel occupied part of the Syrian Golan Heights from which Syria had fired artillery shells at *kibbutzim* in northern Israel. It also occupied Egypt's Sinai Peninsula to make it impossible for the Egyptians to attack from the west without having to encounter Israeli armed forces in the Sinai desert. The net effect was to reduce (but not eliminate) the physical threat to Israel. It made the opposition to Israel by the Arabs even greater than it had been before. The major manifestation of this greater political animosity was the West Bank, where the largest number of Palestinians had taken residence to avoid Israeli rule and found themselves under the Israeli yoke again.

The physical vulnerability of Israel also helps explain the Netanyahu pronouncement that introduced this section of the chapter. The most prominently advocated solution to the current political condition is the establishment of a Palestinian state on the West Bank. In terms of physical vulnerability, a sovereign Palestinian state on this territory would return the situation to the pre-1967 vulnerability experienced by Israel, and this outcome is explicit in many advocacies for a withdrawal of Israel to the internationally accepted boundaries of the Israeli state. This potential situation is intolerable to Netanyahu and those who agree with him, although peace treaties between Israel and both Egypt and Jordan reduce this vulnerability and partially mitigate the concern.

Security is not, however, the only source of Israeli interest in the West Bank. Since 1967, Israel has gradually allowed or promoted the settlement of Israeli citizens and immigrants on West Bank property. Including settlers in East Jerusalem, the number currently approximates one-quarter million Jewish settlers in West Bank land and three million Palestinian residents in an area the size of Delaware. These settlements allow Israel to attract many more Jewish immigrants to the Jewish state, since easily inhabitable territory in pre-1967 Israel is largely unavailable. The international community condemns this colonization and Israel has never publicly admitted that the settlements will form the basis for annexation of the West Bank to Israel. Moreover, a high percentage of the settlers are Orthodox Jews who heavily support Netanyahu. Palestinians have never believed that Israel would abandon the Orthodox Jews as part of any territorial settlement creating a Palestinian state.

Barriers to Progress

These competing preferences define the basic loggerheads confronting any negotiated settlement. Simply put, the current Israeli government will not accept any change in the status of the West Bank that returns Israelis to a position of potential physical peril, and it is not clear whether they are willing to discuss seriously a change in the pattern of Jewish settlements on the West Bank. The Palestinians, on the other hand, insist on their "right" to sovereign statehood, and the only territory available for their state is the West Bank. The key point of incompatibility is *sovereignty*. Palestine cannot be sovereign if it is forced to host Israeli defense forces, and the absence of those forces in Palestine creates an unacceptable existential threat to Israel and its sovereignty. Something must give for any kind of change to occur.

Jerusalem is an integral part of this greater concern. The city is one of the oldest and most highly contentious locations on earth, having changed hands on multiple occasions and even having been physically destroyed at least twice. It has great religious significance to Jews, Muslims, and Christians, and all of them have significant religious monuments and symbols within its boundaries. It is centrally located astride the border between the West Bank and pre-1967 Israel. As part of Palestine, it would be that country's largest urban area; it is the third largest city in Israel. Its current population is about 875,000 (a 2018 estimate from the Israelis), of whom roughly 550,000 are Jews and 300,000 are Palestinian Muslims.

The city has been a major source of contention in negotiations toward a Palestinian state resolution. Both sides have controlled the city (it was forcibly annexed as part of Jordan prior to the 1967 war and has been part of Israel since), and when in control, both sides have excluded the other from access to religious monuments and sites, a source of continuing suspicion and distrust that bedevils proposals for a compromise solution to the city's status.

There are three possible outcomes to the status question. One is continued Israeli possession leading to its declaration as the capital of Israel, an outcome implicitly embraced by the Trump administration. This solution is best served by the continuation of Israeli occupation of the West Bank (the absence of an agreement). The second is annexation of the city to an independent Palestine, which would make Jerusalem the capital of Palestine. This outcome requires the creation of a Palestinian state on the West Bank. The third solution is the division of the city between Israeli and Palestinian jurisdictions. This outcome requires a level of cooperation between the sides that has been missing almost entirely. It also does not solve the question of the location of capitals.

The symbolic international aspect of this disagreement has been the location of foreign embassies in Israel. Until the Trump administration moved the embassy to Jerusalem, all members of the international community (including the United States) maintained their embassies in Tel Aviv, the traditional national capital. Relocating official government representation to Jerusalem symbolically affects the ongoing status on the West Bank, because it denies the Palestinian claim to the city and thus an important element in the conditions of its statehood. As of late 2018, no state had followed the American initiative on the embassy, and many had condemned it.

The contrasting and contradictory ways the Israelis and Palestinians view their mutual predicament make finding a mutually acceptable resolution difficult, if not impossible. Both sides cannot simultaneously achieve their demanded outcomes: Israel secured from possible assault by its neighbors, and the Palestinians a sovereign state to end their statelessness. Their positions are close to being mutually exclusive. Israel with a sovereign Palestine incorporating the West Bank will always have legitimate concerns about its physical safety, and Palestinian self-determination requires fully sovereign control over the West Bank. Israel will not be fully satisfied if it cannot control potentially dangerous threats from Palestine; Palestine cannot accede to these demands and be sovereign. Progress requires that something must change, which means compromises neither side seems willing seriously to entertain.

Political Controversies

The current Israeli position is politically controversial within Israel. Some Israelis (generally of moderate to liberal political persuasions) believe that peace should be the first Israeli goal, and that negotiating an agreement with the Palestinians is a higher order of priority than a more ironclad guarantee of that security based in forward presence on the West Bank. The Israeli nuclear monopoly in the region and the implicit threat that another attack on Israel might prompt the nuclear incineration of the attacking state(s) makes this danger less risky. It is generally assumed that an existential threat to Israel would also be met by an American response, although there is no formal guarantee this would be the case or what that response might be. The position of Netanyahu and other conservatives is that the threat is too great to take the chance on either a settlement that goes bad or a belief in American aid that might prove forlorn. In addition, any agreement that creates a Palestinian state also likely dispossesses the West Bank settlers, and they are a politically indispensable element in the Netanyahu governing coalition.

Palestine clearly wants a sovereign state, but its ability to create it is very limited. It has the official support of the world community in its claim, and its Muslim brethren verbally support it, but there has been virtually no real effort on their part to force the solution to fruition. Palestine's case relies on the good will and effective actions of others, which has not proven to be a very potent form of assistance.

The American perspective is the most conflicted. It is clearly in the American interest for there to be tranquility in the Middle East, and the possibility of war over the West Bank is an American horror scenario for two reasons. The first is that it threatens to spiral out of hand, possibly spreading to inter-sectarian confrontation between Iranian- and Saudi-supported elements seeking to aid the Palestinians. The second is that Israel might feel such existential pressure that it would unleash its nuclear weapons, with unpredictable but potentially cataclysmic results regionally and possibly globally. For the United States, the options in terms of who to support and how to do so reflect the internal debate in Israel: American conservatives tend to back the Netanyahu position, and liberals tend to support a negotiated settlement that results in a Palestinian state. These contrasting approaches by the parties are reflected in preferences for the various policy options available.

Policy Options

Two different outcomes to the Palestinian question, each with two variants and all with different impacts on the Palestinian demand for a sovereign state, have been put forward. Since 1967, the bulk of the debate has been about what is called the "two-state solution," an outcome first proposed by United Nations Security Council Resolution (UNSCR) 242 that year and reinforced by General Assembly concurrence in 1974. The UNSCR is based on the principle of "land for peace" and has attracted the most global support. Its acceptance would result in an independent Palestine on the West Bank. The other proposals deny or attenuate this outcome and result in a single state for the area. They are "one-state solutions," wherein pre-1967 Israel and the West Bank are incorporated into a single sovereign entity presumably forming a "greater Israel," the creation of a semi-autonomous Palestine whose external, and particularly security, functions are controlled by Israel, or the status quo.

One issue lurks in the back of this array of possibilities: the demographic "time bomb" and its effect on maintaining simultaneously a democratic and a Jewish state. It is a factor particularly emphasized by liberal opponents of Netanyahu. The demographics are stark. Israeli statistics from 2018 say pre-1967 Israeli territory is 74.5 percent Jewish, a majority it will continue to enjoy for the foreseeable future. If the West Bank and the Gaza Strip are somehow added to Israel, however, the ratio of Jews to Muslims approaches parity. The time bomb then begins to tick, because the population growth rate among Palestinians exceeds that of Jews, although the Jewish birth rate caught up to Palestinian totals in 2018 (if that birth rate trend continues, it will attenuate the pace of the population trend, something that bears watching). At some point, the Jews will be a minority in the combined state: it would no longer be a truly Jewish state, and the only way the Israelis could maintain control would be as a non-democratic state with weighted political rights favoring Jewish citizens (what former president Jimmy Carter called an "apartheid" state in a 2006 book). These concerns affect all possible outcomes.

Two-State Solutions

The most publicized and internationally supported solution to the impasse has been to create a Palestinian state on the West Bank based on UNSCR 242. There are two variations to this outcome. The most discussed and accepted is a solution in which two sovereign states are created side by side. Netanyahu has proposed a second, contrary variant outside the UN resolution, where the Palestinians would have autonomy on the West Bank for domestic affairs, but where the Israelis would provide security.

The first alternative's international appeal is that it solves both thorny territorial problems of the area: it provides a venue for Palestinian statehood, and it solves international demands for the end of the Israeli occupation of the West Bank. The United States has historically been a chief architect and supporter of this solution because of international concern and because, if it can be implemented successfully, it would remove a major Arab objection to Israel's existence.

The Israeli right has been the chief opponent of this solution, officially because they do not trust the Palestinian Authority and implicitly because of their growing stake in the West Bank settlements for immigrants. The Israeli position is rhetorically accommodating but, especially since Prime Minister Netanyahu assumed office in 2009, has hardened. Cries of "land for peace" have gradually weakened but not disappeared.

On the heels of the Trump announcement on Jerusalem, Netanyahu reiterated a demand that had been made early in his tenure but dropped publicly because of universal international opposition. This demand, as already described, suggests that the only way Israelis can accept any form of Palestinian broad self-rule is if Israel maintains control of security arrangements both to protect Israeli settlers and as a first line of defense against outside invaders. It demands semi-sovereignty for the Palestinians, important parts of whose lives would still be dictated by the IDF and Israeli security forces. This configuration, which Avishai refers to as "confederation," is totally unacceptable to the Palestinians and the international community that supports a Palestinian state.

The prospects for any form of the two-state solution are increasingly bleak to the point that it has been widely suggested that this outcome is effectively moribund. Both sides, with some justification, accuse the other of intransigence in negotiations over contested positions that must somehow be accommodated. Territorially, there is the question of exactly where the frontier between the two countries would be, which means how many of the Israeli settlements along the 1967 border would be incorporated into Israel, and it is accentuated by the disposition of Jerusalem. What would become of the settlers and their security is another issue, particularly given the chaos that accompanied the handover of Gaza to the Palestinian Authority in 2006.

One-State Solutions

Like the two-state solution, this outcome has variants and is, de facto, the preferred Israeli solution. The simplest variant is a continuation of the status quo, in which the West Bank is an effective part of Israel by being included in the occupied territory. This solution serves two important Israeli interests: it means Israel has a "forward presence" in the West Bank, something which the Jewish right considers critical to its security. Second, it maintains the West Bank as part of "greater Israel," and thus part of the space available for greater immigration of world Jewry to Israel. The continuation of the status quo is condemned by the world community because it denies self-determination for the Palestinians. Opposition, however, has not proven so powerful that serious proposals to force Israel to abandon the West Bank have emerged, lending an implicit acceptance of the practice.

The second, and most radical, solution would be the formal annexation of the West Bank by Israel. For those Israelis who favor Israeli expansion, and for settlers who live in the territory, this proposal has some resonance, but it faces two major points of opposition. The first is that it would so enrage world public opinion that it might convince that community to impose the kinds of sanctions on Israel that would have been imposed by now against any other state in a similar situation. Second, this solution would place Israelis and Palestinians in a common political setting wherein the demographic time bomb would tick increasingly loudly.

Of the two one-state solutions, continuing the status quo represents the path of least resistance. Were Israel to annex the West Bank formally, it would face international condemnation, including censure from Arab states with which it has been attempting to develop positive relations but which could not continue to support Israel if doing so openly meant abandoning the Palestinians. The Netanyahu ruling coalition does not have a large majority, and annexation would be opposed by enough of the Israeli electorate that it might cause a crisis in the Knesset (the Israeli parliament) that would drive Netanyahu from power. Any likely replacement for the Likud-led government would probably come from liberal opponents who would try to reinvigorate the peace process leading toward the two-state solution: precisely the outcome Netanyahu and his allies most oppose.

The demographics of the region come into play. In terms of sheer numbers, the populations of Palestine and pre-1967 Israel are today almost the same, and some Palestinian sources argue that Palestinians came to outnumber Israeli Jews in 2017, a ratio that will only get worse for Israel given differential growth rates between the two groups. A single state, in other words, will have a Muslim majority soon, if it does not already. If the Palestinians can vote on an equal footing (i.e., something like one man, one vote) with the Israelis, how long can Israel remain a truly Jewish state? Exacerbating the situation, there is an economic chasm between the two groups. Avishai, for instance, reports the average annual income for Israeli Jews is $37,000, compared to $3,000 for Palestinian Arabs. These figures may not be precisely accurate, but there is a real gap that would lead to real demands from a Palestinian majority in a unified state to rectify. What do the Israelis do about that?

Consequences: What to Do?

What are American interests in managing and resolving the complicated conflict between the Israelis and the Palestinians? At one level, it is part of the overall mosaic of Middle Eastern politics, geographically with Israel on one end of the area and contentious places like Iran and Afghanistan on the other. The American interest in peace and as much stability as possible in the overall region is not served well by the ongoing tension over the fate of the Palestinians. Since Israel became the region's nuclear power, none of the Islamic states can do anything decisive enough about Palestine to provoke a military confrontation with Israeli nukes. In that sense, the Netanyahu demand for a physical presence in Palestine may be overblown or a pretext for undermining the negotiating progress and future annexation.

The United States has a "special relationship" with Israel that creates a special mandate to ensure the continued viability and prosperity of the Israeli state. That interest is historical and emotional, the product of the World War II/Holocaust experience. At the same time, the United States has the largest Jewish population outside Israel, and there is great pressure on Washington from the "Jewish lobby" in Washington as well (see Mearsheimer and Walt). That lobby is not uniform in its views and reflects the division politically in Israel as well. In President Trump, Netanyahu has his closest ally since he came to power.

Any assessment about American national security strategy toward the Israeli-Palestinian conflict begins with two questions. The first is what kind of outcome serves American interests: the United States has been ambivalent on this point, rhetorically supporting the two-state solution but doing relatively little beyond jawboning to push Israel to accept this outcome. The second question is how best to bring about the preferred outcome: American efforts since President Trump took office have represented a significant step backward from the two-state approach and toward the militant resistance of Netanyahu.

A significant aspect of calculating the American strategic aim is the special relationship with Israel. Were Israel not the stumbling block party to its preferred solution, the American interest would be minimal beyond the general concern for regional peace and would, if anything, militate toward support for the Arabs, who have the oil.

The American strategic position has been that the two-state solution is preferable on two grounds. First, it defuses the Arab-Israeli conflict by eliminating the cause of Palestinian statehood from the list of Arab grievances with the Jewish state. Second, the solution would return Israel to a modified form of the 1967 boundaries (the Israelis would certainly be allowed to annex some settlements along the border), and this would ensure a Jewish majority population in perpetuity and thus obviate the Jewish-democratic state conundrum. Netanyahu largely ignores this argument, asserting instead that the dictates of Israeli security override other concerns (as well as allowing additional Jewish settlement on the West Bank that partially mitigates the demographic time bomb). From an American/international viewpoint, this outcome also means Israeli security becomes more reliant on its nuclear arsenal as a deterrent.

None of the other options is truly viable. The "qualified" two-state solution with Israeli security forces occupying Palestine is simply unacceptable to everyone but some Israelis and would further isolate Israel from the international community. Formal annexation of the West Bank would create a similar rejection by everyone else in the international community. The informal prolongation of the status quo, while also unpopular, is by default the least objectionable alternative to the two-state solution. Given the intractability of the situation, it may be the only viable solution if the situation remains as it is.

In the interim, the situation remains unsettled and, for the Palestinians, increasingly forlorn. The simple continuation of the existing deadlock favors the Israelis; it makes the situation appear increasingly permanent and, for Israel, comfortable. Inaction, in other words, works to the advantage of those Israelis who seek to make the occupation permanent in one form or another. Brown summarizes the ongoing situation in a 2017 article in bleak terms (at least from the Palestinian perspective): "The most significant development is not in the occupation itself but in the collapse of all attempts to devise alternatives." In these circumstances, can we expect anything different from the Netanyahu regime than what they are doing?

Is the status quo compatible with what American policy is or what it should be given U.S. interests? If it is not, what can the United States do to force a change in the process and outcome? Promoting the negotiation process has not worked. Should the United States become more proactive—demanding the Palestinians provide some form of ironclad guarantee of Israeli security or threatening to impose sanctions on Israel if it does not relent on its tenacious de facto opposition to settlement? What do you think?

Study/Discussion Questions

1. What is the Palestinian problem? Trace its origins and evolution. On what outcome do the Palestinians insist?
2. What is the status of the Palestinian state situation? Include the status of Jerusalem, the settlements, and demands on both sides in your answer.
3. What are the fundamental differences between Israel and Palestine regarding the West Bank? What

are the basic barriers to progress? Elaborate.
4. What are the options for a settlement to the disagreement? Discuss and evaluate each.
5. Which solution (if any) do you think the United States should advocate to achieve its national security interests? What should it be willing to do to promote those interests? Will any of them work? Why or why not?

Bibliography

Armstrong, Karen. *Jerusalem: One City, Three Faiths.* London: Ballantine Books, 2011.

Avishai, Bernard. "Confederation: The One Possible Arab-Palestinian Solution." *New York Review of Books*, February 2, 2018.

Benn, Aluf. "The End of the Old Israel: How Netanyahu Has Transformed the Nation." *Foreign Affairs* 95 (4) (July/August 2016), 17–27.

Bregman, Ahron. *Cursed Victory: A History of Israel and the Occupied Territories, 1967 to the Present.* New York: Pegasus, 2015.

Brown, Nathan J. "The Occupation at Fifty: A Permanent State of Ambiguity." *Current History* 116 (704) (December 2017), 331–36.

———. "The Palestinians' Receding Dream of Statehood." *Current History* 110 (740) (December 2011), 345–51.

Carter, Jimmy. *Palestine: Peace Not Apartheid.* New York: Simon & Schuster, 2006.

Central Intelligence Agency. *CIA World Factbook 2017.* Washington, DC: Central Intelligence Agency, 2017.

Della Pergola, Sergio. "Israel's Existential Predicament: Population, Territory, and Identity." *Current History* 109 (732) (December 2010), 383–89.

Della Pergola, Sergio, and Rebhun Uzi (eds.). *Jewish Population Identity: Concept and Reality.* New York: Springer, 2018.

Dowty, Alan. *Israel/Palestine.* Fourth Ed. London: Polity Press, 2017.

Ehrenreich, Ben. *The Way to the Spring: Life and Death in Palestine.* New York: Penguin Books, 2016.

Gelvin, James L. *The Israel-Palestine Conflict: One Hundred Years of War.* Third Ed. Cambridge, UK: Cambridge University Press, 2016.

Gilbert, Martin. *Israel: A Revised History.* Revised and Updated Ed. New York: HarperCollins, 2008.

Hammond, Jeremy R. *Obstacle to Peace: The U.S. Role in the Israeli-Palestine Conflict.* New York: Worldview, 2016.

Harel, Amos. "Israel's Evolving Military." *Foreign Affairs* 95 (4) (July/August 2016), 43–50.

Harms, Gregory, and Todd M. Ferry. *The Palestine-Israeli Conflict: A Basic Introduction.* Fourth Ed. London: Pluto Press, 2017.

Korte, Gregory, and David Jackson. "Trump and Netanyahu on Support for Two-State Solution in the Middle East." *USA Today,* February 2, 2017.

Livni, Tzipi. "Anger and Hope: A Conversation with Tzipi Livni." *Foreign Affairs* 95 (4) (July/August 2016), 10–15.

Mearsheimer, John J., and Stephen M. Walt. *The Israeli Lobby and U.S. Foreign Policy.* New York: Farrar, Straus & Giroux, 2007.

Muravchik, Joshua. *Making David into Goliath: How the World Turned Against Israel.* New York: Encounter, 2015.

Ross, Dennis. *Doomed to Succeed: The U.S.-Israeli Relationship from Truman to Obama.* New York: Farrar, Straus & Giroux, 2015.

Said, Edward W. *The Question of Palestine.* Reissue Ed. New York: Vintage, 2015.

Said, Edward W., and Ibrahim Abu-Lughod. *Blaming the Victims: Spurious Scholarship and the Palestinian Question.* London and New York: Verso, 2001.

Shalev, Chemi. "Opinion: The Demise of the Two-State Solution Deprives Netanyahu's Israel of Its Political Iron Dome." *Haaretz,* January 8, 2018.

Shavit, Ari. *My Promised Land: The Triumph and Tragedy of Israel.* New York: Spiegel and Grau, 2015.

Smith, Charles D. *Palestine and the Arab-Israeli Conflict.* New York: Bedford-St. Martin's, 2016.

Snow, Donald M. *Cases in International Relations.* Sixth Ed. New York: Pearson, 2015.

———. *The Middle East, Oil, and the United States National Security Policy: Intractable Problems, Impossible Solutions.* Lanham, MD: Rowman & Littlefield, 2016.

Van Creveld, Martin L. *The Land of Blood and Honey: The Rise of Modern Israel.* New York: Thomas Dunne, 2010.

Vital Statistics: Latest Population Statistics for Israel. Jewish Virtual Library (online), May 11, 2018.

9

America's Longest War
The Afghanistan Trap

In October 2018, the American active combat role in Afghanistan exceeded seventeen years, making it by far the longest shooting conflict in American history. American involvement was begun in October 2001 by President George W. Bush as part of the response to the 9/11 terrorist attacks, was continued by President Barack Obama despite a campaign promise to end American participation in the Afghan Civil War, and has continued under President Trump with his late 2017 determination to increase the American military commitment slightly (by forty-five hundred troops). No end is in sight. Afghanistan is the longest U.S. war; it also seems endless.

The Americans are not the first and will probably not be the last country to try to defeat the Afghans on their own territory. Afghanistan is called, among other things, the "graveyard of empires," a testimony to all the invaders who have attacked and tried to subdue the country and failed. The list of intruders includes historical figures like Alexander the Great and more contemporary aspirants, from the British in the nineteenth century to the Soviets in the 1980s. The Americans are just the latest addition to this list. The others failed (the Mongols were partial exceptions); there is little reason to believe the United States will do better in the long run.

The Afghanistan predicament is a classic case of the vagaries of trying to develop and implement national security strategy. Historically, these two countries have had essentially nothing to do with one another and have shared virtually no common interests or animosities. From an American perspective, Afghanistan was a country half a world away with which it had little contact until the post–World War II period. The major distinguishing features of Afghanistan have been its strategic location in Asia along major east-west and north-south trade routes, its forbidding geography and peoples, and its production of narcotic drugs. It is part of a geopolitically important area in its region, but it is dwarfed by the competitors who have craved access or control of the area. The countries of the Asian Subcontinent, Russia, Iran, and Europeans like the British, but not the United States, have coveted Afghanistan. Its significance is symbolically captured in a 2009 quote by Vice President Joe Biden to Hamid Karzai, the president of Afghanistan (quoted by Mazzetti): "Mr. President," Biden said, "Pakistan is *fifty* times more important than Afghanistan for the United States." Yet the United States has been at war for seventeen years and counting; it merely clashes verbally with Pakistan.

American interest in Afghanistan expanded in the latter part of the twentieth century. In 1980, the Soviet Union invaded Afghanistan to prop up a communist government they had helped come to power. The international community opposed the Soviet action as illegal under United Nations Charter obligations the Soviets had accepted as a UN member. It was viewed as an ominous attempt to use the Afghans as a wedge to extend their influence southward toward India and Pakistan. The United States was one of the countries which came to the aid of Afghan freedom fighters who, with outside assistance, expelled the Soviets in 1988, an event that helped bring down the Soviet Union three years later. It was also indicative of the vagaries of strategy toward Afghanistan: the motive was to cause trouble for the Soviets, but it also inadvertently gave rise to the two groups the United States has opposed there since 2001, the Taliban and Al Qaeda. It also was a harbinger of the monumental task of trying to subdue the Afghans, some of the world's most adept asymmetrical warriors.

The penultimate event in building a national security interest in Afghanistan was, of course, the September 11, 2001, Al Qaeda (AQ) terrorist attack against New York and Washington. That attack was planned and carried out by AQ on Afghan soil, and the terrorists were protected from effective retaliation by their Soviet-era allies, the Taliban government of Afghanistan. When the Taliban refused to remand Osama bin Laden and his cohorts to the Americans, the United States intervened in the ongoing civil war between the Taliban and an insurgent aggregation known as the Northern Coalition. The initial strategic goal was the capture of AQ, and it failed. It did drive AQ out of Afghanistan and into Pakistan, but the United States stayed anyway. At the time it was not clear why; the goal has subsequently been expanded to ensuring the Taliban does not return to power so that it cannot turn the country back into a refuge for AQ. That is where the strategic goal stands today.

If the setting of the strategic objective has been convoluted, translating that goal into an operational strategy has been even more difficult. Afghanistan is an ideal place in which to conduct an asymmetrical campaign to expel outsider invaders and always has been. Its harsh geography and the dispersion and autonomy of the fierce fighters who oppose the invaders make an insurgency-based asymmetrical strategy extremely difficult to defeat, especially by the kind of conventional forces that are the backbone of the military forces of countries like the United States. The Americans have been trying to break the military back of their opponents for years. They have not succeeded and have implicitly admitted they cannot do so.

Perspectives on the Problem

Afghanistan sits in the middle of central Asia, a land-locked country surrounded by major regional powers that include Pakistan, Iran, China, and several of the former Soviet republics, such as Tajikistan, Uzbekistan, and Turkmenistan. It is not a small or insignificant place: its physical size is roughly the same as Texas, and its 2015 population (according to estimates in the *2017 CIA World Factbook*) was over thirty-two million, ranking it forty-first in the world by both measures. Most of the country is mountainous and bleak, but historic trade routes to India and China traverse its territory, creating a geopolitical importance the country would otherwise lack.

An Afghan Sketch

Politically, Afghanistan has always been a difficult place. Although its people and culture date back for millennia, it was not unified into a single state until 1747 by Pashtuns led by Ahmed Shah Durrani, and the Pashtun tribe (which has several sub-tribes) has been dominant ever since. One of the major characteristics of the country is its ethnic diversity: the largest part of its population, currently about 42 percent, is Pashtun, who also are the second largest ethnic group in Pakistan. The Pashtun are not monolithic, basically divided into more urbanized Pashtuns (the Durrani) and rural elements (the Ghilzai). This distinction is important because most Taliban members are Ghilzai Pashtuns, whereas Durrani Pashtuns are part of the Afghan government. Other prominent tribes include Tajiks, Hazara, Uzbeks, and small numbers of other ethnicities. This diversity is reflected in linguistic distinctions: half the population speaks Dari, the roots of which are shared with the Iranians, and 15 percent Pashto, both of which are official languages. The country is predominantly Sunni.

Geography and ethno-tribal diversity both contribute to the combative nature of Afghan society and to the difficulty of dealing with the Afghans militarily. Loyalty tends to be tribal, usually around atomized groups separated by the vagaries of a harsh terrain and environment that makes close interchange difficult at best. These tribal divisions create a strong preference for independence and autonomy and a consequent resistance to central governance. The traditional form of "national" government is the *loya jirga*, a periodic meeting of the traditional leaders of the tribes to discuss and, where possible, resolve differences between tribal groupings. Autonomy is the first value of the tribesmen, and they resist any efforts to create a strong central government in Kabul that can dictate to them. The United States, seeking to create unity and tranquility in the country, has aligned itself both with political elements seeking to create strong central governance and a strong Afghan military capable of enforcing the dictates of the central government; the Taliban has its base in the hinterlands and champions the independence of the rural Pashtuns, which form its support base. Both the government and its Taliban opposition are consistently ranked by outside evaluators as among the most corrupt regimes and movements in the world, thereby not adding to their popularity or support.

The country is also one of the poorest and least developed in the world. Per capita income measured as GDP per capita stood at $1,900 in 2015, 206th in the world, and the leading exports of the country for that year were opium and fruits and nuts. Almost all its economic trade activity was with surrounding countries.

The Afghans have always been a particularly warlike, contentious people who are very difficult to subdue successfully. It is arguably true that Afghans are perpetually in one of two situations. If they are the victims of outside aggression by predatory neighbors—a not uncommon condition given their strategic location—the Afghan tribesmen unite in asymmetrical military opposition until they manage to cause the opposition to give up and go home. As suggested, they have been historically very proficient in this exercise in overcoming invader cost-tolerance. On the other hand, when there is no external opponent, the Afghans retreat into their jealously guarded tribal enclaves and, when the need arises, fight among themselves. Civil conflicts at one level or another are not an uncommon part of the Afghan experience.

This pattern is augmented by a history of regional outside interference intended to gain some ascendancy in Afghan politics to enhance influence in the region. The British fought the Afghans in the nineteenth century primarily to gain enough leverage there to block Russian advances southward toward India and failed. In the late twentieth century, the Soviets managed to help install a communist regime in the country that proved so inept they had to invade the country to prop up communist rule. After eight years of trying, they limped out of the country, the result so traumatic that it contributed to the demise of the Soviet communist regime. Today, Pakistan is a leading interfering party, providing enough assistance to Pashtun Taliban forces to frustrate the government and its American supporters but encountering enough contrary interference from India that it fails to succeed. The United States and its politico-military support for the central government in Kabul is part of the murky mix as well.

The Roots of American Involvement

The American role in Afghanistan is enigmatic. Prior to the 1980 Soviet invasion, it was hard to imagine a more unlikely place for American involvement based in any calculation of national interest. The major reason the Americans came to the support of the Afghan rebels (the so-called *mujahidin*) was to frustrate the Soviets and their historic desire to expand their influence southward toward the subcontinent. In the process, the Americans accidentally triggered the unintended consequence of helping to create the problems that would bring them back into Afghanistan a little over a decade after the Soviet withdrawal. The mujahidin consisted of two loosely coordinated groups: traditional Afghan tribesmen mounting a resistance in the time-honored Afghan tradition, and foreign Muslims who came to assist the resistance. Many of the Afghan tribesmen became the core membership of the Taliban after the Soviets left. The foreigners, known as Afghanis and many recruited through the efforts of a rich young Saudi of Yemeni descent named Osama bin Laden, went on to form Al Qaeda.

American full attention toward and interest in Afghanistan was, of course, a spinoff of the 9/11 attacks. After the Soviets were expelled from Afghanistan, the country's politics descended to its accustomed corrupt chaos, from which a group of young people who claimed themselves to be honest reformers, the Taliban, emerged and managed to gain power in 1996. Many were direct descendants of the mujahidin, had attended fundamentalist schools in Pakistan (the *madrassas*), and promised honest and pious governance. That same year, bin Laden and his Afghani supporters who had formed the core of AQ were expelled from their sanctuary in Sudan (largely at American insistence), and migrated to Afghanistan, where the Taliban granted them the effective sanctuary from which they planned and ultimately launched the 9/11 attacks.

The backlash of the 9/11 attacks brought the two countries into direct conflict. Prior to 9/11, the United States had provided some assistance to the Northern Coalition in the forms of Special Forces and air support. After 9/11, one of the first cries in the American reaction was to bring the AQ perpetrators to justice, and the U.S. government requested that bin Laden and his followers be turned over to the United States. The Taliban refused to comply, and in October 2001, American forces entered the country with the capture of AQ as their major mission.

At this point, the objectives of American actions were clear-cut and part of the general commitment to protection of the homeland. The problem was that, for a variety of reasons, AQ, with the assistance of sympathetic Pashtun tribesmen along the open Afghan-Pakistan border, evaded the dragnet and escaped across the Tora Bora mountains into effective Pakistan exile, which they still enjoy.

The question for the United States was, "what now?" Pursuing and suppressing AQ had overwhelming post-9/11 popular support, but it was questionable how much involvement the American people would support after that venture failed. American air support had helped tip the balance of power in the country toward the Northern Coalition, it continued, and in January 2002, the coalition successfully overthrew the Taliban and came to power, with Durrani Pashtun leader Hamid Karzai as the new political leader. The Taliban retreated to the tribal regions in northern Pakistan to regroup and revitalize their ranks for a return to Afghanistan.

This situation created the need to determine what the future role of the United States should be. The Americans had no durable interest in who governed Afghanistan beyond not wanting the Taliban in power, and, as suggested, had no geostrategic or other stake in the game. Its single discernible interest was in eliminating AQ, which it had failed to accomplish. In early 2002, AQ was not a current Afghanistan problem, since its remnants were in Pakistan, which raised an entirely different set of concerns. It was not at all clear what U.S. interests were adequate to sustain support for a continuing military presence there. The growing plan to invade Iraq diverted public attention from Afghanistan, and the United States remained, eventually leading the formation of a coalition of other states, the International Security Assistance Force (ISAF) to aid in the effort. The rationale for this action, which continues to this day and is the major reason for a continuing American presence is, as Sadat and McChrystal reiterate in a 2017 article, to avoid the "risk (of) turning the country back into the terrorist safe haven it was before 9/11."

Policy Options

The situation in Afghanistan and what the United States should do about it have been matters of concern and disagreement since the United States failed in its initial, and universally supported, mission to capture or kill bin Laden and his AQ cohorts. The United States did succeed in causing AQ to flee the country into the Pakistani tribal areas, where the Pakistanis have proven unwilling or unable to dislodge or suppress them. AQ presence and activity in Afghanistan have not been an operational problem since 2002; the AQ problem as perceived by the United States and as a motivator of policy and strategy is the fear they might return if the Americans left and the Afghan government failed, in which case the worst case is that the country would become a sanctuary and launching pad for future terrorist activity.

This less than totally concrete threat to the real national security problem of terrorism colors perceptions about what American interests are in any given outcome of the Afghan war. If the threat is great and compelling, then a maximum effort is justified. If the threat is possible or even probable, then at least maintaining a status quo in which AQ's return is precluded (regardless of long-term effect on the government's civil war with the Taliban) may be the proper course. If the problem is minimal or could be negated in other, including non-military, ways, then an American withdrawal may be appropriate.

Part of determining the best course depends on the nature of the Afghan environment and thus the likelihood that a strategy will work. There are several obstacles to achieving goals. First, the Afghan government in Kabul is not popular enough to win adequate public support to prevail—or even probably survive—on its own. It represents the tradition of a strong central government, which many Afghans oppose and which forms some of the appeal of the opposition. At the same time, it is thoroughly corrupt, and its presence is not welcome in parts of the country. Second, its Taliban opponents are skilled asymmetrical fighters, meaning their defeat is problematical, especially by outside or outside-supported troops (see Snow, *The Case Against Military Intervention*). On the other side, the Taliban has not proven potent enough to succeed in the civil war with an ISAF presence in the country. In a 2018 assessment, Jones lists five sources of their weakness: an ideology too extreme for most Afghans, over-identification with one tribal base (Ghilzai Pashtuns), the use of brutal tactics to maintain control in areas it occupies, corruption (including association with and profiting from the opium trade), and excessive reliance upon assistance from an outside source (Pakistan).

The situation within which the United States must consider strategy alternatives is thus murky, and the outcome of any choice is either unpredictable or indecisive. There are essentially three alternatives. The first is a major military effort to defeat the Taliban and to facilitate control of the country by the Afghan government, thereby ensuring that the country cannot revert to a terrorist haven (military victory). The second is a maintenance of the status quo, wherein enough force and assistance is made available to prevent the success of the opponent, but not enough is provided to allow the government to prevail (status quo). The third is to decide the entire enterprise is unlikely enough to succeed and the consequences of failure are not so great that staying is impractical and unwise (withdrawal). Each is advocated by some in the strategic community.

Military Victory

The idea of administering a decisive military blow in Afghanistan that will result in a stable, pro-American, anti-terrorist future for the country is the most proactive, "macho" solution to the Afghanistan problem. Partly because of the length and indeterminacy of American efforts to date, it is also the least advocated and the least likely to gain support within the United States—or in Afghanistan.

Whatever merit such an effort might have, it is politically impossible to gain sufficient American public support to mount, an admission even its most ardent supporters accept. Given Afghan history, and most recently the 1980s Soviet attempt to subdue the country, it would clearly take a massive effort even to consider. Even if a plan could be devised that might succeed, it would have to be very large and expensive, and would have problematic prospects of success. The U.S. government does not publicize how much has already been spent in a constrained presence in the country, but outside "guesstimates" are uniformly over a trillion dollars with little to show for it. The expenses of the twenty-first century in military adventures like Iraq and the controversy over the growing deficit (see chapter 14) to which Afghan expenditures have already contributed add to the question of whether *any* reasonable campaign to defeat the Taliban would be worth the cost. In addition, mounting a campaign to impose a regime would meet massive opposition among Afghan tribesmen, who have a long history of rejecting unsolicited blandishments from outsiders.

If it were clear that a military effort to end the civil war could be accomplished with a regime that has popular support and would act as a faithful and honest partner for the United States, there might be more support for and advocacy of this option. More importantly, it would achieve the American goal of ensuring that Afghanistan would not revert to a haven for international terrorism, the most obviously legitimate national security interest for American active involvement in the country. It would not, of course, solve the problem of global breeding grounds for terror, as terrorist organizations would simply move elsewhere to set up shop. Parts of Africa (see chapter 13) seem to be the likely destination point.

Status Quo

Essentially maintaining the status quo is the most enigmatic choice available. It is the compromise solution between the unpopular pursuit of a military victory that might be impossible or too expensive to attain, and leaving, which could make a negative outcome a self-fulfilling prophecy. It is a very difficult position to defend, because it essentially entails supporting a very unsatisfying non-solution to the problem justified by avoiding an even more unsatisfactory outcome if other options are pursued. Sadat and McChrystal summarize the rationale. "Withdrawing would risk turning the country back into the terrorist safe haven it was before 9/11, and drastically ramping up the U.S. presence is a political non-starter," they argue. "That leaves something like the current approach as the only real option. Stuck with doing more of the same, Washington must try to do it better."

The enigma is the strategic interest that the option preserves. Nobody publicly argues that maintaining a shaky Afghan government in power in at least parts of the country fulfills the American stated goal of ensuring that Afghanistan will not become a terrorist haven again in the future. What the policy does accomplish is the diminution of that possibility for as long as American and other ISAF countries are in the country physically to prevent a Taliban victory, which might result in the reintroduction of AQ and others like IS into the country. At the same time, unless the incremental addition of assistance to the Afghan government manages to improve the Afghan National Army's (ANA) capability to the point that it is gradually eliminating that threat to the point of approaching control—a proposition for which there is scant evidence—the commitment is open ended and possibly perpetual. One must ask why the situation has not improved after seventeen or more years of American involvement, and that leads to the further question of what gives us reason to believe that prolonging the engagement will change the situation.

This incremental approach has been the de facto government strategy since President Obama tried unsuccessfully to withdraw American forces as part of his election pledge. Those strategists who maintain a salient American strategic mandate in the country are most loathe to accept withdrawal, partly because of sometimes personal investment in the war and because they believe in the goal of keeping terrorists from returning. They prevailed in the sense that Obama backed away from total disengagement and adopted, with very little public proclamation, the status quo solution.

The matter resurfaced during Trump's first year in office. Like his predecessor, candidate Trump had argued the folly of the continuing war and had vowed to end it when he came to office. During his first year in office, however, pro-continuation voices managed to capture his ear, with two messages. The first was that the war effort was not going well and was in increasing danger of failing if the effort was not reinvigorated. The second was that a relatively modest increase in American troops could stabilize the situation. Trump authorized sending an additional forty-five hundred troops to Afghanistan to augment training the ANA to combat the Taliban. Reflecting general Afghan ambivalence about the centralizing governmental goal underlying their effort, the ANA has not been especially effective in turning the military tide against the Taliban or more recently, Islamic State (IS) infiltrators.

The decision reflects the dynamics of current policy. Nobody advocating the troop increase has maintained that it will in any way be decisive in bringing the war—including American involvement—to a close. When confronted with the likelihood that the increase will not change much in the country, supporters do not bother to make that assertion. Their argument, as reflected by Sadat and McChrystal, is rather a double negative: continuing to do what is already being done will not end the war on favorable terms that translate into any kind of victory for the Afghan or American governments. Rather, the failure to continue to send money and personnel into the battle will make matters worse, up to and including the victory of the Taliban.

This conclusion reflects the nature of Afghan-style asymmetrical warfare. Foreign invaders have tried to subdue the fierce Afghan tribes for a long time. Among the attackers, the Mongols had the most success, occupying and ruling for over a century, but they were ultimately repelled, as were the others. Most asymmetrical warriors are defenders of their territories from outsiders, and a prime asset they can have is a forbidding landscape with which the invaders are unfamiliar but which the defenders can take advantage of. The bleak mountains of Afghanistan certainly fill this description, and it gives them a considerable advantage over invaders. The Afghan tribes, moreover, suspect the motives and desires of their fellow tribes almost as much as they suspect the invaders, but they can put their differences aside to throw out the aliens. The incremental approach is more than vaguely reminiscent of the American approach in Vietnam, where incrementalism eventually failed either to secure victory or to sustain U.S. public support for continuing the effort.

Withdrawal

The third option is akin to the Aiken solution for extrication from Vietnam. Named after Senator George Aiken of Vermont, the senator proposed in 1966 that the United States simply declare victory in Vietnam, leave the country, and let others figure out what winning meant. A similar strategy might apply to Afghanistan, where no one has articulated a coherent, accepted version of what victory looks like. The departure could, also like Vietnam, include the continuation of financial and material assistance for the regime (which was essentially President Richard Nixon's policy prescription for American involvement in post-Vietnam wars), but at heart it would be an abandonment of the mission and an admission that it is an unattainable goal for the United States.

Immediate objections are raised to leaving by supporters of the American mission, as the last two presidents learned when they tried to do so. Part of it is emotional: it means abandoning an ally and admitting the inability to defeat an opponent. This would be a tough psychological problem for the military. Many military leaders realize that prevailing in Afghanistan (which means defeating and evicting the Taliban) without a massive American involvement would be politically impossible and might not succeed anyway—it could be a mission impossible, as it has been until now. Even if decisive action succeeded, Afghan history suggests it would be transitory; if the Americans "won" and went home, the Taliban would just return and the situation would revert to the Afghan norm—tribal autonomy where the tribes bicker among themselves and continue to oppose and bedevil whoever succeeds the American-backed regime.

Would a Taliban return to power after an American departure be unacceptably harmful to American interests? The Taliban did have power in the country for five years, and they harbored AQ during that time as old comrades whom they were willing to protect against the Americans after 9/11. They were driven from power by an Afghan population that marginally preferred the Northern Alliance and simply does not like central governments. In 1996, they were popular reformers because they promised honest governance and minimal intrusion. Those promises proved false and as Jones points out, the Taliban is no longer viewed as heroic or as an attractive alternative to the unpopular regime. It is arguably true that the short-term winner in the competition for control in Afghanistan is the long-term loser.

Two questions are pertinent in assessing the impact of leaving *on U.S. interests*. Neither can be answered definitively because they describe a situation that does not exist: they are hypothetical, not empirical. The first is what difference the outcome will be for Afghanistan itself and thus for the ability of the United States to influence events in the country relevant to *U.S. interests*. That leaves the second question, which is what those interests are. The two are conjoined by what the impact of a withdrawal is on U.S. interests and what, if anything, the United States can do to compensate for any detriments to those interests that different outcomes have on Afghanistan.

Consequences: What to Do?

A great deal of national security planning starts from the framework of *worst-case planning*: trying to determine the worst possible outcome of a situation and what can be done to prevent that outcome from occurring. The future of U.S. involvement in Afghanistan clearly fits into the worst-case model.

Those who wish to continue U.S. policy and strategy as it is or even to expand it to a decisively positive outcome tend to paint the situation in grim worst-case terms that suggest American interests would somehow be grievously damaged by abandoning the war effort and leaving the Afghan government to fend for itself against the Taliban. The predicted damage would be the reversion of the country to its pre-9/11 status as terrorist haven. That is certainly possible, but its severity is softened by two points. The first is that the region is already a haven for the Taliban and its terrorist associates. The United States has brought pressure on Pakistan to suppress this activity, which the Pakistanis are either unable or unwilling to do. Should the Taliban come to power, Pakistan might have to alter its role as it tries to keep its client in power, and more open terrorist activity along and across the border might goad Pakistan into playing a more responsible role. Since a Taliban government would be resisted by Afghan elements, it might also change the relationship between the two countries.

The second mitigating factor is that the United States would almost certainly not honor the sovereignty of Afghanistan if it allowed terrorist use of its territory. Sophisticated drone (see chapter 17) and cruise missile technology could be employed against terrorist locations about which the Afghans could do little. The United States has set the precedent for and gained experience with these kinds of operations in Pakistan. The Pakistanis complain about these actions, which causes the Americans to limit them. The United States would likely feel less inhibition in ignoring the complaints of a hostile Afghan regime, especially if it seemed to be supporting an IS presence in the country.

There are no clear-cut proper or obvious options for future strategy. Analysts disagree about the severity of the problem and how to deal with it. None of the options are good. An all-out campaign is politically impossible among Americans and might well not work. Continuing current policy seems quixotic, futile, and purposeless. Bremmer summarizes the consequences: "The result is a violent, expansive stalemate. If Trump stops sending troops and money, the Afghan government will collapse. If the troops and dollars continue to flow, Washington will be paying to extend the stalemate." Packing American bags and leaving means abandoning an ally and might have some damaging effects on some American interests. None of these are obviously good nor appealing. But can the United States simply make its longest war an endless commitment to a marginal interest? What do you think? What should we do?

Study/Discussion Question

1. Discuss Afghanistan's historical evolution, its importance geopolitically, and its history of dealing with outsiders. What importance has Afghanistan historically had for the United States, especially in national security terms?

2. How and why did 9/11 fundamentally change American national security interests toward Afghanistan? Why did the United States invade the country in 2001? Why did it stay? What is the importance of the decision to remain in Afghanistan?

3. Describe Afghanistan in terms of its attitudes toward outsiders and a strong central Afghan government. Is the current U.S. position compatible or at odds with historic Afghan preference? How important should that be for future strategy and policy?

4. What options does the United States have for dealing with (and especially ending) its war in Afghanistan? Discuss the pros and cons of each alternative.

5. Based on the available options, what do you think the United States needs to do to end its longest war? What are the positive and negative consequences of your choice? Why? Defend your position.

Bibliography

Barfield, Thomas. *Afghanistan: A Cultural and Political History.* Princeton, NJ: Princeton University Press, 2012.

Bremmer, Ian. "Can Donald Trump Accept a Defeat in Afghanistan?" *Time* 191 (5) (February 13, 2018), 12.

Coll, Steve. *Directorate S: The C.I.A. and America's Secret Wars in Afghanistan and Pakistan.* New York: Penguin Books, 2017.

———. *Ghost Wars: The Secret History of the CIA, Afghanistan, and bin Laden from the Soviet Invasion to September 10, 2001.* New York: Penguin Books, 2004.

Ewans, Martin. *Afghanistan: A Short History of Its People and Politics.* New York: HarperCollins Perennials, 2002.

Horton, Scott. *Fool's Errand: Time to End the War in Afghanistan.* New York: CreateSpace Independent Publishing, 2017.

Jalali, Ali Ahmad. "The Future of Afghanistan." *Parameters* XXXVI (1) (Spring 2006), 4–19.

———. *A Military History of Afghanistan: From the Great Game to the Global War on Terror.* Lawrence: University Press of Kansas, 2017.

Jones, Seth G. *In the Graveyard of Empires: America's War in Afghanistan.* New York: W. W. Norton, 2009.

———. "Why the Taliban Isn't Winning in Afghanistan: Too Weak for Victory, Too Strong for Defeat." *Foreign Affairs Snapshot* (online), January 3, 2018.

Kaplan, Robert D. "Man Versus Afghanistan." *Atlantic* 305 (3) (April 2010), 60–71.

Mazzetti, Mark. "The Devastating Paradox of Pakistan: How Afghanistan's Neighbor Cultivated American Dependency While Subverting American Policy." *Atlantic,* March 2018.

O'Connell, Aaron B. (ed.). *Our Latest Longest War: Losing Hearts and Minds in Afghanistan.* Chicago: University of Chicago Press, 2017.

Rashid, Ahmed. *Taliban: Militant Islam, Oil, and Fundamentalism in Central Asia.* Second Ed. New Haven, CT: Yale University Press, 2010.

Sadat, Kosh, and Stan McChrystal. "Staying the Course in Afghanistan: How to Fight the Longest War." *Foreign Affairs* 96 (6) (November/December 2017), 2–8.

Shahrani, M. Nafiz (ed.). *Modern Afghanistan: The Impact of 40 Years of War.* Bloomington: Indiana University Press, 2018.

Snow, Donald M. *The Case Against Military Intervention: Why We Do It and Why It Fails.* New York and London: Routledge, 2016

Tannen, Stephen. *Afghanistan: A Military History from Alexander the Great to the Taliban.* New York: Da Capo Press, 2009.

U.S. Marine Corps. *Afghanistan: Operational Culture for Deploying Personnel.* Quantico, VA: Center for Operational Cultural Learning, 2009.

10

Syria

The Perfect Maelstrom

A maelstrom is a violent whirlpool that, according to legend and heroic literature, can suck ships that venture too close to it to their doom at the bottom of the sea. Most of the world's maelstroms are in the cold waters of the North Sea between Scotland and Norway (the term itself is Norwegian), and their ability to wreak enormous damage is sometimes exaggerated. Possibly the most familiar example for most people is the maelstrom in Epcot Center at Florida's Disney World in the Norwegian pavilion.

The symbolism of the term is of an inexorable force of confusing feelings, ideas, or convictions that draws its victims into a downward spiral from which they ultimately cannot escape. The cascade of events in Syria since it got caught up in the remnants of the Arab Spring of 2010–2011 has spiraled downward into a long, bloody civil war with clear genocidal aspects that include the use of chemical weapons by the Syrian government against rebellious members of its citizenry. The situation represents a virtually perfect international political example of the phenomenon of a maelstrom in action. The tragedy of the civil war is well chronicled in the physical suffering endured by the Syrian people, but it is also a political storm that has affected and been affected by other countries and groups in conflict in the Middle East. Among those hovering at the maelstrom's edge is the United States.

Since the civil war began in 2011, the United States has resolutely attempted to avoid being sucked into the whirlpool. This has meant trying to avoid direct personal military involvement in the fighting within the country, limiting itself to the peripheries of support for forces opposing the government and the Islamic State (IS). It has imposed this self-limit partially because of American public opposition to direct military involvement in yet another Middle Eastern country and because it has few interests in Syria. Its geopolitical stake in the civil war is not great, but the government's chemical attacks against Syrian citizens (which Syria and its patron Russia deny) add another element to the situation: so-called humanitarian interests in the welfare of humanity. The prosecution of war criminals (anyone who employs chemical weapons is a war criminal) further complicates the situation.

The maelstrom swirls deeper and harder because the many parties have different and often contradictory interests in the civil war's outcome. Many countries (including the United States) prefer different outcomes that affect their interests in different ways. For the United States, the ideal outcome is for the war to end, for peace to be restored, and for healing and reconstruction and reconciliation to begin, for instance. That would begin to solve the humanitarian crisis associated with chemical weapons use. It matters critically, however, who prevails.

If, for instance, peace is achieved with the Syrian Alawite minority government of Bashar al-Assad still in power, American interests could still be frustrated because that might well mean that the Russians remain a major player in Syrian politics (as noted in chapter 11, Russia has a major naval base in the Alawite region of the country). Given the state of American-Russian relations and apparent Russian expansionist policies, this outcome would not please the Americans. At the same time, the Alawites are Shiites, and much of their assault on their own people has been directed at the Sunni majority, and it is difficult to reconcile them to a continuing Assad regime. This is particularly true regarding the nearly twelve million Syrian refugees, who must be enticed to return home, a difficult "sell" if Assad remains in power. Those countries and groups like Iran and Hezbollah that support the Assad regime because they are fellow Shiites clearly do not want to see Assad overturned and replaced by a Sunni government and find themselves in de facto but unnatural alliance with the Russians.

This example is a microcosm of an even more complicated, arguably convoluted set of circumstances and motives that different countries and groups, including the United States, have in the outcome of this situation that gives articulate meaning to the descriptor "byzantine." Like many other countries, the United States has been reluctant to get too close to the edge of the maelstrom for fear of being pulled into its downward swirling spiral. Trying to sort out and reconcile the myriad contradictions, however, remains central to determining American national security interests in Syria.

Perspectives on the Problem

The civil war has raged in Syria since 2011. It is one of the most vicious, barbaric, and violent conflicts in the world today, rivaling some of the worst atrocities in remote African states. It is at heart an inter-confessional contest between the two major sects of Islam, the majority Sunnis (about 74 percent of the population), and Shiites led by the Assad government dominated by a minority Alawite tribe (about 13 percent). It is hard to distinguish whether religion or ethnicity was the most important factor in creating the uprising in the first place, but it has been so intense and embittering that it is even more difficult to conceptualize how it can or will end. The attempt has devolved to finding, in the subtitle of Ford's *Foreign Affairs* article, a "least bad option."

It is an incredibly intricate conflict with, as already suggested, a broad spectrum of parties with strong and mostly mutually incompatible interests in the outcome. Since 2013, the U.S. government, at the time directed by President Obama, has tried to keep the United States out of the physical fray because, as Hennigan rightly asserts, "a U.S. President has no attractive option in Syria." Frustrated like his predecessors, President Trump declared on March 29, 2018, "We are coming out of Syria, like very soon. Let the people take care of it now." The chemical weapons attacks in April 2018 demonstrated the declaration was easier said than done. Understanding that difficulty requires looking at the crisis itself and particularly how the crisis has created an apparent triumph for the Assad regime.

Syria and the Civil War

Syria has always been something of a wild card in Middle East politics. During the Cold War, it was one of the leading opponents of Israel and proponents of Arab nationalism and non-commitment to one side or the other in the Cold War. To this end, it joined Egypt, whose leader Gamal Abdul Nasser was a leading neutralist, in forming a political union, the United Arab Republic (UAR) in 1958. The UAR surrounded Israel in the north and south, and it propounded the neutralist philosophy. National egos broke the union apart in 1961, and an attempt to recreate it in 1963 with the addition of Iraq failed to materialize. Syrian distinctiveness remained.

The Syrians became Russia's major foothold in the region. In 1971, Russia and Syria agreed to allow the Soviets to establish a naval base on the northern Syrian coast at Tartus. It was the first Soviet naval base outside Soviet territory, and it remains an important link between the Putin regime and the Assad regime of Syria, since the base is in the Alawite region and would be in danger should anti-Assad forces claim power in Syria.

Prior to the outbreak of the civil war, Syria lived in a peaceful but obviously precarious political situation. The country had between seventeen and eighteen million people in 2014 according to the 2017 *CIA World Factbook*. Syria is physically about 1.5 times the size of Pennsylvania, and about 90 percent of its population is Arab. By religion, it is 87 percent Muslim, predominantly Sunni. The largest Shiite group is Alawite, which is the ethnicity of the ruling Assad family. For decades after Hafiz al-Assad, the patriarch of the Alawite government, came to power in 1970, the working arrangement was that the Alawites dominated the government and the military, Sunni businessmen controlled the economy, and they collaborated to keep Syria running. This arrangement, of course, proved to be tenuous, and it injected a Sunni-Shia element into the civil war that, among other things, helps define which Middle Eastern states and movements support the government or the rebels in the civil war. Notably, most of the support for the regime comes from Shiite sources like Iran and Hezbollah, although others support it for other reasons discussed in the next section.

The civil war was one of the numerous spinoffs of the so-called Arab Spring that began in December 2010 in Tunisia and rapidly spread throughout the region in 2011. The major theme of the movement was a conscious attempt by mostly young Muslims to democratize the political systems of decidedly undemocratic states. This included Syria, where the mantle of power had passed from Hafiz al-Assad to his son Bashar. Pro-democratic demonstrations erupted in March 2011, demanding political reforms and the replacement of Assad as president. Those efforts were met with increasingly violent opposition from the regime. The spark that ignited violence occurred when teenagers in several cities defaced buildings by spray-painting pro-democracy, anti-government slogans on them. The police reacted violently, arresting and detaining fifteen boys, who were tortured by government security forces. One teenager was subjected to particularly brutal torture from which he died. This incident sparked much larger demonstrations that rapidly devolved into the Syrian civil war.

What distinguishes the Syrian uprising from other phenomena associated with the Arab Spring is the ferocity, duration, physical destruction, and suffering it has caused the Syrian people. The war has been raging for over seven years, and it has virtually destroyed much of what pre-war Syria represented. Statistics on the war are imprecise, but the UN Commission on Human Rights offers some tantalizing estimates. *Al Jazeera* reports that as of February 2018, an estimated 465,000 Syrians (about 5 percent of the population) had been killed in the war. In addition, refugees who have fled the country are estimated at 5.5 million, and the number of internally displaced persons is over six million. That means more than two-thirds of the pre-war population is either dead or have been forced out of their homes by the war. The chemical weapons attacks of 2012, 2013, and 2018 only accentuate the horror that is modern Syria.

The economic and physical consequences are equally terrible. The economy is ruined. Gross Domestic Product (GDP), for instance, fell from an estimated $97.5 billion in 2012 to $55.8 billion in 2014, a drop of almost two-fifths, and the physical effects of the war have destroyed much of the infrastructure necessary to recuperate from those losses. The statistics are no more than estimates, of course, but most predictors suggest that the cost of economic recovery will be at least $1 *trillion*, roughly twenty times the size of the economy today. Once the war is concluded, the human and physical task of trying to reconstitute Syria is virtually incalculable. It is not clear where the funding will come from to undertake the task, especially since some potential benefactors will be alienated by whoever "wins" the civil war.

Why the Government Is Winning/Has Won

As of mid-2018, the physical war seemed to be dying down, as the government and its associates had largely destroyed organized resistance in virtually all Syrian communities. A reasonable question is how this has been possible: how could such a small percentage of the population (the Alawites) impose their will so thoroughly (if brutally) on the rest of the population? There are several contributing factors.

The major source of government advantage in the civil war arises from its control of both the government and the military. Although there was discontent with the Assad regime before the war broke out, it was not organized in either a political or military sense. The result was virtually total disorganization among the rebels in the face of joint military operations by an organized and disciplined government. The result was that multiple groups formed, but they were independent of one another, uncoordinated, often in opposition to the others, and unable to agree on a political program or joint military opposition. The Assad regime did not have to divide and conquer the opposition; it did so to itself. The Alawites, by contrast, had established themselves in leadership roles in both the government and the military for generations, and thus were prepared organizationally for the task.

This division minimized the effective rise of forces against the Alawite regime, and it also frustrated outsiders who opposed the regime but were frustrated by the inability to identify factions they could support. The United States was particularly reluctant to support groups whose dedication to democracy was suspect, a form of "intervention shock" from the Iraq intervention. The emergence of IS as a major opposition group tainted and further complicated the problem of developing support for a unified opposition.

Second, the regime had an advantage in attracting effective outside assistance, despite its general unpopularity internationally. That support came from two very different quarters. One was Putin's Russia, which was in the process of reasserting itself as a world power (see chapter 11) and wanted to cement its relationship with the Syrian regime, both because of its naval base at Tartus and because Syria represents its one real foothold in the region. More importantly, since the Alawites are Shiite, they received support from other Shiite sources, notably Hezbollah and Iran. The Iranians have been particularly helpful because, as Ford points out, "The Iranian government has assembled tens of thousands of Shiite fighters from Afghanistan, Iran, Iraq, and even Pakistan" to augment government forces.

The Sunni rebels, by contrast, have received relatively little help from Sunni states, and in the case of Kurds who oppose the regime, their success is openly opposed by other Sunni countries, notably Turkey. This opposition to the Kurds even creates an affinity between the Assad regime and countries like Turkey because, as Ford also points out, "The Syrian government has already rejected the legitimacy of the Syrian autonomous region, known as Rojava." He adds, "The Turkish government would cheer Assad's repression of the Syrian Kurds."

Third, there has been a notable lack of sustained outside assistance for those opposing the Assad regime. The United States was in no mood to initiate another Middle East intervention in 2011, especially in support of Syrian opposition (Sunni) movements of dubious provenance or that, like IS, might prove more of a problem than the Assad regime itself. In the volatility of the Arab Spring, most Western states were waiting for the dust to settle around that phenomenon. Throwing forces or sizable support into Syria seemed risky and likely to fail. Only when Syrian refugees began to flee the country in large numbers—many headed for Europe—did outsiders become interested. By then, it was largely too late.

Fourth, consensus quickly congealed around the proposition that there was probably no good solution to the Syrian problem. This was certainly true of the geopolitical situation. What outsiders desperately wanted to find was a viable, virtuous, democratic faction that had some chance of uniting the disparate rebel factions and producing an alternative to Assad worthy of support by the major powers. The post-occupation evolution of governance in Iraq served as a cautionary note. Despite considerable efforts, no such movement could be identified. The only groups that looked like they might challenge the regime were the Kurds or IS, which were bitterly opposed to one another because the Kurds claimed northeast Syria as the heart of Rojava and IS claimed the same ground for the caliphate. As a result, resistance remained atomized and localized, allowing the government to engage in bitter, highly destructive actions to isolate and destroy pockets of resistance.

This progression has added to the humanitarian dimension of the conflict and raised questions about whether the protection of mankind represents a vital interest of the world community. Is there a central place in national security policy for what I (among others) have called in *Thinking about National Security* humanitarian intervention, the purpose of which is to relieve human suffering? The situation in Syria clearly qualifies: the volume of displacement and death offers a compelling rationale, as does the massive destruction of the country on a scale of Russian destruction of the Chechen capital of Grozny in the 1990s, an analogy that may or may not be coincidental.

Policy Options

In many ways, the slaughter in Syria is an extreme microcosm of the savagery that so often marks Middle Eastern conflict, and as is so often the case, the region itself seems incapable of resolving the difficulties and thus relieving the slaughter. Part of the reason is that there is no country or reliable combination of countries there capable of intervening and imposing a settlement. In turn, that problem arises from the multiplicity of interests and prejudices that dominate the area and are often so contradictory that they preclude rational progress toward solving the problem. That means that any attempts to resolve matters must fall to outsiders who either lack the interest level or means to impose solutions.

This description clearly applies to Syria. What the Syrian government is doing to its citizens defies virtually all definitions of civilized behavior. The Syrian "civil war" is a humanitarian disaster of the first order, and it will continue until the Assad regime violently suppresses the last of its opposition or is overthrown. Except for supporters of the regime, no one defends what the Syrian regime is doing, but no one is doing much about it. The reasons intermix the geopolitical and humanitarian interests of the various parties, and geopolitical factors are prevailing at the expense of extreme human suffering.

The United States has minimal geopolitical interests in Syria. It has always had proper but cool relations with the Syrians, largely because of Syrian-Israeli tensions centering on the Golan Heights. The United States has some humanitarian interests that militate toward a policy that would bring the carnage to an end, but it is reluctant to try to create that situation by recourse to American force, an option that is virtually universally opposed in the United States. It has been unable to bring together a coalition of regional actors to pursue the cause of peace. The combination of personal reluctance and the inability to identify and aid regional partners very greatly circumscribe American options.

Regional Geopolitical Barriers

The relationship of two major regional actors demonstrates vividly the complicated nature of dealing with the Syrian civil conflict. Neither is an accepted state actor, but both oppose the government of Syria and have claims against

Syrian territory. These two entities are the Islamic State and the Kurds. Both are important in different ways and for different reasons, and this expands geopolitics to Turkey, which logically seems a candidate for mediation but has not emerged in that role.

IS and its claims as a caliphate is a direct artifact of the civil war. IS began as Al Qaeda in Iraq (AQI) during the American occupation of that country. It was largely dispatched in 2007. It did not disband, but rather went underground, many of its members and activities moving to remote parts of eastern Syria. AQI is Sunni, and thus found itself in opposition to the Shiite Assad regime as various rebel groups were forming around the country. Unlike many others, IS had previous (if not terribly successful) combat experience, which put it ahead of many forming rebel factions. Moreover, most of its early activities were in eastern sections of the country, the pacification of which was a lower-order government priority. The organization burst upon the international scene in 2013 and 2014, and it was quickly identified as one of the more militarily effective arms of the resistance. As an AQ terrorist legatee, it was also viewed as part of the problem rather than the solution by outsiders anxious to help anti-government forces.

No state in the region or elsewhere took up the IS cause. Once the IS leadership declared its intent to form an expanding independent state (the caliphate) out of the territory of surrounding states, it became a potential threat to the rest of the region, and particularly Sunni states who might otherwise have been sympathetic and supported them as part of an anti-Shiite effort in Syria. IS has received private aid from conservative Sunnis (mostly Wahhabis, with whom they share common religious views), but even conservative Sunni states could not embrace them as the caliphate was expanding. The status of IS was greatly diminished by military engagements in 2017 and is not currently a major concern. Its continuing existence, however, forms the rationale for the stationing of between one thousand and two thousand American forces in eastern Syria.

The Kurdish situation is different. As already noted, there is a Kurdish enclave (Rojava) in eastern Syria that is part of what Kurdish nationalists hope will eventually form part of the independent state of Kurdistan. The idea of such a state is opposed by every regional state with a Kurdish region, but the Kurds were also by far the most effective fighting the advance of IS and effectively led the regional resistance that halted and began the reverse of the expansion of the caliphate. Lost in most analyses at the time was Kurdish motivation: much of the territory in both Syria and Iraq being devoured by IS was in fact Kurdish territory. The Kurdish defense forces (the *pesh merga*) who became famous for their engagement with IS were in fact self-defense forces stopping and expelling IS from what they consider their own lands. When it was suggested (in the United States, among other places) that the Kurds might become the armed leaders of the broader campaign against IS, they demurred. The same is true of supporters of Rojava today.

All this is directly related to the Syrian conflict and particularly outside attitudes toward it. Among regional powers, for instance, Turkey stands out. Given its common boundary with Syria and the fact it is Sunni, one would expect the Turks to support anyone opposing the Assad regime as well as opposing IS, whose occupation of northern Syria put the terrorist organization on its borders. The Turks, however, are obsessed with the Kurdish "problem," since 20 percent of its population is Kurdish, and there is a Turkish secessionist group with ties to Syrian and Iraqi Kurds in its boundaries. The Turks worry more about the Kurds than about the slaughter in Syria, and it creates contradictions. The Turks oppose IS but do not entirely want it to be destroyed, because that would strengthen the Assad regime. At the same time, it is not entirely supportive of overthrowing Assad, because the result could create a power vacuum that Rojava supporters might exploit, to the delight and encouragement of Iraqi, Turkish, and even Iranian Kurds (thereby creating a weak link between Turkey and Russia, Syria's primary patron).

U.S. Options

The United States has been one of several frustrated outsiders trying to ameliorate conditions in Syria. American direct geopolitical interests in Syria have always been minimal and mostly adversarial. Interactions between the two countries in areas such as trade have been very small, meaning there is relatively little with which the United States can threaten the Syrians if they do not comply with American preferences. The countries that support the Syrian regime uniformly have a greater stake in the Syrians than the United States has in its opposition. Syria is Russia's foothold in the region, and Russia is Syria's primary protector in forums like the United Nations. Iran, as the largest Shiite state in the world and as a country seeking to enhance itself as a regional power, finds support natural. Even states with some ambivalence toward the situation like Turkey—which opposes the Shiite Alawite regime but fears the Kurds will benefit if Assad is overthrown—are of little help.

The United States is in a serious quandary trying to fashion a traditional security strategy for the Syrian conflict. What outcome does the United States want? Since American geopolitical interests are minimal, there is not a great deal either to protect or promote in Syria. Essentially, those interests are limited to continued support for Israeli security and minimizing expanded Russian influence beyond Syria's borders. The Golan Heights, which forms the major Israeli military concern with Syria, is secure, with over twenty thousand Israeli settlers living in occupied areas of Golan. The Russian foothold in Syria is clearly more important to Russia than its denial is to the United States, both because of the naval base and because it is Russia's only real entrée into the region. All the United States can realistically do with Russia is continue to decry its denial of accusations of Syrian chemical weapons employment in forums like the United Nations.

A strong case can be made for serious American humanitarian interests in Syria that are the result of Syrian chemical attacks against its population in 2012, 2013, and 2018. Although the Syrians and their Russian advisors deny it, Syria has used chemical weapons against its citizens in towns and cities still under rebel control to break that resistance and allow the government to extend its authority without engaging in bloody urban warfare that would attrite its own forces in addition to rebels. These attacks are strictly prohibited by the 1997 Chemical Weapons Convention (CWC). Syria has been a signatory of the agreement since 2013, an accession that was part of its agreement to destroy its stockpiles after its attacks of that year. The treaty prohibits the development and stockpiling and especially the use of chemical agents against humans, and its violation is a "crime against humanity" (a war crime) that can be prosecuted by the International Criminal Court (ICC) at The Hague, Netherlands.

The problem is that humanitarian interests, the vitality of which is extolled rhetorically, rarely rise to the level of actual enforcement when such actions would be opposed—especially violently—by accused perpetrators. The only way that the chemical ban could be enforced would be to arrest and try those responsible for authorizing and carrying out chemical attacks and putting them before the ICC docket. That group would include Bashar al-Assad who, if convicted, would spend the rest of his life behind bars. If anything, that prospect means prevailing in the civil war is more important to the regime than it might otherwise be.

The available list of other actions the United States can undertake is circumscribed and unlikely to cause significant change. The calculation begins with what the United States seeks to accomplish. The traditional answer is to remove and replace the existing regime, but no one is advocating that solution. For one thing, it is probably unachievable. As Ford summarizes, "hopes of getting rid of Assad or securing a reformed government are far-fetched fantasies, and so support for antigovernment factions should be off the table." It is not clear how such a goal would be attainable except through massive intervention, which would almost certainly fail if attempted (see my *The Case Against Military Intervention*) and not serve basic American interests not based in humanitarian concerns.

Moreover, although many Syrians favor trying, a successful overthrow would not please many others in the region. Turkey, which is no friend of the Alawites, prefers Assad in power because he blocks the establishment of Rojava, and the Russians rightly fear a successor government would not cooperate with them. Shiite countries like Iraq and Iran do not favor a Sunni replacement, and the Sunni Arab states have not been exactly zealous in promoting Syrian Sunnis. If intervening in a civil war is not about replacing the government in power, what is the point?

That leaves smaller, more symbolic gestures that do not greatly enhance U.S. interests or help the situation very much. Military options beyond the small Special Forces teams in the country are no longer seriously contemplated, which is probably good from an American viewpoint but does not improve a situation in which it appears Assad will retain control over a badly diminished Syria in desperate need of major rebuilding. It has even been suggested that the best thing for the United States would be to let the Assad regime prevail (which they probably will anyway) and leave it to the Russians to help them recover and rebuild.

Consequences: What to Do?

The Syrian civil conflict provides a cautionary note for national security planning. It clearly represents a human disaster of the first order. Millions of people have been killed or displaced, and bitterness and hatreds that have been created by the destruction and atrocities like the chemical weapons attacks will take years, even generations, to heal, if they ever do. The cities and countryside have been decimated to the point they will require massive rebuilding once the guns are finally stilled. It is not clear where the resources will come from to try to accomplish the massive task. It is even fair to ask if Syria as the world knew it will ever be totally reconstituted.

The disaster is cautionary in two senses. First, it points to the limits of the willingness of the international community, including the United States, to do anything effectively positive in this situation. American traditional geopolitical calculations suggest Syria is not a place in which the United States can or should invest its resources. The prospect of gain is simply not present, and this evaluation is shared by other powers. Russia, with some vested interests, is an exception. The only concrete interests the United States and the rest of the international order has are humanitarian, and they have proven inadequate to produce more than comfort for some suffering Syrians. The mounting refugee crisis in Europe has not been enough to impel a political solution the contours of which are not clear in any case. Ford may be right in his summary: "for the time being, it [aid to refugees] is the best the United States can do."

Consider the situation in mid-2018. By most measures, the regime had won. As Stein points out, it has routed the insurgency, consolidated control of Syria's most important region (the west), and it has solid support from Moscow and Tehran. But has it really won? Two-thirds of the population remain refugees, and the country cannot be "whole" under those circumstances. Yahya, however, reminds us that most refugees are so fearful of the regime they will not return home if Assad remains in power. The tragedy continues.

Second, the disaster may be a harbinger—a dark model—of the dilemmas of national security strategy for the future. Syria is a highly publicized instance of developing world atrocity and disaster, but it is hardly alone. Situations of equivalent tragedy or even worse are happening in other developing world areas, notably Africa, and some of these are described in chapter 13. Outside inaction in Syria may be the harbinger for similar disregard.

The maelstrom continues to swirl. Millions have been drawn into its vortex and either been killed or escaped to internal or external exile. The world community stands as far from the edge as it safely can to avoid being consumed by it, and in the process, nothing is done to try to ease the force of the whirlwind. On April 22, 2018, the maelstrom expanded to the capital of Damascus. Government planes attacked a refugee camp at Yarmouk, where IS operatives were said to be hiding. No place in Syria escapes the storm. No one knows how to surmount it.

Should the United States be rethinking its view toward Syria and similar kinds of human disasters? Should humanitarian *vital* interests, as some of their champions propound, be elevated in the hierarchy of national security interests?

Alternatively, does the existence of chaos that may prove impossible to relieve in Syria suggest the United States should retreat from poking its national head in the business of other people? Or is the answer somewhere in between? If so, where? What do you think?

Study/Discussion Questions

1. Describe how the Syrian civil war began. Relate it to the Arab Spring and differences within Islam.
2. What are the major internal and external groups involved in the civil war in the country? How does this constellation, individually and collectively, make resolution so difficult?
3. Why is the Syrian government winning the war despite international opposition to how they are waging the war? How do regional geopolitical factors contribute to this outcome? Include a discussion of IS and the Kurds in your answer.
4. What is the basic U.S. position on the war in Syria? Why has the United States not become more involved? Include the impact of regional dynamics in the U.S. decision process.
5. Are all American options regarding the Syrian civil war bad, as they are generally portrayed? If the United States lacks sufficient geopolitical interests for involvement, what about humanitarian interests? What should the United States do? Why?

Bibliography

Abboud, Samer N. *Syria.* Hot Spots in Global Politics. Cambridge, UK: Polity Press, 2015.

Abouzeid, Rania. *No Turning Back: Life, Loss, and Hope in Wartime Syria.* New York: W. W. Norton, 2018.

Ajami, Fouad. *The Syrian Rebellion.* Palo Alto, CA: Hoover Institution Press, 2012.

Bellamy, Alex J. *Responsibility to Protect.* Cambridge, UK: Polity Press, 2009.

Evans, Gareth. *The Responsibility to Protect: End Mass Atrocity War Crimes Once and for All.* Washington, DC: Brookings Institution Press, 2008.

Feaver, Peter. "The Just War Tradition and the Paradox of Public Failure in Syria." *Foreign Policy* (online), August 22, 2013.

Ford, Robert S. "Keeping Out of Syria: The Least Bad Option." *Foreign Affairs* 96 (6) (November/December 2017), 16–22.

Goldsmith, Leon. *Cycle of Fear: Syria's Alawites in War and Peace.* London: Hurst Publications, 2015.

Hashemi, Nader, and Danny Postel. *The Syrian Dilemma.* Cambridge, MA: MIT Press, 2013.

Hennigan, W. J. "The Syrian Gamble: Can the U.S. Deter War Crimes without Going to War?" *Time* 191 (15) (April 23, 2018), 26–29.

Hisham, Marwan. *Brothers of the Gun: A Memoir of the Syrian Civil War.* New York: One World, 2018.

Lukyanov, Fyodor. "Putin's Foreign Policy: The Quest to Restore Russia's Rightful Place." *Foreign Affairs* 95 (3) (May/June 2016), 30–37.

McHugo, John. *Syria: A Recent History.* London: Saqi Books, 2015.

Nardin, Terry. "The Moral Basis of Humanitarian Intervention." *Ethics and International Affairs* 16 (1) (March 2002), 57–70.

Nasr, Vali. "Iran Among the Ruins: Tehran's Advantage in a Turbulent Middle East." *Foreign Affairs* 97 (2) (March/April 2018), 108–18.

Phillips, Christopher. *The Battle for Syria: International Rivalry in the Middle East.* New Haven, CT: Yale University Press, 2016.

Schmidinger, Jordi. *Rojava: Revolution, War, and the Future of Syria's Kurds.* London: Pluto Press, 2018.

Snow, Donald M. *The Case Against Military Intervention: Why We Do It and Why It Fails.* New York and London: Routledge, 2016.

———. *The Middle East, Oil, and the U.S. National Security Policy.* Lanham, MD: Rowman & Littlefield, 2016.

———. *Thinking about National Security: Strategy, Policy, and Issues.* New York and London: Routledge, 2016.

Stein, Aaron. "A U.S. Containment Strategy for Syria: To Beat the Russians, Let Them Win." *Foreign Affairs Snapshot* (online), March 15, 2018.

"Syria's Civil War Explained from the Beginning." *Al Jazeera* (online), February 16, 2018.

Tabler, Andrew J. "Syria's Collapse: And How Washington Can Stop It." *Foreign Affairs* 92 (4) (July/August 2013), 9–15.

Tejel, Jordi. *Syria's Kurds: Politics and Society.* New York and London: Routledge, 2008.

Trenin, Dmitri. *What Is Russia Up to in the Middle East?* Cambridge, UK: Polity Press, 2017.

Van Dam, Nikolaos. *Destroying a Nation: The Civil War in Syria.* London: I. B. Tauris, 2017.

Weiss, Thomas G. *Humanitarian Intervention.* Cambridge, UK: Polity Press, 2012.

Yahya, Maha. "What Will It Take for Syrian Refugees to Return Home? The Obstacles Are Significant." *Foreign Affairs Snapshot* (online), May 28, 2018.

Yassin-Kassab, Robin, and Leila Al-Shami. *Burning Country: Syrians in Revolution and War.* London: Pluto Press, 2018.

11

Russia

Dealing with a Long-Term Rival

The politico-military confrontation between the United States and the Union of Soviet Socialist Republics (USSR) dominated the international system for nearly a half-century between World War II and the implosion of the Soviet Union in 1991. Largely because of their mutual possession of massive thermonuclear arsenals capable of decimating one another and possibly all of humankind, they were the world's "superpowers," a designation designed to capture their primacy among sovereign states. They opposed one another across the broad range of international politics based on their ideological opposition and evangelical obsession to spread their ideologies to the rest of the world.

The symbol of that relationship was the Cold War, the geopolitical name given to the competition for supremacy. Managing the Cold War was the chief national security priority of both, particularly as the nuclear-based military balance demonstrated progressively that a military conclusion was both mutually senseless and suicidal. Until they peered over the edge at the possibility of Armageddon during the Cuban Missile Crisis of 1962, war had seemed the likely, fatalistic outcome of the Cold War. After 1962, avoiding that disaster became their mutual fixation.

Neither side, however, knew how to end it. The situation may have dictated peace born not of compassion but out of fear of the consequences created (what I have called a "necessary peace") that was uncomfortable, expensive, and time- and energy-depleting, but nobody knew how to make it end without a nuclear fireball. The Cold War could not be allowed to become "hot," and that meant its perpetuation. It ended when the Soviet Union and most of the rest of the communist world collapsed between 1990 and 1992, and the national security landscape had been fundamentally changed. We are still trying to devise a new paradigm for understanding basic world politics and how national security strategy must adapt to the new reality.

The change has been dramatic and dynamic. The most traumatic effects have been on the Russian Federation, the major successor to and core of the Soviet Union. The most visible concrete change was the physical breakup of the *union* of Soviet republics, whose parts rapidly seceded and formed their own independent sovereign states. The core, Russia, was also decimated. The most obvious manifestations have been political and demographic. Following the eviction of the Communist Party of the Soviet Union (CPSU) from the Kremlin, the country began a long, contentious process of adjustment and reconstitution from which it is still emerging. Democracy emerged in the 1990s with Boris Yeltsin as its symbol, but it failed. Since then, the country has attempted to find an appropriate format and leadership. The popular dictatorship of Vladimir Putin is the current solution, but it is transitory: Putin was elected to a new term in 2018 and can, under the Russian Constitution, only serve until the conclusion of that term in 2024. There is no successor on the current horizon.

The most dramatic, and in the long term consequential, trend is demographic, and it bodes poorly for Russia's and Putin's pretensions for returning Russia to the ranks of leading world powers. During the Cold War, the USSR was the world's third most populous country (after China and India); the United States was fourth. In 1990, the Soviet population was about 291 million, compared to roughly 249 million Americans. Population size was part of the Soviet claim to superpower status.

The fall of communism savaged that total, in two ways. First, almost half the population seceded as the former Soviet republics left the union and formed independent governments. Second, there was a ticking demographic time bomb in the form of a negative population growth rate that reflected both a negative ratio between births and deaths (which is, according to the 2017 *CIA World Factbook*, currently at –0.4 percent) and discouraging population characteristics. Joffe, for instance, reports that one in four Russian males dies before the age of fifty-five.

The result is a shrinking Russian population base. Comparative population figures from 2015, for instance, show the 1990 population of Russia has been more than halved at 142 million, whereas the American population has risen to 321 million. When population trends are projected into the future, the results are even grimmer for the Russians. Biden and Carpenter report that the Russian population will decline by 20 percent between today and 2050 to about 128 million; the U.S. population is expected to expand to 438 million.

These negative trends form the geopolitical context for a Russian state and leader desperate to reassert the relevance and primacy of their country as an international actor. It is a difficult prospect for the Russians, who have fought for centuries to establish themselves as a world power and who achieved that goal during the Cold War, only to have it snatched away as the USSR evaporated. It began a traumatic descent from superpower to arguable secondary power, which greatly troubles the Russian population. As Lukyanov summarizes, "Neither Russian elites nor ordinary Russians ever accepted the image of their country as a mere regional actor." Among those most dismissive of decline and most dedicated to the reassertion of power is Vladimir Putin. Dealing with a Russia seeking to reestablish its major power status is the major American national security problem in U.S.-Russian relations and, in a world where both Russia and America still maintain huge nuclear arsenals, the existential core of security.

Perspectives on the Problem

Relations between the United States and Russia have varied largely in terms of the degree of assertiveness of the Russian government and the extent to which Russian actions have impinged on U.S. interests. Russia is a diminished actor compared to its Soviet predecessor, but it is still a formidable rival and a country that wants to expand its interest and power in the world. Unfortunately for Russo-American relations, Russian assertiveness is expansionist, as it has been for centuries, and its attempts to broaden its influence and power collide with the American worldview and interests.

The Roots of Conflict

The modern contours of the relationship were honed during the Cold War period. Soviet communism sought to expand its ideological foundation and to extend its physical presence and control globally. At its most basic level, the Cold War was a competition between Western-style political democracy and capitalist economics represented by the United States and Leninist authoritarianism and Marxist socialist economics represented by the Soviet Union. The hard edge of that competition was military confrontation. The ultimate expression of the military rivalry was nuclear weapons, which ultimately convinced both sides that the rivalry could not be decided by war without destroying both sides. At the same time, the Soviet model proved to be uncompetitive, especially in the economic sphere. That failure helped lead to the collapse of the Soviet Union.

The American strategy for dealing with the communist threat was *containment*. Crafted in the latter 1940s when communist expansionism was at its zenith, the heart of the strategy was that the communist domain had to be prevented from expanding beyond its existing frontiers through the further conversion of non-communist to communist states. A containment "line" was drawn on the global map beyond which communism attempts to expand would be resisted and defeated. The policy was first implemented when American and other Western states intervened in North Korea's invasion of South Korea in 1950. The strategy was premised on the deterrence of Soviet aggression, initially by maintaining a large U.S. standing military force during peacetime after the Korean experience to dissuade Soviet adventurism. Many believed the competition was perpetual and its maintenance as a "cold" war became supreme.

The heart of the need for containment was Russian expansionism adorned with communist ideology. It is difficult to determine how much of that desire to push the boundaries of Russian influence and control came from communist ideology and how much from Russian expansionist nationalism that had been a Russian obsession during the days of the Tsarist Russian Empire. Both were present in some measure.

Communism has, of course, virtually disappeared as an operational politico-economic phenomenon; only four states (China, North Korea, Vietnam, and Cuba) remain putatively communist, and their purity of attachment to Marxism-Leninism has been diluted in the process. Russia's Putin was a colonel in the Soviet Committee on State Security (KGB) and a loyal communist, but one no longer hears direct reference to that communist past. Instead, it is more common to hear the Russian president referred to as the new "tsar," a Russian nationalist pursuing expanded Russian influence the way his predecessors did. He operates, however, in a very different world environment.

The Russian Condition

A large measure of the Russian predicament in trying to project itself as a major power is that Russia is a preeminent state in terms of military might but not by virtually any other measure except physical land mass (even after the dissolution of the Soviet Union, Russia does remain the world's largest physical state). The claim of great power status has been an obsession for centuries, but Russia has never been completely accepted as a great power except after World War II when it achieved superpower status because of its enormous nuclear arsenal.

By almost every non-military measure, Russia is a state in decline, and a central element of Putin's rule has been both to arrest that decline and to project an image that denies its existence. Much of its claim to major power status remains based in its nuclear arsenal, however. The Russian Federation retained virtually the entire Soviet arsenal, and although arms control agreements reached with the United States have reduced the size of both countries' nuclear holdings, their relevance to the claim of great power status has not been entirely diminished. It was, after all, nuclear power that paralyzed the Cold War, and it is not clear who the Russians can credibly threaten with their nuclear might without running the risk of committing suicide.

Shorn of the nuclear distinction, Russia's only obvious claims as a great power are geographic. The sheer size of Russia still makes it the largest country in the world physically, its girth spans from boundaries with European countries to the Bering Straits, and under its soil and some of its territorial waters, it has enormous stores of natural resources the world needs, especially in energy. The result is a Russian state that is at best a regional power, the non-energy economy of which is structurally more like that of a developing country. During the Cold War, the USSR was sometimes described derisively as a "frozen banana republic with nuclear weapons." Much of that depiction is still true, if for different reasons. The result is to raise serious questions about Russian aspirations to great power status.

Along with states like Nigeria and Venezuela, Russia has become a classic example of what the columnist Thomas Friedman identified in 2006 as a "petrolist" state. The designation refers to a state that becomes so dependent economically on revenues from oil and natural gas that it distorts and molds the country's economics and politics.

Petrolism affects a country in at least two ways. First, it skews and distorts the economy. Under communism, the economy was controlled by the state and its Communist Party managers. When the Soviet Union collapsed, these mechanisms and most of the personnel were displaced, leaving little in their place and effectively creating a state of economic anarchy which new Russian "entrepreneurs" dominated by the Russian Mafia and former members of the CPSU (including Putin) occupied. The economy was in free fall, to the detriment of the Russian population. During the 1990s, economic life and the situation of most Russians declined precipitously, as did Russia's status as a world power.

Oil came to the rescue, as the new rulers began to expand aggressively the great energy wealth of the vast Russian landmass. Led by state-owned Gazprom, Russia rapidly expanded production of oil and gas, rising in 2014 to the world's leading producer with an estimated production of 10.84 million barrels per day (mbd), and to second place as an exporter at 4.97 mbd. After the decline of oil prices in the early 2010s, that stimulus declined precipitously. Kotkin reports that Russian GDP contracted from $2 trillion in 2013 to $1.2 trillion in 2016. These early revenues allowed stimulation of the economy, effectively buying political support with petrodollars (a prime characteristic of petrolist states). The exports in turn provided leverage with states to which petroleum-based products were sent, notably natural gas for heating in Europe and some former Soviet states like Ukraine. Oil, however, boosted the importance of Russia, provided fuel for expansionism, and cemented support for the Putin regime. Still, Bremmer points out that "today's Russian economy is smaller than that of Canada."

The dependence on petroleum had other, not so favorable impacts. The second impact was to promote government corruption, including its export. The Russian post-communist economy lacks mechanisms to regulate economic activity (under communism, these were not needed, since the state controlled everything), and that void promoted widespread corruption within Russia that has prompted the widespread depiction of Russia as a "kleptocratic" state (also a characteristic of petrolist states). This flood of illicit monies has spread abroad to financial institutions in the West, where "staggering amounts of illicit Russian money" are regularly laundered according to Biden and Carpenter. This latter phenomenon has been a factor in the complex of alleged Russian interference in the 2016 election.

The effect of petrodollars is clearly a double-edged sword. It provides the government with a source and stream of revenue that allows the government to operate and to create a higher level of prosperity for the country and its citizens than was possible before it became dominant. At the same time, there has been so much unaccounted money in the system that it has created the incentives for and reality of a high level of government corruption and kleptocracy, a charge that extends all the way to Putin himself. It has also provided funds for the Russian attempts at resurgence in foreign affairs, providing funding, for instance, for Russian efforts in places like Syria and to support Russian nationalists in Ukraine. Without petroleum-derived funds, the Russians simply could not afford to try to re-create a prime place for themselves in international affairs.

All of this has come with costs. The effect has also been to leave Russia vulnerable to fluctuations in world prices for petroleum. When the price of petroleum cratered in and around 2013, so did the revenues and profits from petroleum to fund other priorities. This is one of the negative consequences of a petrolist state; it is subject to the vicissitudes of fluctuations in the economy, and the result is often political instability as support is eroded from the deprivations that down cycles produce.

The problems attaching to a petrolist state will not go away anytime soon. As Russia looks to augment market-based budget deficiencies by utilizing its conventional and unconventional reserves like shale oil, the dependence on energy production and export will increase, especially if the Russians want to use government wealth to reassert Russian preeminence in the world. The major limitation that they have faced in expanding their energy sector is technological deficiency in energy recovery, and the major source of the expertise they need has been in the United States. This fact provides a potential lever for the United States as it explores the options it has for dealing with the problem of Russia.

Policy Options

In its ongoing relationship with Russia, the United States must keep three considerations in mind. The first of these is the nature of American interests in Russia and how they evolve: how important is Russia to the United States? The second is Russian actions and motivations in an evolving world order in which Russia seeks to reassert its place in the international order while simultaneously accommodating clear evidence of decline: what can the United States do to influence Russian policy in ways most congenial to American interests? Third is the question of what kind of relationship with Russia the United States wants and what it is willing and able to do to pursue that orientation and its consequences. This concern has become particularly relevant since the assumption of the U.S. presidency by Donald J. Trump. The answers to these questions help frame American options for dealing with the current sources of conflict between the two countries.

The Nature of American Interests in Russia

Given their history of disagreement, Russian-American relations have always had an adversarial tone except during World War II, when they had a common interest in defeating Germany. Both countries are large and naturally consequential places, and the question is how adversarial their relationship is or needs to be, and how to modulate it has always been the central concern for both.

The Cold War relationship helped form the strategic answer. Geopolitically, it was conceptualized as a zero-sum confrontation, where one side prevailed at the other's expense. Militarily, this translated into both sides being essentially armed camps with very large, lethal armed forces prepared for something like a repetition of the combat in World War II (see chapter 13). The situation both reflected and contributed to Cold War tensions and was only moderated when both sides realized the disaster and folly of war because of its possible nuclear consequences. The Cold War confrontation set the tone of U.S.-Russian relations that persists to the present. The geopolitical conflict has abated but has not disappeared, as reflected by ongoing conflicts between them. The military balance between them continues at a lower level of arms that are generally not directly aimed at one another but remain a key element in strategic planning for both, especially in the nuclear weapons area. The two sides are still adversaries.

Is it in the American interest to try to moderate the animosity between the two countries? Most American leaders have acknowledged that reduced tensions and even cooperation with the Russians would be desirable in areas where interests overlap, such as in parts of the Middle East. Still, interests do not coincide—Russian-American accord on limited parts of the campaign against the Islamic State were possible, but the two countries are at basic odds over

Syria. Russian defense of the Assad regime and denial of its brutal treatment of its citizens in Syria offends Americans who want to isolate and bring down that regime, but is that opposition important enough to the U.S. national interest to take actions that could lead to a military confrontation with Russia? The United States has encouraged and sponsored the deployment of NATO troops to Baltic countries on the Russian border, a practice the Russians strongly oppose, but their response has been to move Russian troops closer to those frontiers and nothing more.

The United States also has an interest in the tenor of Russian political development. The American government was a major supporter of Russian democratization in the 1990s and provided monetary and political support for the Yeltsin presidency, which foundered because of the great upheaval and resulting instability in the Russian economy and weakness in the democracy movement. The United States watched the rise of Putin and his nationalist agenda riding astride a wave of petrodollars and tried to moderate his impact. Prosperity and his appeal to national glory has made Putin an overwhelmingly popular figure in Russia. Many of Putin's policies are anti-American in purpose or effect, but the United States has proven powerless or unwilling to oppose those policies effectively.

American interests also come into direct conflict with the interests of the Putin regime. Putin has, with increasing aggressiveness, pursued an expansionist policy intended to restore Russian prestige and power in its region and beyond, and time is not on his side for demographic and political reasons. The effect of complying with American preferences helped make Russia accept a more modest status in the world after the Cold War, but the tsarist tendencies of Putin will not allow him to avoid resisting that fate. Americans want to limit Russian expansion, and Putin wants to extend it. These positions are at basic odds with one another. What can the United States do?

The third part of the puzzle is what the United States can and is willing to do to shape Russian behavior into something more to its liking. The Russians know the United States opposes their expansionist, adversarial behavior, but it is not clear to them (and many Americans) what the United States is willing to do to make the Russians comply. Direct military action has been "off the table," even though the United States does not freely admit that. Prior to the Trump administration, the strategy had been escalating economic sanctions against Russia, and the Congress overwhelmingly passed comprehensive sanctions in 2017 to tighten the screws on the Russian economy. The Trump administration has refused to implement these sanctions, and a Republican-controlled Congress has not pressed the administration strongly enough to force his compliance. The president has instead relied on what he views as the reasonableness of Putin and his personal relationship with the Russian president to create influence. Which strategy (if either) will work is a matter of debate.

Policy Conflicts and Alternatives

The conflict between American and Russian interests has been manifested in a series of ongoing issues and disputes. The heart of these disputes is about what kind of Russia is desirable, and it is reflected in the countries' interests and world-views. The United States wants Russia to act as a more "normal" (which is to say less aggressive) state, and Russia clearly wants to reassert the glory of Russia as a great power. Constructed in this manner, the two views are mutually exclusive in important ways represented by two ongoing and one future source of disagreement. The two current problems are Russian physical expansionism militarily and politically and Russian meddling in electoral processes in the United States and other democratic systems. The future problem is American cooperation or enmity in the development of Russian energy resources that are vital to any pretensions the Russians may have about maintaining their place in the world.

Russian Expansionism. The proclivity to try to expand Russian boundaries and influence is nothing new for the country. Whether it was expansion out of the original enclave of Muscovy, the outward movement of the Tsarist Empire into parts of central Asia and eastern Europe, or the acquisitiveness of the Soviet Union, Russians have historically considered the annexation of new territories as part of their national destiny and as a major avenue toward establishing themselves as a global power. The collapse of the Soviet "Empire," which Putin has famously described as the most negative event of the twentieth century, reversed that trend and was the most outwardly obvious, humiliating geopolitical effect of the breakup of the Soviet Union. It symbolized a severe reversal of the Russian/Soviet mandate of greatness and prestige. It is not at all surprising that a leader like Putin would arise and reassert the Russian destiny and use petrodollars to finance this reassertion. It is also unsurprising that, as noted earlier, he would find a ready supply of Russian public support for his advocacy and efforts.

The major instances of this assertion are well known. In the 1990s, the Russian government acted brutally to suppress Muslim separatists in Chechnya and Dagestan in the Caucasus to arrest further deterioration of post-Soviet Russia. In 2008, they used alleged Georgian abuses against Abkhazia to attack Georgia and add former Soviet territory back to Russia. With Putin firmly in power, Russia occupied strategically vital Crimea (a peninsula jutting into the Black Sea and the traditional home base of the Russian Black Sea fleet at Sevastopol) in 2014, seizing the territory from Ukraine, to which Crimea had been annexed by Nikita Khrushchev. This was followed by support for Russian nationals living in eastern Ukraine, the purpose of which appears to be annexation of that territory to Russia. It has also acted to spread its domain into the Middle East by befriending Syria's Bashar al-Assad in return for extending Russian access to the naval base at Tartus, an arrangement that goes back to 1971.

The salient characteristic of these moves is that they are quintessentially Russian. If the history of Russian expansionism is any indication, they will continue for as long as the Russians are able to get away with them, particularly under Putin's rule. To this point, the American counterreaction has been limited to the imposition of escalating economic sanctions, most of which, in mid-2018, the Trump administration had chosen not to enforce.

Russian expansionism extends beyond the physical acquisition of territory or specific regional influence. It is part of the reassertion of Russian greatness and consequence in international relations. As such, it has the explicit purpose of reasserting the kind of parity it had with the United States in the Cold War, and its primary instrument is military power. The Russians have, for instance, moved with great fanfare to upgrade their nuclear arsenal, and on February 28, 2018, Putin announced the perfection of a new "doomsday machine," a nuclear weapon that, if employed, could spread enough deadly radiation to leave large parts of the globe uninhabitable for a long time. Such a device was part of the theoretical policy debate of the Cold War, but the obviously suicidal impact such a weapon implied made most analysts discard it as an impractical device, making Putin's announcement odd and beyond the assertion of some sort of Russian machismo.

Russian Meddling. Russian interference, largely electronic in nature, with the American national elections in 2016 has been a major irritant between the two countries and a divisive element in American national politics since (which is a probable purpose of the Russian actions). The accusations, which include cyber attacks like hacking and the use of bogus social media manipulation, have been categorically denied by the Russians but are universally accepted within the U.S. law and intelligence communities. Political controversy has surrounded a tepid Trump administration response to the accusations that reflects speculation that their pursuit may undermine the credibility of the president's election.

Accusations have extended to the 2018 election and have been widely assumed for the 2020 election season as well. All involve the use of cyberspace exploitation, a dynamic addressed in chapter 16, and represent arguable infringements on the national sovereignty and thus security of the United States and the integrity of its political institutions. The Russians deny commission of these acts, and they accordingly offer no explanation of their origins and purposes, but the most obvious motivation is to demonstrate the power and capability of Russia to project itself internationally against the United States and other countries. As noted, the U.S. Congress has passed comprehensive sanctions against Russia in retaliation and to get them to cease these operations, but the White House had not implemented them as of late 2018.

Development of Russian Energy Reserves. Petroleum wealth has formed the resource platform on which Russian resurgence has been based. It has provided the base on which the Russian economy has been improved sufficiently to form much of the foundation of Putin's popularity and support, and it has provided the money to revive the Russian military and allow Russia to move more aggressively in the international arena than it otherwise could.

That wealth, as noted, can be a two-edged sword. It distorts Russian politics, leaving Russia a highly unstable petrolist state. Putin has exploited petroleum wealth to help revive and reassert the Russian state, but the cratering of petroleum prices worldwide demonstrated the vulnerability dependence on a single natural resource can create. In the Russian case, it also appears that riding on a petroleum "high" has suppressed attention to other forms of development, including economic diversification and political development. Like most petrolist states, politics in Russia is highly personalized around its leader, whose power is based on his ability to reward and effectively bribe the citizenry into support. The problem is that Putin is getting old, his constitutionally prescribed term is up in 2024 when he will be seventy-two, and there is no successor in the wings. What happens then? No one knows.

The dependence on oil creates another, possibly exploitable, source of vulnerability. Russia became the world's largest producer through aggressive exploitation of readily available, easily exploitable petroleum sources, and these sources are dwindling. Russia has vast reserves in its northern regions in Siberia and the Arctic, but it lacks the technology to mine these effectively. Because of its experience in Alaska, the American oil companies have that expertise. Trying to guarantee that access may help explain much Russian exploitation of American vulnerabilities in areas like cyberspace and even the American electoral process. This Russian need provides the United States with considerable leverage with the Russians if it decides to exploit it.

Consequences: What to Do?

U.S.-Russian relations are at a low point. The situation is not as dire or as geopolitically charged as it was during the Cold War, but after the near-thirty-year period of Russian recovery from the dissolution of the Soviet Union, it has become more assertive in its foreign policy, and much of its greater activism has been directed at its old Cold War adversary. The major foci of this renewed rivalry are evident in Russian expansionism into parts of the old Soviet Union and elsewhere and in Russian interference in the American electoral process. Recently, the Russians have engaged in significant saber-rattling in the form of claims about how they have enhanced their nuclear arsenal.

None of these actions are new from a Russian government. The actions and rhetoric of Putin represent familiar themes of Russian history. There are contextual differences: Russia's emergence as a prime petrolist state and the demographic nightmare that will serve as a brake on Russian capabilities in the future. One way to think about this iteration is as a process of adjustment, where Russia seeks to reinvent itself as a major force from a position of growing weakness in areas other than military. Could it be, for instance, that Russia's nuclear posturing is motivated by the same kind of model followed by North Korea as an otherwise lesser state made important by weapons of mass destruction?

What should the American response be? The basic strategic alternatives are either to engage positively with the Russians or to adopt tough, negative postures intended to bring them to heel by offering negative incentives to noncompliance. Both approaches have been tried, and elements of both are part of current policy. Strict economic sanctions have been adopted toward Russia and restrictions on oil exploitation technology loom in the future. At the same time, the Trump administration refuses to enforce some sanctions, and Trump continues to praise Putin. Still, Exxon (whose former CEO is former secretary of state Rex Tillerson) withdrew from an oil exploration deal with Russia on March 1, 2018, to avoid sanction penalties from the U.S. government.

It is not an easy call. Forcing the Russians to abandon their historic outward drive is certainly a key part of it, but it also involves human frailties as well. Biden and Carpenter assert that it also is "motivated by the Kremlin's desire to protect its wealth and power," and Putin's reported wealth (some estimates suggest he may be the world's wealthiest person) is a prime example. Even if they are right that Russian "power remains brittle at the core" and that, as Kotkin adds, the country is "in structural decline," it remains consequential. Rumer, Sokolsky, and Weiss offer the basic rejoinder: "history shows that such states can cause considerable damage on their way down." How can the United States be firm without pushing them to cause that damage? What do you think?

Study/Discussion Questions

1. Trace U.S.-Russian relations since World War II. How have they changed yet remained the same?
2. Discuss the "Russian condition." How does it help shape current Russian policy and U.S. dealings with it? Include a discussion of oil and petrolism.
3. What are U.S. interests in Russia? What conditions the ability to realize those interests?
4. What are the main sources of concern in Russian-American relations? Describe each, as well as the Russian energy quandary.
5. How should the United States deal with Russia: as a normal state with which it can deal conventionally, or as a rival that must be treated accordingly? Why?

Bibliography

Biden, Joseph S. Jr., and Michel Carpenter. "How to Stand Up to the Kremlin: Defending Democracy Against Its Enemies." *Foreign Affairs* 97 (1) (January/February 2018), 44–57.

Bremmer, Ian. "Putin Won. But Russia Is Losing." *Time* 191 (13) (April 2, 2018), 41.

Committee on Foreign Relations, United States Senate. *Strategic Assessment of U.S.-Russian Relations.* New York: CreateSpace, 2018.

DaVargo, Julie, and Clifford A. Grammich. *Dire Demographics: Population Trends in the Russian Federation.* Santa Monica, CA: RAND Corporation, 2007.

Dawisha, Karen. *Putin's Kleptocracy: Who Owns Russia?* New York: Simon and Schuster, 2014.

Friedman, Thomas L. "The First Law of Petropolitics." *Foreign Policy,* May/June 2006, 28–36.

Gorbachev, Mikhail. *The New Russia.* Cambridge, UK: Polity Press, 2016.

Isikoff, Michael, and David Corn. *Russian Roulette: The Inside Story of Putin's War on America and the Election of Donald Trump.* New York: Twelve Books, 2018.

Joffe, Julia. "Putin's Game." *Atlantic* 321 (1) (January/February 2018), 68–85.

Kotkin, Stephen. "Russia's Perpetual Geopolitics: Putin Returns to the Historical Pattern." *Foreign Affairs* 95 (3) (May/June 2016), 2–9.

Legvold, Robert. *Return to Cold War.* Cambridge, UK: Polity Press, 2016.

Lukyanov, Fyodor. "Putin's Foreign Policy: The Quest to Restore Russia's Rightful Place." *Foreign Affairs* 95 (3) (May/June 2016), 30–38.

Mearsheimer, John J. "Why We Shall Soon Miss the Cold War." *Atlantic Monthly* 266 (2) (November 1990), 35–50.

Myers, Steven Lee. *The New Tsar: The Rise and Reign of Vladimir Putin*. New York: Vintage, 2015.

Nalbandov, Robert. *Not by Bread Alone: Russian Foreign Policy Under Putin*. Washington, DC: Potomac Books, 2016.

Nance, Malcolm. *The Plot to Hack America: How Putin's Cyberspies and WikiLeaks Tried to Steal the 2016 Election*. New York: Skyhorse Publishing, 2016.

Rumer, Eugene, Richard Sokolsky, and Andrew S. Weiss. "Trump and Russia: The Right Way to Manage Relations." *Foreign Affairs* 96 (2) (March/April 2017), 12–19.

Snow, Donald M. *Cases in International Relations: Principles and Applications*, Seventh Ed. Lanham, MD: Rowman & Littlefield, 2018. (See chapter 2: "National Interests and Conflict: Russian Oil and U.S.-Russian Relations," 23–42.)

———. *The Necessary Peace: Nuclear Weapons and Superpower Relations*. Lexington, MA: Lexington Books, 1986.

Stent, Angela. *The Limits of Partnership: U.S.-Russian Relations in the Twenty-First Century*. Princeton, NJ: Princeton University Press, 2015.

Toal, Bernard. *Near Abroad: Putin, the West, and the Contest over Ukraine and the Caucasus*. Oxford, UK: Oxford University Press, 2017.

Treisman, Daniel. "Why Putin Took Crimea: The Gambler in the Kremlin." *Foreign Affairs* 95 (3) (May/June 2017), 47–54.

Trenin, Dmitri. *Should We Fear Russia?* Cambridge, UK: Polity Press, 2016.

Tsygankov, Andrei. *Russia's Foreign Policy: Change and Continuity in National Identity*. Fourth Ed. Lanham, MD: Rowman & Littlefield, 2016.

12

China

Dealing with a Frenemy with a New Face

The balance of world politics, and thus the configuration of power and influence in the world, is rapidly changing. The old Euro-centered balance of power no longer dominates geopolitical concern, and even a militarily dangerous Russia occupies a lesser role than it did in the last century. Global politics has moved eastward. As Henry Kissinger, one of the chief architects of the opening of China, put it in a 2016 interview with *The Atlantic*'s Jeffrey Goldberg, "Our relations with China will shape the international order in the long term. The United States and China will be the world's most consequential countries." Campbell and Ratner add, "Washington now faces its most dynamic and formidable competitor in modern history."

The importance of the relationship with China for American national security and foreign policy is difficult to overestimate. It is commonplace for observers to refer to the twenty-first century as the "Asian century," and the most dramatic venue of that emergence is in East Asia and the Pacific regions, where the chief contestants for influence and power are the traditional land giant of Asia—China—and what has been since the twentieth century the major Pacific power—the United States.

China and the United States stand at the center of the unfolding drama. Chinese policy under Xi Jinping is aimed at reestablishing the preeminence of his country regionally and in terms of global influence, and the success of much of that effort may come at the expense of American influence and prestige. For the United States, the priority is the preservation and strengthening of the network of alliances and friendships that it developed after World War II as a hedge against another Pacific war like that of the 1930s and 1940s. The new visions are not entirely incompatible, but they do come into conflict in places as diverse as the Korean Peninsula and the South China Sea. China and the United States are central frenemies, part friend and part enemy.

The relationship is decidedly different than that with America's other principal Cold War rival, Russia/Soviet Union. For two decades after the ascendancy of the Chinese communists in 1949, China did not officially exist in American policy. The premise was that the legitimate government of the Chinese mainland was the Nationalist government of Taiwan, the contestant that had lost the Chinese civil war and fled across the Taiwanese Straits, where it remains in power. That relationship changed when the Nixon administration opened relations with the People's Republic of China (PRC) in 1972, and it accelerated after the country's founder, Mao Zedong, died in 1976 and was replaced with a less doctrinaire Marxist regime that began to incorporate elements of capitalism that have formed the base of the Chinese economic miracle, fueling Chinese ascent and an intimate economic relationship with the United States that former U.S. treasury secretary Lawrence Summers (quoted in Beeson) once referred to as the "balance of financial terror." The basic idea is that the two countries are so economically intertwined that any major change in their political relationship could be economically calamitous for both.

During the Cold War, Russia and China were the matching thorns in the attainment of America's national interest in building a world of liberal capitalist democracies. The Soviet and Chinese Communist Parties and movements vied for the leadership in the world's challenge to the Western order, at least until the death of Mao. The successors of Mao did not abandon authoritarian rule by the Communist Party, but they did embark on an economic revitalization incorporating capitalist elements that lit a Chinese economic fire that still burns brightly today.

The Chinese ascent has not been uniform, and it has gone through several generations of leaders with somewhat different ideas. Deng Xiaoping was the most important of the early leaders, and his vision and direction have been passed along. The West now faces a very "new face" in power in Beijing in the person of Xi Jinping, who in February 2018 proposed that the constitution of China be amended to remove term limits, a move apparently designed to place him in power indefinitely. How this change affects the world and U.S.-Chinese relations is an important new factor in American national security policy.

The relationship is more complex than American security policy with other countries. The United States has developed and nurtured a network of alliances and relationships along the Pacific Rim in places from South Korea and Japan to Taiwan and the Philippines, the maintenance and nurturing of which remain major national security priorities. China's focus remains on East Asia, as Chinese policy always has, but the two powers rub against one another in places like the Korean Peninsula and over Taiwan. The positive, moderating force is the enormous economic intertwining of the two countries, the extent of which makes fundamentally antagonistic behavior too expensive—the financial terror. At the same time, the ascent of Xi Jinping is an aggressive wild card in the equation. The result is a relationship with two strong but different emphases: the geopolitics of the Asia-Pacific region and a newly fractious economic partnership.

Perspectives on the Problem

China is the world's oldest continuous civilization, and its population has been the world's largest until Indian population growth threatened that distinction. The longevity of its existence as a political entity and civilization has endowed the Chinese with a unique perspective on their place in the world, the primary attributes of which are a sense of superiority to all others and a preference for isolation and fealty from the rest of the world. To many Chinese, the Han Chinese live in a world that consists of themselves and the "barbarians." The Great Wall was built to keep the barbarians out and thus to avoid diluting their superiority by lesser outsiders. To the extent that contact with the outside world was to be tolerated, it was that of superiors to the inferior others. Properly understood, it was the role of the outsiders to pay tribute, literally and figuratively, to their superiors in a suzerain relationship.

Xi Jinping seeks to reestablish China's traditional role of superiority in East Asia and to expand Chinese power and influence more widely. The effort is not so overt as to try to reinstate anything as overtly humiliating as the *ketow* (or Kow Tow), wherein leaders of vassal states were forced physically to visit the Chinese capital and to prostrate themselves physically as they paid their tribute (taxes) to the emperor. Rather, the regime seeks to intermix military superiority and economic prowess to establish the traditional regional relationship. On the global stage, they seek to use economic incentives and a growing military presence to influence the global system—often at the expense of the United States. It is a startling reversal of China's image in the last century, and the international system is struggling with how to deal with this new Chinese "dragon." China was the suzerain (ruler or sovereign) of Asia before; it is a role that Xi Jinping and his associates would seemingly like to reassume.

Decline and Resurgence

The problem of the traditional system was that it isolated China from the rest of the world. The premise was that Chinese civilization was so superior to everyplace else that there was essentially nothing China could learn from others and that the presence of others in other than subservient roles would pollute the purity of the Chinese nirvana. Excluding the barbarians (essentially anybody who was not Han Chinese) was the prime value, and its symbol was the Great Wall. The problem of self-imposed isolation was that China did not enjoy the benefits of advances being made in the outside world, and it gradually fell behind the other, evolving civilizations to the point that, by the nineteenth century, China had become a backward and uncompetitive civilization that was too weak to protect itself from the incursions of the outside world.

The result was something known in China as the Century of Humiliation. It began when the West (notably Britain) occupied parts of China in the Opium War of 1839–1842, and it continued until the end of World War II and the expulsion of the Nationalist government of Chiang Kai-Shek from the mainland to Taiwan. The worst humiliation was associated with the invasion of northern China by another Asian power (Japan) during the 1930s, an event so traumatic that the opposing pretenders to Chinese control, Chiang and Mao, paused their ongoing civil war and cooperated in trying to repel the invaders.

The Chinese communists, of course, came out of the struggle for control victorious and have remained in power since. During the early Cold War period, China was militantly communist and expansionist, holding special animosity toward the United States and its continuing support of the Nationalists on Taiwan as the legitimate government of the mainland and Taiwan. China expressed this antagonism physically in the winter of 1950–1951, when it infiltrated over two hundred thousand "volunteers" into North Korea who effectively stopped the physical reunification of the peninsula by the Americans. Internationally, it supported communist movements on its periphery—often in competition with the Soviets—in places like Southeast Asia. Domestically, it attempted to purge recalcitrant elements of the population with Maoist-inspired purification efforts like the Great Leap Forward.

Things began to change in the early 1970s. The first major event was the opening of relations between the United States and China in 1972. Engineered behind the scenes with the help of Pakistan, Richard Nixon, the most militantly anti-communist president of the Cold War period, and Henry Kissinger orchestrated the breakthrough, ending the fiction that had existed about who ruled China that had been in place since 1949. It was capped by Nixon's state visit to China in 1972. The process was completed when President Jimmy Carter formally recognized the Communist regime in Beijing in 1979.

The other major event was the death of Mao in 1976 and his succession by the diminutive Deng Xiaoping. Mao's death ended the militantly ideological phase of Chinese rule and allowed China to begin the transition to a more normal status with the rest of the world, including the United States. Deng brought with him a desire and plan to transform China into a major world power. The instrument for accomplishing this goal was the so-called Four Modernizations, the individual and collective purposes of which were to assert China's return to major power status.

The Four Modernizations

Deng's purpose was to end once and for all the degradations of the Century of Humiliation by reestablishing a vibrant and powerful Chinese society that could compete with the rest of the world. Unlike the previous model that presumed Chinese superiority to be protected against outside infection, Deng chose instead to emulate the productive capacity of the world by borrowing and emulating its bases and, in effect, outdoing the barbarians at their own game. His weapon of choice was economic power.

The Four Modernizations—agriculture, science and technology, economic, and military—are areas where China needed to change to compete and succeed in the global system. It began with agricultural reform by dismantling the terribly inefficient collective farming system in the countryside, home of three-quarters of the Chinese population, by allowing peasants to lease land from the state to grow and sell food. Without quite admitting it, the regime injected market principles into production, a process that became known euphemistically as "socialism with Chinese characteristics." The second thrust was science and technology; Deng's government tacitly admitted the Chinese system had fallen behind the rest of the world and that the only way to close the gap was to send Chinese students abroad to study these subjects in the West. In the process, these students observed and absorbed Western political ideas that they took back to China.

The most consequential modernization was the economy. Under Mao, the country had employed militantly doctrinaire Marxist economic principles, and like other places where they were tried, they failed abjectly. When Deng succeeded Mao, the heart of his reforms was in the economic area, generously adding capitalist principles to Marxist practices and transforming the country into the economic powerhouse that challenges the United States today.

The heart of the economic reforms was the creation of a series of Special Economic Zones (SEZs) in major urban areas in southeastern China. The SEZs involve the formation of joint ventures between the Chinese government and foreign businesses to set up operations in China where the ventures could benefit from very low Chinese labor costs and China could benefit by making their citizens more affluent and could learn from Western capitalists. The SEZs have been wildly successful and have provided almost all the fuel for the Chinese resurgence in the world. They have also included the seeds of some current controversy. Emulation, for instance, has sometimes manifested itself in perfecting intellectual property theft, a venerable Chinese practice.

The fourth area has been military modernization. Under Mao, China had maintained a very large but technologically backward military force. Its chief function and capability was as a self-defense force capable of repelling another foreign invasion like that of the Japanese in the 1930s. The Chinese economy was so poor that it could not provide adequate resources for a military force with other capabilities: the Chinese military challenge was effectively self-limiting. Economic wealth produced has allowed expansion, especially into more sophisticated weapons systems that progressively have increased the ability of the regime to project military power beyond its borders. The extent and intent of this expansion are matters of national security policy concern for the United States. At the same time, much of the Chinese military budget comes from profits from the so-called State-Owned Enterprises (SOEs), which have been less successful than China's more capitalistic economic endeavors.

Anchors That Weigh

China's continuing growth and power is impressive, but it has also not been unqualified, and the future of the Chinese "miracle" is not inexorable or its direction entirely predictable. There are some matters on the Chinese horizon that could slow—act as an anchor on—overly optimistic projections, even with the rise of Xi Jinping as the country's energetic, visionary, but seemingly autocratic new leader.

The Chinese economy has slowed in recent years. As the SEZs came to dominate the manufacture of many goods—primarily in the consumer sector incorporating foreign technology—the Chinese economy grew in double digits for over two decades at the world's fastest rate. That growth has slowed somewhat, and although the Chinese are awash in wealth produced by their prosperity, their growth rate is also down. The 2017 *CIA World Factbook*, for instance, reports a 2015 GDP growth rate of 6.9 percent, still impressive, but no longer the world leader. A cardinal part of Xi's plan and intent is to increase it once again.

There are several confounding sources of this relative decline. Part of it is the balance in the economy between SEZ-driven economic dynamism and the comparative stagnation of the SOEs. These government-owned and Communist

Party–controlled industries employ approximately 70 percent of the industrial workforce in the country but are responsible for only about 30 percent of productivity. In purely economic terms, dismantling the SOEs and reorienting them toward the capitalist economy makes sense. Shirk, however, points out that Xi sees "the sprawling state-owned companies" as the "economic base of Communist Party rule," which some like Rudd argue is its primary value. It leaves the state in the quandary of opting for a solution that might promote economic growth at the expense of party security or of keeping the Communist Party strong at the expense of maximized Chinese growth.

China has other limits on its growth (see Economy and Levi). One is demographic. Like most developed countries, the Chinese population is aging, and the demographic repercussions of the one-child policy of the 1980s mean there is a smaller cohort entering the workforce. Unlike countries like the United States that have historically dealt with manpower shortfalls through immigration of young workers, China is unlikely to follow this path for racial reasons. At the same time, China is energy deficient. It has huge reserves of shale oil and gas, but it lacks the technology and transportation capacity to exploit them, which is a potential leverage point for the United States and helps explain Chinese intransigence in the South China Sea (under which there are huge petroleum deposits). At the same time, China has a water problem as well: China's water tables are dangerously low in many areas, fully one-fifth of agricultural land has gone out of use since 1949, and the problem is continuing. These latter problems are interactive: China needs to exploit shale deposits, but that exploitation requires fouling large quantities of water. China is still ascendant, but as Hale and Hale reported over a decade ago, China still suffers from some of the "dragon's ailments."

Policy Options

The term *frenemy* is often used to describe the relationship between the United States and the PRC. Comedian Stephen Colbert used the word on his *Comedy Central* show expressly to describe the Sino-American relationship, but it has a longer history. The late columnist Walter Winchell originally suggested the term (he called it *frienemies*) to describe Soviet-American relations in a 1953 column. The 1953 depiction was of relations considerably more adversarial than friendly; the current context features more of a balance between the two characteristics.

Levels of the Relationship

Chinese-American relations are multifaceted, complicating national security policy more than if it were between friends *or* enemies. It can be thought of as existing on at least three overlapping levels. The heart of the relationship since Deng has been economic. It is a relationship marked by the "balance of financial terror" described by Summers. Operationally, this means the two countries' economies are so intertwined that any adversarial actions by one could have serious, even catastrophic economic effects on both. Simply put, China needs a stable, prosperous United States because the United States owes it so much money in loans and investments that a severe downturn would be extremely harmful to both. China, on the other hand, has been the lender of choice for the United States, providing the funds that have made the accumulation of national debt seem tolerable. If Chinese lenders stop providing funds (or demand repayment of loans), the American economy would suffer greatly, with enormous consequences for both.

The economic relationship conditions the other elements, both of which are more familiar in national security terms. Militarily, the two countries have the largest armed forces in the Asia-Pacific region, including large nuclear arsenals. Fortunately, they only confront one another tangentially and can, if they desire, largely avoid one another. Chinese military power, while expanding, is largely continental in Asia, and its goal, in Beeson's terms, is "restoring what most Chinese see as their country's rightful place at the center of regional, if not global affairs." American military interests are largely defined as support for its allies along the Pacific Rim, and it has been a cardinal (if occasionally violated) principle of American security to avoid land wars in Asia. Chinese military concentration is on the continental Asian aspect of the Asia-Pacific region; American interest is in the Pacific aspect. These relations only become abrasive when the United States ventures onto the Asian mainland, as in Korea, or when China collides with American Pacific interests, as in the South China Sea. If each honors the other's area of preeminence, there is little basis for direct military confrontation for strategic or, possibly more importantly, economic reasons.

The third level of interaction is political, and it has two basic facets. On the one hand is the question of political supremacy in the region and beyond. Beeson capsulizes the Chinese interest: "Recognition of China's status by other major powers, especially the United States, is a central goal of China's foreign policy." The United States recognizes this aspiration but wants to moderate it and to exact as many concessions as possible for accepting it. This leads to the second facet, which is Chinese cooperation in matters of mutual concern; the nuclear crisis with the Democratic Republic of Korea is currently the test of that part of the relationship.

What marks all these levels of the relationship is that they are illustrative of frenemies in a competitive but not necessarily volatile interaction. Chinese economic power is growing, and China is using its excess wealth to promote its interest and presence in, among other places, the Middle East and Africa, and it is constructing a military force with more global reach than that associated with a purely regional power. Politically, China's leadership has also become more assertive in places like wresting the leadership in the global climate change movement away from the reluctant leadership of the United States and taking over the lead in climate change–mitigating technologies like solar panels.

Flash Points

Too much and too little can be made of the issues that divide the two countries. China poses a long-term challenge to the United States in the sense that China is clearly intent on reestablishing China's historic role in the world, and as Allison points out "Chinese leaders are strategically patient: as long as trends are moving in their favor, they are comfortable waiting out the problem." That patience undoubtedly is reflected in Xi's move to eliminate term limits on his presidency: it may take longer than the two terms mandated in the constitution to achieve his goals. The shape of the long-term competition is thus a matter of how patient and vigilant the United States will be—not historically an American strong point.

The strategic conflicts between the two countries are concentrated on the jagged line of Asian versus Pacific supremacy. None of these are necessarily critical or have great escalatory potential, although each could have. The three major conflicts are over the status of Taiwan, the South China Sea, and the DPRK. Each is idiosyncratic but important to the overall relationship between the two countries.

Taiwan. The United States has been a champion and guarantor of the independence of Taiwan from the PRC since the Chinese Nationalists fled there following their defeat in the Civil War in 1949 and reestablished the Republic of China (ROC) there. Until 1972, the United States recognized the regime in Taipei as the legitimate ruler of both the island and China proper. When the regime in Beijing threatened to invade or otherwise militarily harass the Taiwanese, the United States interposed the Sixth Fleet in the relatively narrow Taiwan Straits to prevent a takeover. American recognition of the PRC has meant loosening its ties to Taiwan.

The PRC and ROC regimes have been moving unevenly toward resolving the conflict. Both agree that mainland China and Taiwan are both parts of China and should be united. Taiwanese investment in China is greater than that of any other country, and the ROC and the SEZs are tightly related. Reunification seemed inevitable a few years ago, but the ROC has had concerns about the terms of a similar uniting of Hong Kong to the PRC, in which Hong Kong has emerged as less independent of Beijing than they initially expected, a fear shared by Taiwan. In the meantime, the ROC and PRC remain divided but with the prospect of peaceful reunification.

South China Sea. The South China Sea washes the east coast of China, and countries touching on it include the Philippines, Vietnam, Malaysia, Brunei, and the highly contested Spratly Islands. It has become a flash point in the U.S.-PRC relationship because of increasingly aggressive Chinese activity in the body of water. The controversy centers on two major issues: transit through this vital link between East Asia and the Middle East, and Chinese proprietary claims regarding rightful control of it.

The issues have a common thread: petroleum energy. The South China Sea has enormous reserves lying under it that are vital to the energy-deficient states of the region, including China and Japan. An indication of the potential is the fact that the Sultan of Brunei (a tiny state on the coast of Borneo) was once purportedly the wealthiest person in the world due to oil revenues. At the same time, Middle Eastern petroleum is transported to East Asia through the Straits of Malacca from the Indian Ocean into the South China Sea on its way to Asian ports. Control of the South China Sea routes is thus critical to energy access.

The Chinese have sought to assert control over the sea and its petroleum. Their visible vehicle has been building artificial islands in shallow parts of the sea, over which they claim sovereign control, including territorial waters. If honored, these claims would make the sea a virtual Chinese lake with a potentially intolerable stranglehold over the naval well-being of American close allies. The United States thus rejects the Chinese claims and regularly violates the conditions with naval and air assets that impinge on the claims. The Chinese protest these actions but do little more. Were they to try to enforce their claims with armed force, however, the result could be dangerous.

DPRK. The final national security issue is American insistence that China do more to restrain the DPRK. The spotlight issue is the North Korean nuclear force, but there is a significant Asia-Pacific aspect as well. The Korean Peninsula, after all, is the only place on the East Asian mainland where the United States maintains a physical military presence, thereby rubbing against the PRC's historically based values. In the past, China has guarded the DPRK from American supposed predations, but Mastro maintains that this has weakened, saying "China has tired of North Korea's insolent behavior and reassessed its own interests on the peninsula." This reassessment includes consideration of a unified Korea. Instead, Mastro contends, "China's chief concern remains the prospect of U.S. forces in a reunified Korea." If this is true, it recasts the prolonged American complaint that China is not doing enough to rein in the North Koreans.

The implication of this possibility may be that an American agreement to renegotiate the presence of American forces in their last real foothold in East Asia may be the cost of changes in a nuclear North Korea that could even provide the condition for dismantling the DPRK nuclear force. The de facto acceptance of the Chinese vision of Asia-Pacific influence distribution could be the price, with vital impacts on America's Pacific Rim allies. Indeed, this could be the most profound national security issue between the two countries.

Consequences: What to Do?

Relations between the United States and China are complex and difficult, and their management will be an increasing concern for American national security in the years ahead. The two countries are geopolitical and economic rivals, but they also share common interests and perspectives on the world, chiefly in avoiding the deterioration of their relationship in the direction of armed conflict. As Shirk puts it, "Both countries would lose if it provoked a trade war, an arms race, or a military confrontation." Economic ties—the balance of financial terror—make militarization of their relationship bad business, and thus their relationship is constrained: they remain frenemies, but the "enemies" part of that designation is more muted than with a country like Russia, with which similar ties do not exist.

China still poses a national security problem for the United States. Chinese reclamation of its historic place in Asia does rub against American interests. The economic relationship, including U.S. indebtedness to China and the consequent ability of the Chinese to wave the economic instrument of power under the noses of other countries, is a concern, and the two confront one another uncomfortably along the imaginary Asia-Pacific boundary that defines the limits of their areas of influence or control. The most important traditional national security questions between them are along that frontier: in North Korea, Taiwan, and the South China Sea. How to handle these is the major national security question for the United States.

The relationship is not one for which orthodox divisions between "tough" or "soft" have much resonance or relevance. Both sides would like to improve their status and leverage with the other, but not at the expense of jeopardizing a relationship from which both basically benefit. In Kissinger's terms, this basic position is clearly true regarding the present leadership. For Xi, he says, "confrontation is too dangerous." The rise and consolidation of power by Xi Jinping may, as analysts like Fallows suggest, mark a reversion to a more authoritarian Chinese society, but it probably does not imply a deterioration in the government-to-government relations between the countries.

The competition for world supremacy between the two countries is likely to be a major feature of this century. Kissinger is correct: they are the "world's most consequential countries," and that is unlikely to change. The United States emerged from the last century as the most powerful state in the world—the sole superpower—and that singularity is being challenged by a Chinese worldview of itself as the rightful possessor of premier global status. Beeson captures the heart of China's aspiration in the competition: "recognition of China's status by other major powers, especially the United States, is a central goal of Beijing's foreign policy."

The interplay between aspirations and national egos is thus a major factor in dealing with the Chinese-American relationship. Because they are competitors geopolitically (the Asia-Pacific divide) and economically, there will always be different interests that rub against one another and ensure they will always have a partially adversarial relationship. They will be frenemies, not friends. The question is how to mute the possibility of their becoming enemies. How does the United States enlist China to ensure the latter does not occur? What do you think?

Study/Discussion Questions

1. Define and describe the concept of "frenemy." In general terms, how is the concept useful in understanding the basis of the U.S.-China relationship?

2. Describe the broad contours of the Chinese historical experience and how it conditions the Chinese view of the world. Include a description of Deng Xiaoping and the Four Modernizations and their import on the current Chinese condition.

3. What negative factors have an impact on conditioning the problems that China poses for the United States and China's expanding role in the world?

4. At what three distinct levels does the Chinese-American relationship exist? Describe each, how it forms a parameter on the overall relationship, and the "flash points" in the current situation between the two countries. Include a discussion of the Asian and Pacific ori-

entations and positions of the two countries.

5. Using the flash points as examples of issues between the two countries, is China more friend or enemy? Should the United States accept the de facto notion of Chinese dominance on the East Asian landmass and U.S. preeminence in the Western Pacific as the basis of the national security relationship between the two and American allies in the region? How, in other words, should the United States deal with China? Why?

Bibliography

Allison, Graham. "China versus America: Managing the Next Clash of Civilizations." *Foreign Affairs* 96 (5) (September/ October 2017), 80–89.

———. *Destined for War: Can America and China Escape Thucydides's Trap?* Boston: Houghton Mifflin, 2017.

Beeson, Mark. "Can the United States and China Coexist in Asia?" *Current History* 115 (782) (September 2016), 203–18.

Brown, Kerry. *CEO China: The Rise of Xi Jinping.* London: I. B. Tauris, 2016.

Campbell, Charles. "China Steps Closer to Despotism as Xi Becomes Leader for Life." *Time* 191 (10) (March 12, 2018), 5–6.

Campbell, Kurt M., and Ely Ratner. "The China Reckoning: How Beijing Defied American Expectations." *Foreign Affairs* 97 (2) (March/April 2018), 60–70.

Chen, Gregory T. "China's Bold Economic Statecraft." *Current History* 114 (773) (September 2015), 217–23.

Christensen, Thomas J. *The China Challenge: Shaping the Choices of a Rising Power.* New York: W. W. Norton, 2016.

Economy, Elizabeth. *The Third Revolution: Xi Jinping and the New Chinese State.* New York and Oxford, UK: Oxford University Press, 2018.

Economy, Elizabeth, and Michael Levi. *By All Means Necessary: How China's Resource Quest Is Changing the World.* New York: Oxford University Press, 2014.

Fallows, James. "China's Great Leap Backward." *Atlantic* 318 (5) (December 2016), 150–56.

French, Howard W. *Everything Under the Heavens: How the Past Helps Shape China's Push for Global Power.* Reprint Ed. New York: Vintage, 2018.

Garver, John W. *China's Quest: The History of the Foreign Relations of the PRC.* Oxford, UK: Oxford University Press, 2016.

Gill, Bates. *Rising Star: China's New Security Diplomacy.* Washington, DC: Brookings Institution Press, 2007.

Goldberg, Jeffrey. "The Lessons of Henry Kissinger." *Atlantic* 318 (5) (December 2016), 50–56.

Goldstein, Lyle G. *Meeting China Halfway: How to Defuse the Emerging U.S.-China Rivalry.* Washington, DC: Georgetown University Press, 2015.

Hale, David, and Lyric Hughes Hale. "China Takes Off." *Foreign Affairs* 82 (6) (November/December 2003), 36–53.

Heilmann, Sebastian. *China's Political System.* Lanham, MD: Rowman & Littlefield, 2016.

Lanteigne, Marc. *Chinese Foreign Policy: An Introduction.* Third Ed. New York: Routledge, 2015.

Li, Cheng. *Chinese Politics in the Xi Jinping Era: Reassessing Collective Leadership.* Washington, DC: Brookings Institution Press, 2016.

Mastro, Oriana Skylar. "Why China Won't Rescue North Korea: What to Expect If Things Fall Apart." *Foreign Affairs* 97 (1) (January/February 2018), 58–66.

McGregor, Richard. *Asia's Reckoning: China, Japan, and the Fate of U.S. Power in the Pacific Century.* New York: Viking, 2017.

Paulson, Henry M., Jr. *Dealing with China: An Insider Unmasks the New Economic Superpower.* New York: Twelve Books, 2015.

Pei, Minxin. *China's Gang Capitalism: The Dynamics of Regime Decay.* Cambridge, MA: Harvard University Press, 2016.

Rudd, Kevin. "How Xi Jinping Views the World: The Core Interests That Shape China's Behavior." *Foreign Affairs Snapshot* (online), May 10, 2018.

Shambaugh, David. *China's Future.* Cambridge, UK: Polity Press. 2016.

Shirk, Susan. "Getting to Yes with China." *Foreign Affairs* 96 (2) (March/April 2017), 20–27.

Snow, Donald M. *Regional Cases in U.S. Foreign Policy.* Second Ed. Lanham, MD: Rowman & Littlefield, 2018.

Sutter, Robert. *Chinese Foreign Relations: Power and Policy Since the Cold War.* Lanham, MD: Rowman & Littlefield, 2016.

13

Africa

The New Battleground?

A merican national security policy toward Africa is different than it is toward other places. All the other chapters in this section deal basically with American interests and policies toward individual countries, whereas Africa is a continent currently composed of over fifty sovereign countries that are remarkably diverse by virtually any measure and toward which a single national security orientation and policy cannot be applied. At the same time, policy and strategy toward Africa has been at the virtual bottom of the priority list for the United States. African problems are widespread and growing more so, but they have historically not engaged American policy prominently because of their diversity, the lack of tangible vital American interests at risk in most African situations, and the low likelihood crises in African countries will affect the United States.

The United States was never a colonial power in Africa, so it lacks the residual ties that countries like Great Britain and France have toward former possessions. Roughly one of every six American citizens can trace his or her ancestors to somewhere in Africa because of chattel slavery, but the kindred spirit that African Americans feel toward their African roots has never been a significant influence on U.S. foreign policy.

Africa represents a sizable part of the globe. It is physically the second largest continent with roughly 11,495,000 square miles of territory (20.4 percent of the global total). By contrast, the largest physical continent is Asia, which occupies 21.4 percent of the world's landmass; North America is fourth at 14 percent. Its population is also the second largest in the world at 1.22 billion (16.5 percent of the world's people). Asia is first with over 4 billion people (59.5 percent of the total). By 2025, the African population is expected to rise to almost 1.5 billion.

Africa is the world's most diverse continent, which is a major reason it is so difficult to capture it as an entity. Most of its countries are multinational, composed of many tribal groupings that speak different languages, practice different religions, and have very diverse, often conflicting ethnicities and cultures. Estimates vary according to classification criteria, but between 1,250 and 3,000 languages and dialects are spoken by different African people. Nigeria alone, the continent's most populous state, has citizens who speak around 500 languages. Essentially all African states are multilingual. Attempts to create "national languages" are strongly resisted. Imposing Arabic on the population of Sudan, for instance, was a major source of the civil war that has effectively torn that country apart (see discussion below). By contrast, almost all North American citizens speak English or Spanish, and English is almost universally understood in Australia.

African problems have only periodically engaged Americans, and even in those cases there has generally not been any sustained level of commitment. Between 1967 and 1970, a brutal civil war centered in Nigeria's oil-rich province of Biafra created widespread suffering and atrocity against its Christian majority Ibo tribesmen, and the horror produced, among other things, death by starvation of between five hundred thousand and two million Biafrans. In 1995, Watusi tribesmen went on a literal rampage against the Hutu in Rwanda, over a half million were slaughtered, and the International Criminal Court tried the most egregiously guilty. The Sudanese government attacked rebellious fellow Muslims in Darfur, and that slaughter produced a regional response by the Organization of African Unity (OAU) under U.S. auspices to protect the survivors. In 2011, the Republic of South Sudan successfully seceded from Sudan with some American encouragement, and in less than a year, a vicious, genocidal civil conflict broke out that continues to the present.

What these incidents share is tepid world, including American, response to them. In each instance, there was international appall at the atrocities and suffering these incidents produced that created gasps of horror and some humanitarian response, but not sustained effort to stabilize and rectify situations so that they could not recur. There is an uneasy status quo in Nigeria, the bloodletting has ended in Rwanda, there is an uneasy, probably unstable peace in Darfur, but South Sudan continues to burn without an end to its bloodletting in clear sight. Why? These situations are difficult, idiosyncratic, and their outcomes are not sufficiently vital to the outside world, including the United States, as are events in other parts of the world.

In these circumstances, Africa has been the most marginalized continent internationally and in U.S. national security planning and concerns. The major manifestation of American concern is the Africa Command, a small military command established in 2007. It is headquartered in Stuttgart, Germany, and is the smallest unified command. Its major emphases have been on suppressing terrorist expansion and activity in Africa and in promoting regional peace and stability, not easy tasks but also not high on the global list of American security concerns.

Perspectives on the Problem

African national security marginality reflects the relative isolation of the continent from much of the rest of the world, as well as its political turmoil and instability and the relative inconsequence of what goes on in most African countries for international politics. That marginality may be changing slowly because of demographics and international political trends like the movement of international terrorist organizations and activity out of the Middle East to Africa. The world has ignored Africa and seems to prefer continuing that attitude; it may or may not be able to sustain that position.

The Colonial Legacy

What makes Africa so difficult to understand is its enormous atomization. Prior to the incursion of European colonialists mostly beginning in the sixteenth century, it was politically and economically underdeveloped. Loyalties and political jurisdictions, such as they were, were largely tribally defined, generally associated with finite territories that were further divided by language and religion. When the Europeans arrived, they arbitrarily carved the continent into colonial jurisdictions that ignored whatever preexisting boundaries might have existed. In many cases, these divisions were the result of ignorance of the existing arrangements or European indifference to those distinctions. The result was to overlay the atomization with a completely arbitrary set of political distinctions that placed multiple competing tribal units into larger political entities and often divided tribal lands with boundaries that left members of tribal groups in different colonies.

Other factors exacerbated these artificial sources of political confusion. One was the slave trade. Various European countries participated in the process subjecting Africans to chattel slavery. The typical method was for the European slave traders to establish themselves along the coast, where they would recruit and arm compliant tribes to venture inland, where they would capture members of other tribes and bring them to the coast for sale to the slave traders. In partial payment, the slave traders would pay tribesmen in additional arms to facilitate further slave procurement. Among the more egregious examples of this practice was the trade operating out of Sudan, which sent mercenaries inland into what is now South Sudan.

Another roiling factor was religious conversion. Prior to colonialism, most Africans worshipped indigenous, often animist deities. Part of the window dressing surrounding the rationale for colonizing was to convert Africans to Christianity, and missionaries were active in large parts of the continent. Muslim missionary efforts were established in northern, including Saharan, Africa, and gradually have spread southward toward central Africa. One of the major sources of friction in places like Nigeria is the collision of Christian and Islamic tribal converts, a collision that is partly caused and exacerbated by the terrorism associated with some Islamic movements.

A cacophony of upsetting influences mostly rooted in the colonial experience confronted Africa when independence movements began to emerge after World War II. Very little if anything had been done by the colonial rulers to prepare natives for political freedom; the purpose of colonialism, after all, was profit, not political education and emancipation, which only would have contributed to the fostering of independence movements and thus been bad business. Any efforts that different European colonizers might have expended on "crash courses" in political independence or trying to reimpose colonial rule were compromised by the economic devastation of the war on their economies. Faced with unpleasant facts and trends, the Europeans mostly acquiesced in the demands that they relinquish control. An old standing joke was that the British foreign minister traveled from colony to colony with blank independence treaties in his briefcase that only required filling in the name of the country and finding some natives to sign it. The era of colonial domination came to an informal end when Portugal, the last holdout against decolonization, relinquished control of its remaining colonies in 1978.

The result, in many cases, has been political chaos. Most of the new countries created by decolonization inherited the boundaries of the old colonial unit of which they were a part, and those boundaries had little or nothing to do with the desires or political realities of the indigenous populations. Because development and preparation for statehood had not been colonial priorities, no group within the population had been educated in the skills either to govern or administer the political system, and there was a shortage of educated "natives" to perform other societal tasks. In Portuguese colonies, for instance, it was normal for Africans to receive a primary education but no more. When the Belgian Congo (later Zaire, now the Democratic Republic of the Congo) was granted its independence in 1960, a dozen of its thirty million indigenous inhabitants had college degrees.

Multinationalism

The result was an environment with two basic characteristics that endure to some degree. The first was *multinationalism*, the situation in which multiple national groups inhabit the same state. Nationalism refers to the political unit with which one has primary affiliation and toward which people have their primary loyalty. It has numerous definitions and characteristics (e.g., ethnicity, language, religion, historical experience), but it can be captured in how people answer the question, what do you consider yourself to be? In the state system, the answer is supposed to be the name of the country in which one resides: "I am a Frenchman" or "I am an American," for instance. In a multinational society, on the other hand, the answer is likely to be some more physically narrow form of identification. A Nigerian may answer the question "I am a Hausa" or "I am an Ibo," and a resident of South Sudan may say "I am a Dinka" or "I am a Nuer." The examples are not randomly chosen: the Hausa and Ibo were the major combatants in the Nigerian Civil War of 1967–1970, and the Dinka and Nuer are the major antagonists in the ongoing genocide in South Sudan. When the primary loyalty is to the state unit, violence between subnational groups is less common and people are likely to sublimate their more parochial differences to the interests of the country of which they are a part. In multinational countries, politics is often the struggle between these subnational groups and about the ascendancy of one group over the other.

Multinationalism is virtually universal in Africa, and it is the overwhelming reason for violence and instability in virtually all the countries where it is present. It some cases, it is exacerbated by *irredentism*, where political boundaries bisect traditional tribal lands and leave some members in one state and others in another. This situation exists in places like Nigeria, Niger, and the Cameroons, and can be exacerbated when religious factors make the divisions more fervent. In parts of central Africa, for instance, the Muslim Hausa, who have migrated from northern Africa, have become militant antagonists in political systems and the desire to unite ethnic groups becomes overlaid by religious proselytization.

The ubiquity of multinationalism helps define the pattern of violence and instability on the continent. Most of the continental problems with violent, national security import or content tend to be internal to countries where major rivals are trapped in a common state where they do not trust and often fear and hate their neighbors. The result is that most African violence comes in the form of often desperate, bloody civil wars.

Economic Development

The other source of instability is developmental. Africa is the least developed continent in economic terms. Prior to colonialism, almost all of Africa (other than a few places like Egypt) was underdeveloped in the classic sense of village-based economic units that produced some goods and services for local consumption but did not have an economic structure that was geared to economic growth. Illiteracy was the norm, natural resources were scarce and their exploitation minimal, and tribally based societies did not encourage interchange or interaction.

When European colonists arrived, they changed this situation somewhat, but generally not to the great advantage of the indigenous Africans. Primary motivations for the colonial rulers included the prestige of empire and the intention (often unachieved) of profit. Prestige meant ruling as large swaths of the map as possible at minimal costs. The public rationale of colonization was "civilizing" the natives, which required some social investment in missionary activity and minimal levels of education, but not to the degree that would nurture an independent sense of entrepreneurship in the population. Some economic transformation was necessary to exploit natural resources, transport them back to the mother country, and to ship goods to the colonies to sell to colonial subjects, but it was intended to maximize profits and not to prepare the colonies for a prosperous independent existence.

The new regimes were not only poor and structurally underdeveloped. Exacerbating their poverty and suffering was (and still is) a culture of corruption within society that has allowed politicians and others to skim what few economic resources exist for personal aggrandizement or to promote the interests of their tribal group at the expense of others. The problem is especially rampant in countries with natural resources like petroleum. Nigeria and the Sudans are both victim to this form of debasement. Some activists like the actor George Clooney see this problem as a cornerstone to improving the African situation.

The bottom line was that the post-1945 movement toward independence in Africa occurred with virtually no prior preparation. Independence was granted to colonial administrative units that were almost entirely arbitrary and artificial, institutionalizing the multinationality of the territories granted their national freedom and leaving many unprepared governments with difficult and sometimes insurmountable problems trying to develop unifying senses of nationalism that could aid in the transition to stable statehood. The building blocks of economic prosperity that could have made that transition easier—an educated population and more than the rudiments of a primitive infrastructure—were also absent in many countries. That the result would be a chaotic, violence-prone collection of over fifty independent states was almost entirely predictable. What to do to improve that situation, and the motivation to try in a concerted manner, was not clear.

Policy Options

The diversity of Africa makes the delineation of continent-wide policies extremely difficult. Almost any general strategy that one can devise is so vague and general that it cannot be universally applied. If a formulation can be crafted that is applicable to some parts of Africa, it will almost certainly not be relevant to other places and problems. Strategic formulation toward individual countries is hard; toward the world's second largest and most populous continent, it is next to impossible.

With that rejoinder in mind, one can attempt to discuss American national security policy and strategy toward Africa in two sequential steps. The first is to try to assess both what American strategic interests are, including how important they are relative to other interests in the world. This assessment both forms the parameter for assessing how important the interests are and how much and what kind of effort is justifiable to try to secure those interests. The second involves trying to specify and discuss recurring problem areas in different parts of Africa. To this end, three problem areas will be identified and explored through prominent examples.

Interests and Priorities

American national security interests in Africa are less well developed than in any other major part of the world. African countries have not, by and large, played a major role in the international system, and most people equate Africa with massive human-caused suffering in places like Rwanda and Darfur. There is a limited amount of trade and other forms of economic activity between the United States and Africa. U.S. direct investments in Africa in 2016 were lower than with any other continent at about $4.3 billion, and nearly two-thirds of that total was with South Africa (about $2.9 billion). U.S. Department of Commerce statistics for that year reveal that no African countries were among the top twenty-five trading partners of the United States and that among trading regions, the only two ranking lower than Africa were the Caribbean Free Trade Area and the Central American Common Market. The United States has historically nurtured relations with Nigerian petroleum interests as a hedge against the vicissitudes of dealing with Middle Eastern sources, but even that relationship has shrunk with decreased American reliance on foreign oil.

Traditional national security interests have also been largely absent. During the Cold War, there were limited Soviet attempts to gain a foothold in places like Zaire, but since the Soviet Union dissolved, Chinese economic penetration in Djibouti has been the major geopolitical challenge on the continent. The recent movement of displaced terrorist organizations out of the Middle East has become a concern, as has concern for internal violence and atrocity in places like the Sudans.

All this creates a crazy quilt of less than central national security concerns for the United States. The problems that exist are often horrendous and heart-wrenching, but they are almost all internal with limited dangers of spreading far beyond the boundaries of existing states—international terrorist organization intrusions are a partial exception. In terms of their national security relevance to the United States, these concerns pale in immediacy compared to other problems discussed in these pages. It is difficult, if not impossible, to imagine an African situation that would invite American military involvement beyond its current parameters in the form of training and equipment provision and limited Special Forces activity in places like Niger.

Policy Examples

The diversity of Africa makes it impossible to examine instances of continental problems that fully capture the phenomenon: there are simply too many idiosyncratic elements amid the geographic and human diversities for that to be possible. It is, however, possible to suggest some of the more pressing matters with potential national security implications and to provide examples that may help suggest patterns and possible directions. This section explores three of these: petroleum-induced instability and corruption in Nigeria, the growing problem of terrorist intrusion in the northern half of the continent (notably Nigeria and Niger), and the extreme internal violence of Sudan (including Darfur) and South Sudan.

Resources and Petroleum-Based Instability

Given the poverty of so much of Africa, the infusion of additional wealth could act as a palliative to the instabilities and violence that selectively plague the continent. African poverty is endemic in most countries, and where there is some wealth, there are competing claimants whose major purpose is personal or group (usually tribal) enhancement rather than the greater good of a state to which many have minimal loyalty anyway. In these circumstances, the countries that have more resources are often more chaotic and violent than those who do not because there is more money to be gotten than in very poor locales. In African terms, those resources are often in the form of exploitable natural bounties, of which petroleum is the most obvious case.

Nigeria is the most extreme case in point. As noted in chapter 10, Nigeria is one of the quintessentially petrolist states. It sits astride the coastline where the Niger River delta empties into the Gulf of Guinea, and under the delta are vast stores of petroleum that comprise the tenth largest reserves among countries at 37.2 billion barrels (2013 estimate). In 2012 (before the oil market collapsed), it produced 2.54 million barrels a day (mbd), of which it exported 2.41 mbd, fully 95 percent of its production. This revenue funds virtually the entire government, and oil revenues also make Nigeria among the most corrupt, kleptocratic countries in the world.

What should the United States do about these conditions? Except for the need for petroleum products, there are virtually no American vital interests in the internal disorder of African states, including its most prominent members. There is internal violence in Nigeria, as in many states where multinationality has a strong religious basis in intertribal cleavages. For the most part, instability remains regionalized with limited short-term expansionist possibilities. If one projects demographic trends forward, however, African marginality may become centrality. As an example, the U.S. population in 2016 was 323 million, and it is expected to rise to 438 million by 2050. Nigeria's 2016 population stood at 186 million; it is projected to be 391 million in 2050. The difference, in other words, will shrink from 137 million to seven million.

Are these trends important to the United States and the rest of the world? They clearly do not have the immediate national security consequences of contemporary Middle East instability, but unless they are moderated, could they become more pressing in the future? How does one make the African transition to major global importance smoother and the results more positive? Development and greater national integration are keys, and they require developmental assistance efforts in areas like reducing corruption (see Clooney and Prendergast). These are not problems for which traditional national security emphases on the military have much obvious salience. The traditional American attitude has been, in Dowden's 2009 words, to "shrug off Nigeria's all-pervasive corruption, happy to talk softly and never waving a big stick."

Terrorist Intrusions

The face of religiously based international terrorism is evolving. The setbacks to landmark terrorist organizations like Al Qaeda following the assassination of Osama bin Laden in 2011 and the essential eviction of the Islamic State (IS or ISIS) from its self-proclaimed caliphate in 2017 are examples. One aspect of the change that has received little publicity has been that many displaced terrorists and their organizations have migrated southward into Saharan and increasingly into sub-Saharan Africa, where they receive a more welcoming environment than they get in the Middle East that spawned them. In turn, these terrorist organizations intermingle and make common cause with home-grown African terrorist groups like Somalia's Al-Shabaab and Nigeria's Boko Haram. This new violent element can further destabilize situations with violent repercussions.

Most Americans were largely unaware of American participation in trying to contain this phenomenon until early October 2017, when news erupted that four U.S. Special Operations Force (SOF) members had been killed in an apparently unauthorized mission in Niger along the boundary between that country and Mali. Those forces have been in place, offering training and assistance to native forces for over a decade (they were originally authorized in 2001 as part of the War on Terror following 9/11). They are not a major element in American national security nor in the campaign against terrorism, but their existence does point to some national security concern with the region—albeit one of which the American public has been largely ignorant. A similar incident occurred on June 8, 2018, in Somalia, when an SOF soldier was killed in a firefight with Al-Shabaab while on a training mission with Somalian forces.

Terrorist penetration of Africa also includes the actions of more indigenous groups that have ties to Middle East terrorists. Al Qaeda (AQ) was, for a time, headquartered in Somalia, but left because, ironically enough, it considered conditions there too lawless and chaotic. After the American intervention in Somalia in 1992, chaos reigned in that country, and the vacuum was partially filled by

Al-Shabaab, an organization with indigenous roots but ties to AQ, from which some of its members continue to operate. Boko Haram, which came into existence in Nigeria largely as a reaction to alleged anti-Muslim activities by the government in Abuja, is most famous for its kidnapping of young teenaged girls and holding them incommunicado while attempting to convert them to Islam. In March 2018, the organization released all the girls except one, who reportedly was a Christian who refused to convert.

The Boko Haram case both helps explain the nature of the terrorist problem on the continent and American interest in it. Although there are internal African terrorist groups, the broader threat comes from the intrusion of more dangerous and larger movements like AQ and IS, where the lack of governmental control allows these organizations to set up effective sanctuaries from which to organize and launch terrorist attacks elsewhere. Part of the dynamic has been for foreign terrorists to try to infiltrate and take over indigenously based movements. This has occurred within Boko Haram, the leadership of which has successfully resisted the increased radicalization such a takeover implies. Trying to blunt and reverse this penetration explains most of the motivation the United States has shown in places like Niger, which has a significant land border with more geopolitically significant Nigeria. These operations had flown largely under the radar before the Special Forces killings in Niger, which was the first awareness many Americans—including members of Congress—had that such operations existed.

Internal Violence and Atrocity

The most spectacular and gruesome examples of African geopolitical instability have been committed by deeply divided population elements in African states. Some, like those in the former Belgian Congo and Nigeria and the genocide in Rwanda, were widely publicized when they were ongoing and elicited impassioned calls for Western, including American, intervention on humanitarian grounds. In contemporary African affairs, none of the continental conflicts comes close to the long civil war that broke out in Sudan almost immediately after independence and which continues to this day, now mostly concentrated in the Republic of South Sudan.

The state of Sudan has been almost constantly at war with itself since the country became independent in 1956. The original country, now divided into Sudan and South Sudan, was an extraordinarily diverse place and almost the caricature of the phenomenon of an artificial state (a country that has no natural centripetal forces to cause it to be a single unit). Natsios reports that at independence, the country contained 597 distinct tribes that spoke 133 languages. The northern part of the country was essentially Muslim, with about 40 percent of the population. The population of the southern part of the country, which essentially became South Sudan, was primarily Christian and animist, and the northerners, who ruled from Khartoum, attempted to impose Arabic and Islam on the southerners. The result was civil war in 1956 that plagued the country until the secession of the South in 2011.

Sudanese violence and atrocity has had two basic faces, both of which are centrifugal because, as Williamson describes, "No vision unites Sudan, no sense exists that various groups share a stake in the nation, no agreement pertains on what it is to be Sudanese." One of these divides Muslim and non-Muslim Sudanese. Its symbolic face is South Sudan. The other is intra-Islamic and centers on different levels of piety among Muslims. Its signature symbol is Darfur. Collectively, these conflicts have resulted in the slaughter of three to five million Sudanese since 1956.

The question of Islamic fundamentalism, which infects all of the Muslim world, has its Sudanese manifestation in the division between the northern, fundamentalist tribes that live around and control the central government in Khartoum and other less fundamentalist Muslims. Their signature source of controversy is insistence on the absolute primacy of Koranic virtue, meaning the imposition of Islam, Arabic language, and *sharia* law. This position has made them natural allies of conservative Middle Eastern states and some terrorist groups.

The Darfur crisis pits the central government against more liberal Muslims in the areas removed from Khartoum, notably Darfur Province along the Chad border. Attempts at imposed Islamification have resulted in violence in 1987–1989, 1995–1997, and 2003–2007, at which time an armistice was reached that is largely enforced by Organization of African Unity (OAU) forces. The notorious *Janjaweed* raiders who forced many Darfuris into exile in Chad were the symbol of government violence. The Chad exile has put the Darfuris outside government control, allowing widespread publicity of the violence that has left an estimated four hundred thousand dead.

The far more hideous violence has been between Sudan and South Sudan. Civil war broke out over the forcible attempt to convert non-Muslim southerners in 1956, and the war raged until a 1972 cessation when a Khartoum regime relented in its campaign. It reignited in 1983 with another attempt to impose sharia and continued until 2005, when outsiders helped negotiate a Comprehensive Peace Agreement (CPA) leading to South Sudanese independence in 2011 following a referendum. An estimated 2.4–4 million perished over the fifty-five-year extent of the war. Since independence, South Sudan has been engaged in genocidal conflict led by the Dinka and Nuer tribes that has cost over a million more deaths and exiles. There is no clear end in sight.

Consequences: What to Do?

The three cases briefly described here are very diverse and offer extreme examples of the problems plaguing African states and those who must interact with them. Their differences have three characteristics. First, they represent very different kinds of phenomena in very different countries. Second, although they have tragic elements in terms of human suffering, their salience as national security concerns for the United States varies considerably, as do the consequences (or absence thereof) attaching to American assessments of those interests. Third, what (if anything) the United States can or should try to do about each of them is uncertain. How does the U.S. government contribute to a reduction of corruption in Nigeria? What are the consequences of not doing anything but exhorting the Nigerians? In places like Niger, the United States African Command attempts to assist indigenous forces seeking to contain or threaten terrorists, but how important is that limited effort? Since it can occasionally produce tragic results (the Special Forces killed in Niger in 2017), how hard should we try? The situations in Sudan (Darfur and South Sudan) are clearly horrific and cry for palliative responses, but what are those responses? Is the United States going to send forces into the fray? That seems very unlikely, so what do we do?

The African examples offer internal contrasts and differences from the other national security concerns in this section. All the others are more concrete, detailing U.S. efforts with countries and regions more immediately important than the African problems. U.S. interests are more clearly defined and generally more important in all those cases. They represent more important geopolitical concerns than the individual African cases, and U.S. national security interests in most of them are marginal or nonexistent. Can the United States have a coherent national security strategy that it can apply to the African continent? If so, what might it be?

Study/Discussion Questions

1. Why is it more difficult to make national security strategy and policy for Africa than for other areas in this book? Why is Africa especially different and difficult?

2. How are many African problems the direct legacy of colonialism? Specifically, discuss the problems of multinationalism and development.

3. What are the major American interests in the problems of Africa? What level of priority do these interests have for American national security policy?

4. The difficulty of forming national security policy toward Africa is the result of its diversity. Discuss that diversity in terms of the three examples discussed. Are there common threads around which to base policy? How did the 2017 Niger incident raise awareness of Africa in U.S. national security concerns?

5. Are there identifiable bases around which to devise a U.S. national security strategy and policy toward Africa? What do you think those bases and policy might be? Why?

Bibliography

Arnold, Matthew, and Matthew LeRiche. *South Sudan: From Revolution to Independence.* New York: Oxford University Press, 2012.

Buss, Terry, Joseph Adjaye, Donald Goldstein, and Lewis Picard (eds.). *African Command: Viewpoints on the U.S. Role in Africa.* West Hartford, CT: Kumerian Press, 2011.

Campbell, John, and Matthew T. Page. *Nigeria: What Everyone Needs to Know.* Oxford, UK: Oxford University Press, 2018.

Chivvis, Christopher S. *The French War on Al Qai'da in Africa.* Cambridge, UK: Cambridge University Press, 2015.

Clooney, George, and John Prendergast. "The Key to Making Peace in Africa: Fighting Corruption Can Help End Conflict." *Foreign Affairs Snapshot* (online), March 14, 2018.

Cockett, Richard. *Sudan: The Failure and Division of an African State.* Second Ed. New Haven, CT: Yale University Press, 2016.

Collins, Robert O. *A History of Modern Sudan.* Cambridge, UK: Cambridge University Press, 2008.

DeWaal, Alexander, and Julie Flint. *Darfur: A New History of a Long War.* London: Zed Books, 2008.

Dowden, Richard. *Africa: Altered States, Ordinary Miracles.* New York: Public Affairs Books, 2009.

Englebert, Pierre, and Kevin C. Dunn. *Inside African Politics.* Boulder, CO: Lynne Rienner, 2013.

Falola, Toyin, and Matthew M. Heaton. *A History of Nigeria.* Cambridge, UK: Cambridge University Press, 2008.

Hentz, James. *Routledge Handbook of African Security.* New York and London: Routledge, 2017.

Johnson, Hilde E. *South Sudan: The Untold Story from Slavery to Independence.* London: I. B. Tauris, 2016.

Jok, Jok Madut. *Sudan: Race, Religion, and Violence.* London: Oneworld, 2015.

Kendhammer, Brandon. "Nigeria's New Democratic Dawn?" *Current History* 114 (772) (May 2015), 170–76.

Lavinder, Kaitlin. "Niger Delta Militants Compound Nigeria's Security Crisis." *Cipher Brief* (Council on Foreign Relations online), August 4, 2016.

Natsios, Andrew S. *Sudan, South Sudan, and Darfur: What Everyone Needs to Know.* New York: Oxford University Press, 2012.

Rolandsen, Oystein H., and M. W. Daly. *A History of South Sudan: From Slavery to Independence.* Cambridge, UK: Cambridge University Press, 2016.

Snow, Donald M. *Cases in International Relations.* Sixth Ed. New York: Pearson, 2015; Seventh Ed. Lanham, MD: Rowman & Littlefield, 2018.

———. *Regional Cases in U.S. Foreign Policy.* Second Ed. Lanham, MD: Rowman & Littlefield, 2018.

Thomson, Alex. *An Introduction to African Politics.* New York and London: Routledge, 2016.

Thorston, Alexander. *Boko Haram: The History of an African Jihadist Movement.* Princeton Studies in Muslim Politics. Princeton, NJ: Princeton University Press, 2017.

U.S. Department of State. *Country Note: South Sudan.* Washington, DC: U.S. Department of State, 2016.

———. "U.S. Relations with Nigeria." U.S. Department of State Bureau of African Affairs, June 20, 2016.

———. "U.S. Relations with South Sudan." U.S. Department of State Bureau of African Affairs, September 16, 2015.

Williams, Paul D. *War and Conflict in Africa.* Second Ed. Cambridge, UK: Polity Press, 2016.

Williamson, Richard S. "Sudan on the Cusp." *Current History* 110 (736) (May 2011), 171–76.

III

POLITICAL CONTEXT

The first two parts of this book have dealt with concrete national security problems. In Part I, the topics were challenges to national security arising from different system dynamics like forms of warfare (e.g., asymmetrical war and terror) or questions surrounding nuclear weapons. Part II dealt with challenges inherent in concrete relationships in the world, from the Middle East to traditional rivals like Russia and China to a possible mandate to think about emerging challenges on the African continent.

Part III has a different focus. It looks not so much at the geographically based problems the country faces as it does at the circumstances and resources available to meet those challenges. The topics are more contextual than substantive and are directed at the policy level of how the country can deal with strategic priorities through policies and capabilities. The first two cases examine the parameters of the resources available generically to meet national security challenges; the third and fourth cases look at specific environmental challenges and opportunities.

The discussion begins with the broad question of how many resources the country needs to realize its national security needs and the budgetary resources available to match strategic needs to threats from the environment in chapter 14. The two concerns are related and sequential. Answering how much is enough requires assessing what threats exist and then determining what monetary resources are available to counter them. Both are subjective processes where not all information is available all the time. For military aspects of dealing with these problems, the question of military personnel is the subject of chapter 15. The heart of the discussion is that the All-Volunteer Force (AVF) concept by which military personnel have been procured since 1972 has been adequate for a relatively non-stressful environment, but if more difficult tasks requiring larger numbers of troops arise, the AVF might prove inadequate and create the need for other methods of procurement, including conscription.

The other two chapters deal with conditioning factors. Chapter 16 addresses the question of cybersecurity, the impact of computer information collection, management, and security from hostile others. Its central theme is that the general cyber phenomenon is not unique, but that it is the latest way in which many traditional tasks are performed. The field is evolving so rapidly that its assessment and direction are necessarily tentative and subject to change. Chapter 17 looks at a specific technology, drones, and how their use has revolutionized some aspects of warfare. It also raises ethical questions about whether some uses of drones, especially in terrorist sanctuary locations, may constitute a form of terrorism of their own.

14

How Much of What Is Enough?

What Kinds, Levels, and Costs of U.S. Force?

The nature and quality of threats the United States encounters are changing and will continue to do so. One of the most significant changes in the international environment and American response to it has been the increased militarism of the American role. Before World War II, the United States assiduously avoided a large military establishment; since 1945, a signal characteristic of America's role has been its persistent position as the world's most powerful country militarily. For over forty years, the creation of the "national security" state featuring a central military element was necessitated by the military challenge from the Soviet Union. The Cold War transformed America and American attitudes toward military force as the prime tool for securing America's security.

That primacy includes a willingness to fund a large standing military force to protect America's security. It has created a prominence and acceptance of American military might that would have appalled the founding fathers. One major reason for enacting the Second Amendment to the Constitution, after all, was so citizens could protect themselves from a U.S. military that might try to deprive them of their freedom.

In 2018, a budgetary agreement was reached greatly increasing defense spending to ensure American primacy. The increase would allow broad spending on new and more lethal weapons systems across the spectrum to ensure the United States remains the world's most powerful military actor in a national security environment that has changed greatly since the turn of the twenty-first century. The focus is no longer on major power conflicts that could lead to the global bloodletting symbolized by the two world wars. The European plain, the historical arena for mass warfare, is militarily tranquil except at the intersection with the old Soviet Union, and no one can conjure a situation in which war would break out on the continent. Asian geopolitics remain active, but other than on the Korean Peninsula, there is little likelihood of violent clash. Almost all observers agree that the age of massive international war is over, at least for the foreseeable future. This change affects both the national security problem and how one prepares to manage it. The question is the extent to which the implication of that change has been translated into levels and kinds of military preparedness. This question is central to the chapter's title, a variation on the theme of "how much is enough?" originally raised by Alain Enthoven during the Vietnam War and no less relevant today. The imbedded question is how much the country should be willing to pay for it.

Questions about defense preparedness are becoming politically charged for three reasons. One is the extensive pattern of deployments of American forces in this century. America has been at war continuously since 2001, and there is no apparent end to the Afghanistan involvement. These deployments have been expensive in terms of American blood and treasure, and there is reason to question whether this level of force deployment should continue. Second, since 2013, something called the "sequester" has limited the amount of funding available for military matters, a condition that affects future security preparations. Current deployments like Afghanistan have to some extent come at the expense of investing in capabilities that may be needed for future contingencies and have contributed to burgeoning deficits and accumulated governmental debt. Third, President Trump managed, as part of the March 2018 budget deal, to get sequester-driven defense cuts largely erased, with a budget of $700 billion that he promised would include provision for defense investments across the board.

Perspectives on the Problem

The question "how much is enough?" raises at least three other questions. The first is "enough to do what?" The second is "enough of what?" The third is at what cost? The model laid out in Chapter 1 suggests the first question is primary and should provide direction for answering the second question, which in turn should guide the third question. This rational, deductive model is not, however, always paramount, because the dictates of national security intermix with political considerations inside the national security community and in national politics more generally.

National Security Needs

The question of how much for what begins with an assessment of national security needs driven by assessing the pattern of threats the country faces. Promoting American interests starts with a determination of what forces in the world imperil American interests globally and thus what needs to be done to protect those interests.

The landscape has changed dramatically. The most basic national interest is the physical survival of the country and its people. All other interests pale in comparison with it. For the United States, the only survival threat is an attack on national soil by nuclear weapons, making nuclear deterrence the ultimate U.S. national security priority. The end of the Cold War relaxed this threat. Russia retained the old Soviet arsenal (although it has shrunk) and remains physically capable of destroying the American homeland, but it lacks the incentive to do so. Russian nuclear force modernization is a concern the United States must monitor and work to negate, as is growth in the Chinese nuclear force. This primacy also provides the rationale for great American concern about nuclear proliferation by North Korea and potentially by Iran.

The rest of the national security environment is also different. Big threats like a war with the Soviet Union have been replaced by a shifting environment of smaller threats. The old structure of an overwhelming military opponent that had to be deterred, and if deterrence failed, fought and defeated dictated strategy and forces. It was a menacing environment; it was also intellectually orderly. Everyone knew the nature of the threat and how to deal with it.

That structure has largely disintegrated from a traditional national security military perspective. Its premises are no longer relevant. Russia is a menace of sorts, but it lacks the capability to launch a major conventional military thrust into Europe. Europe is basically stable, with no pressing national security threats. By extension, American interests in maintaining a free European partner are also no longer threatened the way they were when the Iron Curtain separated communist and non-communist Europe. The division of primary interests in the Asia-Pacific between China and the United States is the major issue in East Asian geopolitics, but it is a conflict with very little military potential (see chapter 12). The era of large wars between the most powerful countries is indeed over for now.

Anomalies and Mismatches

These changed conditions have resulted in anomalies that the national security policy process has not clearly resolved. Two sequential changed dynamics introduced in chapter 2 stand out. The first is the *interest-threat mismatch*. During the Cold War, interests and threats were aligned: America's most important interests were threatened by the Soviets, thereby offering direct guidance to strategy and policy. Today, however, there is a mismatch: America's most important interests (e.g., Europe and East Asia) are hardly threatened, and the places where there are threats are much less important to the United States (e.g., Africa).

The other anomaly is the *threat-force mismatch*. This construct refers to the major holdover from the Cold War, when American forces were geared primarily for use in a large ground war in Europe or elsewhere in the Eurasian land mass. The model for force composition and structure was World War II. The result is an American force structure clearly attuned to fighting in that environment where interests are great; in the contemporary environment, the threat for which they are prepared is not the places for which it is most appropriate. Most real threats are in the developing world, for which the forces were not designed.

Existing threats are also structured differently. Most current instabilities come from internal wars in developing countries (the DWICs identified in chapter 2). In these circumstances, it is not clear that the kind of force structure developed for the Cold War is particularly appropriate. Warfare between the two Cold War rivals would have been "heavy"—using large firepower-intensive weapons platforms like artillery and tanks. Tanks operate optimally on relatively flat terrain (especially with roads); they cannot operate effectively in the mountainous landscape of a place like Afghanistan. At the same time, the air battle in Europe would have featured extensive air-to-air combat between Soviet and American fighter jets. Hardly any developing country has an air force of any note. The last time American fighters were engaged in dogfights with a hostile air force was in Vietnam.

Budgetary Sleight of Hand

There is an old, unattributed truism in Washington politics: policy is what gets funded. It makes a fundamental distinction about the political world between the rhetoric that surrounds contentious public issues and the actual allocation of resources to define and implement public policy. Virtually everything that the government does involves the expenditure of public monies, so the existence and distribution of public funds is a more accurate indicator of *actual* governmental priorities than even the most impassioned but unfunded advocacies of policy directions. A corollary is that how and to what extent the government funds different activities is the most reliable indication of real policy directions. Advocacy devoid of spending consequences is a much hollower indicator of priorities than the things on which one spends the people's money.

There is no category of federal activity where this observation is truer than in national security policy. National security is one of the most expensive activities of the national government. Armed forces are expensive, and the larger and more capable they become, the more they tend to cost. At the same time, the development and deployment of military accoutrement is very dynamic, meaning the demands for new, more effective, and more expensive weapons is an ongoing process. It is also competitive, because those against whom weapons are devised engage in the same process.

The dynamics and import of this characteristic are difficult to overstate. During the Cold War, the United States spent more on national defense than any other budgetary category. In the Eisenhower administration of the 1950s, the defense share of a federal government less encumbered with entitlement spending was around half the total budget. Today, it is the third largest category, following entitlements (e.g., Social Security and Medicare/Medicaid) at about two-fifths of the budget and service (interest) on the national debt at almost one-quarter of the budget. Defense spending has hovered at about one-fifth, but that could increase. Many of the increases have been caused by constant overseas deployments since 9/11, and increases could also be the result of deploying new weapons systems deferred by the sequester (see below). The budget increase for 2018 is from $549 billion to $700 billion.

How these funds are invested will have considerable impact on the strategy the country can follow in the future. As a purely intellectual exercise, the military capability of the country should derive deductively from national security strategy. Once a strategy is chosen, the defense establishment should produce the weapons and other capabilities to support that strategy. In fact, these considerations are often inverted: available capabilities dictate strategies and thus the relevance of strategy rather than the other way around. Whether the process will become more rational with added funding remains to be seen.

The current "gusher" of defense spending is the result of the de facto rescinding of something called the *sequester*. It was the result of a piece of legislation called the Budget Control Act of 2011, the purpose of which was to reduce governmental deficits. Under its provisions, these reductions would be divided equally from the defense and non-defense discretionary budgets (funds that must be renewed annually). This plan required a bipartisan agreement that was problematical in Congress. To guard against inaction, a provision was included that if Congress could not reach accord on reductions, the cuts would be made automatically from the defense and non-defense budgets—sequestration. This prospect was viewed as so draconian and unacceptable that congressional conferees (a so-called Super Committee) would reach an acceptable agreement rather than impose the consequences. They failed, and sequestration began in 2013. It is scheduled to run until 2021 and save the government $1.1 trillion.

The sequester has been very unpopular within the national security community, since it has meant little money available for research, development, and deployment of new weapons systems and the replacement of damaged or worn-out equipment because of multiple U.S. military deployments. When the Congress (with presidential agreement) passed a $1.3 trillion continuing resolution to fund the government (and keep it open until September 2018) in February 2018, it effectively (but not officially) rescinded the sequester and restored much national security spending. The defense budget rose by $151 billion to $700 billion under its provisions. It thus increased the ability to cover more security contingencies; it also increased the deficit and the accumulated national debt.

Policy Options

As the bonanza of an apparent budgetary hemorrhage on defense spending looms in the American political debate, this prospect creates an opportunity for the country to reassess its basic national security posture. With the communist threat dissipated, the closest thing to a strategy-guiding event has been 9/11 and international terrorism as the overarching threat of the 2000s. That threat, however, is qualitatively different from the Cold War: at heart, it lacks the existential nature of its predecessor, and as a result, the old construct does not provide much guidance for the future.

Parameters of Discussion

National security strategy is an emotional, contentious topic. The emotion is largely the result of the personal and national vitality of the subject. National security is, after all, about keeping America and Americans safe from harm, even death. Other policy areas do not have this life-and-death aura about them: disputes over fisheries policy do not have discernible existential consequences for the American people.

This character of national security gives it a conservative bias partially captured in the idea of worst-case analysis. The conservative bias reinforces the predilection to accept the direst possible occurrences and to prepare through the expenditure of public resources to negate these sources of risk. This is the heart of the idea of worst-case analysis: one looks at the most cataclysmic possible threat in a policy environment and prepares to negate that. The assumption is that doing so either deters the opponent or creates the capability to defeat the threat if deterrence fails. Since major responses often involve weapons developments that take a long time to develop and deploy, the failure to act in advance may leave the country powerless to deal with a threat for which advance preparation has not occurred. Given the potentially horrendous consequences of some threats, prudence dictates covering as many potential risks as one possibly can. The operative idea is "better safe than sorry."

The conservative bias reinforces the argument for a strong defense strategy, but it has limits. The most obvious, of course, is expense: is it physically possible to fund the capabilities that can negate all the risks posed by all potential threats? This problem is real because, as noted in chapter 1, threats are subjective. All people are not threatened by the same things, and the list of potentially threatening situations is virtually infinitely expansible. Those who want to increase resources for national security argue for expansion based on the premises that create the conservative bias. Others who feel less threatened will argue some threat projections are either bogus, highly unlikely, or outside the bounds of legitimate national security imperatives. Better safe or sorry?

A further problem comes from an imbedded assumption of worst-case analysis: the *lesser-included case*. Worst case defenders argue that if one prepares for the worst possible case, one has in the process also prepared for smaller versions of it. This assumption is misleading unless the so-called "lesser cases" are isomorphisms of the worst case: essentially smaller versions of the same phenomenon. If they are, then preparation for the worst case prepares for the smaller case and is cost-efficient—a kind of two (or more)-for-one sale. The problem is that situations are often not so similar that a solution designed for one contingency applies to what may appear to be a smaller apparent copy. In an obvious case, money spent on nuclear weapons to deter Russia has no utility in deterring regional wars in the Middle East or internal African civil wars. The reasoning of lesser case inclusion was basically applied in Vietnam. The United States inserted a conventional force into the asymmetrical war there in 1965 on the assumption it would prevail against a lesser Vietnamese challenge, and it did not work.

All these matters are controversial, and there are articulate spokespeople who argue any side of all of them. In many cases, the differences reflect partisan political positions based in ideology (liberal-conservative) or party lines (Democratic-Republican). Often, patriotic appeals are also attached to debates, and the net effect not infrequently is to promote a more conservative, expansive interpretation of how much is enough.

Policy Choices

There are two ways to view solutions to the national security risk equation. The objective is always how to reduce risk to a minimum or to negate it altogether, if risk is the difference between the threats one encounters and the capability to deal with those threats that was introduced in chapter 1 (Risk equals Threat minus Capability). It can be approached by manipulating either of the factors on the right side of the equation. One can attempt to reduce risk, expand capability to counter that threat, or one can try to fashion some combination of the two. Much of the determination of how much is enough is really about the relative weight one gives to either element.

One must recall basic understandings of the concepts. Risk is a *variable* concept. It depends on a subjective determination of what threatens the national security. Threat is the "motor" of national security analysis in the sense that the degree and ways in which threat is manifested define the problem for which capability is the solution. These calculations are often either unstated or not explicitly addressed in national security conversations. What kind and level of threat to the United States is posed by various outcomes of the civil war in Afghanistan? Do those threats justify the continuing American military presence there, and how does that capability reduce risk to the United States? The same analysis can be applied to dealing with the situation in Syria discussed in chapter 10—but it rarely is.

Modulating risk begins from one's basic geopolitical orientation about the American role and interests in the world. How much is enough is a composite of the answer to three questions. The first is where are there sufficient American national security interests to justify the possible deployment and employment of American armed forces? This is a geopolitical question that flows from America's assessment of its place in the world and how active it wants to be in enforcing its interests. The second is the nature of the military challenge one is likely to face in those places where it might feel the need to use force. The historical answer was a large, heavy, lethal force capable of conducting European-style warfare. That contingency has largely disappeared. The third question is how much force is needed in any of these situations. Included in that calculation is how much that force costs.

The literal answer to each of these questions is "we don't know." Military preparedness always exists in an environment of some uncertainty, largely because circumstances change, and opponents seek to frustrate one's preparations, adding to difficulty of prediction. An old military saw says even the most elaborate prewar plans disappear after the first encounter with the enemy. Who, for instance, believed in 2010 that something like IS would pose a threat suggesting the possible need for American force in 2014? The conservative response to uncertainty is to prepare not only for predictable but also unpredictable threats. The fear of a dangerous unknown which suddenly appears and for which there is inadequate time to prepare is at the core of the worst case, and it gives enormous advantage to those with a fulsome response to how much is enough.

Dealing with Uncertainty

One cannot perfectly know or even anticipate the national security future, but that also does not mean one is powerless to plan for something less than everything bad that can happen. The goal of national security planning is risk elimination, but uncertainty means that goal is unlikely to be achieved. The more practical goal is to maximize risk reduction, and the three questions asked above can help channel efforts to do so.

The question of where to fight derives in large measure from the vision the country has for its role in the world. The broader and more activist those goals are, the greater the likelihood one will need larger and more capable military forces to achieve them. Conversely, the more modest and physically bounded the goals are, the less demands are made on capabilities. In turn, that assessment has an impact on the size and price of the capabilities one needs to have "enough."

The first step in the assessment process is the general orientation toward the environment. Since the end of World War II, the basic American stance has been that, as a world leader with global interests, these interests must be enforced with force if necessary. There are three variants in the current debate, and each predisposes its adherents to different levels of national security activism.

Two of the alternatives are expansive. The first and most prevalent position has been *internationalism*. Its basic underlying idea is that the United States has global interests and is the de facto world leader, but that it must work in concert with other countries and entities like alliances and international organizations (e.g., the United Nations) to produce a world order of its liking. Internationalists prefer using diplomacy and negotiation to solve international conflicts, but they recognize that robust American forces provide an incentive for others to listen to the U.S. position and that the recourse to military force is always an option that will sometimes be necessary. The internationalist position tends to be associated with political liberalism, but it has been accepted by realists and conservatives who believe that a more aggressive approach is counterproductive or outside the political tradition of the country.

The other expansive position is *interventionism*. It is basically a more militarized variant of the internationalist philosophy, agreeing the United States has interests that must be protected and promoted but more willing to invoke the recourse to American arms to achieve their goals. The internationalists and the interventionists do not disagree on the basic role of the United States in the world; they diverge on the relative emphasis on political/diplomatic or unilateral military means for solving problems. The greater willingness of interventionists to rely on military power is sometimes equated with the philosophy of conservatism.

The third general orientation is *isolationism*. People who advocate this position believe the United States should limit its involvement in the world, and they are especially reluctant to invoke the American military option unless truly vital American interests are threatened. This orientation, most forcefully advocated by Kentucky senator Rand Paul, is that most foreign involvements do not fundamentally affect the United States. Moreover, the isolationist position requires the smallest amount of physical investment. A central tenet of isolationism is that direct homeland security is the only pure function of those forces. This position is often associated with fiscal conservatives.

The positions are more distinct in theory than in practice. The rhetoric of President Trump during the 2016 campaign and after was decidedly isolationist, but he has shown some interventionist tendencies in situations where American avoidance or withdrawal would be pure isolationist postures. At the same time, most internationalists have some sympathy for the interventionist position: President Obama, for instance, was willing to leave American forces in Afghanistan when diplomatic efforts to end the conflict there failed.

The second step is determining what kinds of forces one needs to cover what kinds of contingencies. One's general attitude toward the world affects how and when to use force. The traditional American realist position has been that force should only be used in defense of America's most vital interests. In today's world, that is a restricted list: other than nuclear attack, the most vital interest, homeland integrity, is not threatened at all, and traditional overseas vital interests (Europe, East Asia) also are not militarily threatened. Since 9/11, the list of places in which force may be contemplated has expanded to developing-world locations in the Middle East and elsewhere whose security was not traditionally considered vital to the United States, and this has expanded both the quantity and quality of forces the United States must have under arms. This expansion, and particularly deployments arising from it, also expands the definition of how much is enough.

The final step is the size commitment one needs to realize its interests. Clearly, the longer and more diverse the list of places where one might contemplate using force expands or contracts the requirement. This is true regarding the likely size and composition of forces and the ways in which they might be called on to fight. The military is still centrally configured to conduct hostilities on the model of the worst case, which means a concentration on large-unit, conventional warfare—the European model. The United States has not, however, fought that kind of war since Korea (Operation Desert Storm to remove Iraq from Kuwait in 1990 and 1991 is an exception). All other encounters have been in developing world locales where traditional forces are not particularly proficient or appropriate.

Budgetary Legerdemain

The third step brings the discussion back to the central point of spending: how many monetary resources must the United States devote to its security? Most Americans have only a general—and sometimes erroneous or misleading—idea of how much is involved beyond "a lot." Publicly available estimates are generally lower than reality: if all the money expended on national security–related matters were lumped together, the result would be staggering and would shock the public.

There are several reasons for and manifestations of this phenomenon. The standard reason for incomplete estimates begins with the "black budget": money spent by government to fund priorities that are secret, either because what is being funded is a secret or because acknowledging expenses would reveal activities the government wants to hide from adversaries. A second manifestation is assigning arguable defense obligations in other agencies' budgets so that they are not counted against the national security burden. The costs of veterans' care, for instance, is not included in the Department of Defense (DOD) budget; instead the Department of Veterans Affairs has its own separate budget. Similarly, much of the cost of nuclear weapons is in the Department of Energy budget. If all arguably defense spending was publicly linked to national security per se, it would dwarf the $700 billion appropriated in 2018 and raise significant budget-balancing questions in the public debate.

Understanding the real parameters of how much national security costs is further obscured by forms of legerdemain that minimize the appearance of spending.

Since 2001, a popular variant has been Overseas Contingency Operations (OCOs). Sometimes referred to as the Pentagon's "slush fund," OCOs were authorized after 9/11 as part of an open-ended Authorization of the Use of Military Force (AUMF) to allow emerging expenditures for military operations in the War on Terror when there was inadequate time to legislate a direct appropriation by Congress for the needed task. Their basis was in the longstanding tradition of supplemental appropriations, the authority to make emergency expenditures in the event of national disasters like Hurricane Katrina in 2005. Under practices going back to the 1790s, these expenses would be reimbursed in the next budget cycle.

The OCO process has arguably been abused. OCOs have been the primary source of funding for American wars in Iraq and Afghanistan that hardly qualify as emergency national disasters. Their advantages are that they do not require specific allocations and detailed justifications in advance and that they do not appear as defense expenditures per se in the defense budget. It is also not clear that all OCO expenditures are compensated in subsequent budget cycles, meaning they disappear into the federal deficit without clear acknowledgment that they are the result of national security spending. If the expense of these involvements were directly accounted in defense spending, its impact would be in the trillions of dollars.

Consequences: What to Do?

Determining the answers to questions about how the country should prepare to defend its interests is clearly more complicated than is possible in an examination of this length. The debate about military equipment, capability, and the like is clearly technical, and classification of characteristics of weapons guarantees that outsiders cannot fully assess claims about things like the capabilities and worth of very expensive weapons systems. What one can do is pass some judgment on where and for what reasons the country should be prepared to fight and how much it is willing to spend in the process.

The basic determination is the extent of American interests and which of those the United States should be prepared to defend with military force. Situations are, of course, unique, but one can render general national security force judgments about where which force should be contemplated. In contemporary circumstances, this judgment revolves around levels of interventionist activity in the DWICs. Since 9/11, these have been concentrated on the Middle East because of its connection to terrorism, but it can be extended to Africa (e.g., South Sudan) or parts of Asia (e.g., the Rohingya of Myanmar and Bangladesh; see chapter 18). These kinds of involvements can be expensive, as in Afghanistan, and there is always some question about their advisability in terms of U.S. interests.

The budgetary process distorts the rational process of translating strategy into policy in another way. Due to the political gridlock in Washington, the United States has not passed a general budget reflecting an assessment of current policy and strategic needs since 2009, because it cannot agree on national priorities, including national security. Instead, the government is kept open and functioning through what is now a familiar device: the continuing resolution. When congressional authorizations to spend public monies are about to expire, the Congress passes a "CR," as they are known. This device allows the government to continue spending in the amounts and for the purposes it has previously authorized for a specific period (always less than a year). This means that determinations of how much is enough are based on how those judgments were made under the previous resolution. Since this has been the appropriation method since 2009, this means the policy costs of current strategy were determined in that year. By extension, this means the effective, operational national security strategy of the United States is what it was determined to be in 2009. Has anything changed in the world?

In an era of skyrocketing deficit spending, spending on national security is, or should be, an important part of the national security debate. What is enough for what purposes is the result of how many negative assaults on national interest one is willing to endure (i.e., the risk one will accept), and that determination affects where and what amounts one will be willing to spend. Lurking in the background of the debate is the realization of uncertainty: there will always be unanticipated contingencies that could imperil the country's security. It is a difficult set of calculations. How do you think it should be approached? Some of the implications are discussed in monetary terms in the next chapter.

Study/Discussion Questions

1. What is the basis for the question "how much is enough?" Trace the question and answer historically and in the current environment, including the elements in framing the question.

2. Break down "how much is enough" into sub-questions: "enough to do what?" and "enough of what?" Apply to national security needs and conceptual problems like anomalies and intellectual mismatches. How do budgetary concerns affect and factor into the process?

3. What parameters help define the national security debate on American military needs? How do these parameters complicate discussions of the topic?

4. Frame national security policy choices in terms of risk and risk reduction. How does uncertainty affect these calculations? How do factors like defense expenses influence the process?

5. What are the three basic orientations toward American national security activism and the effects of each on the answer to "how much is enough?" With which position do you most closely agree? Why? What are its implications for answering the central question, "how much is enough?" To what degree should matters like the cost of defense factor into the calculus? What do you think?

Bibliography

Adams, Gordon, and Cindy Williams. *Buying National Security: How America Plans and Pays for Its Global Role and Safety at Home.* New York and London: Routledge, 2010.

Art, Robert J., Peter Feaver, Richard Fontaine, Kristin M. Lord, and Anne-Marie Slaughter. *America's Path: Grand Strategy for the Next Administration*. Washington, DC: Center for a New American Security, 2012.

Aydin, Aysegul. *Foreign Policy and Intervention in Armed Conflicts*. Palo Alto, CA: Stanford University Press, 2012.

Bacevich, Andrew C. (ed.). *The Short American Century: A Postmortem*. Cambridge, MA: Harvard University Press, 2012.

Brzezinski, Zbigniew. *Strategic Vision: America and the Crisis of Global Power*. New York: Basic Books, 2012.

Candreva, Philip J. *National Defense Budgeting and Financial Management*. Charlotte, NC: Information Age Publishing, 2017.

Demarest, Heidi Bracken. *U.S. Defense Budget Outcomes: Volatility and Predictability in Army Weapons Funding*. New York: Palgrave Macmillan, 2017.

Enthoven, Alain C., and K. Wayne Smith. *How Much Is Enough? Shaping the Defense Program*. Santa Monica, CA: RAND Corporation, 2016.

Haass, Richard M. *Intervention: The Use of American Force in the Post–Cold War World*. Washington, DC: Carnegie Endowment for International Peace, 1994.

Hentz, James J. *The Obligation of Empire: United States Strategy for a New Century*. Lexington: University of Kentucky Press, 2004.

Levitsky, Steven, and Daniel Zilblatt. *How Democracies Die*. New York: Crown Publishers, 2018.

McMaster, H. R. *Dereliction of Duty: Johnson, McNamara, the Joint Chiefs of Staff, and the Lies That Led to Vietnam*. New York: Harper Perennials, 1998.

O'Hanlon, Michael E. *The $650 Billion Bargain: The Case for Modest Growth in America's Defense Budget*. Washington, DC: Brookings Institution Press, 2016.

O'Hanlon, Michael E., and David Petraeus. "America's Awesome Military and How to Make It Even Better." *Foreign Affairs* 95 (5) (September/October 2017), 10–17.

Pfaff, William R. *The Irony of Manifest Destiny: The Tragedy of America's Foreign Policy*. New York: Walker, 2010.

Sandstrom, Karl. *Local Interests and American Foreign Policy: Why International Interventions Fail*. New York and London: Routledge, 2013.

Snow, Donald M. *The Case Against Military Intervention: Why We Do It and Why It Fails*. New York and London: Routledge, 2016.

———. *Distant Thunder: Patterns of Conflict in the Developing World*. Second Ed. Armonk, NY: M. E. Sharpe, 1997.

———. *National Security*. Sixth Ed. New York and London: Routledge, 2017.

———. *When America Fights: The Uses of U.S. Military Force*. Washington, DC: CQ Press, 2000.

Snow, Donald M., and Dennis M. Drew. *From Lexington to Baghdad and Beyond: War and Politics in the American Experience*. Armonk, NY: M. E. Sharpe, 2010.

Thornberry, Mac, and Andrew A. Krepinevich Jr. "Preserving Primacy: A Defense Strategy for the New Administration." *Foreign Affairs* 95 (5) (September/October 2017), 26–35.

Williams, Lynn M., and Susan B. Epstein. *Overseas Contingency Operations Funding: Background and Status*. Washington, DC: Congressional Research Service, February 2, 2017.

15

Military Personnel
Where Do the Soldiers Come From?

ost Americans, and virtually all U.S. citizens since 1972, have had to give little thought to who will serve, fight, and possibly die in military service to their country. The reason is simple: at the end of 1972, the United States suspended the practice of forcing young men into the military service of their country against their express will: the draft ended. Involuntary service has long, if episodic, roots in the American experience at war, but became unpopular during the Vietnam War. Since 1972, the only people who have worn the American uniform have volunteered to do so. No one choosing not to join the military has had to fear being coerced into military service through conscription, known more colloquially as the draft. Most Americans have chosen to avoid that service; since Vietnam, their country has endorsed that preference.

There has always been a national tension about the basis for military service that has balanced the needs of state with the personal peril in which service members are placed. For most of American history, all voluntary service has been the norm when the country has not been engaged in a major war. There has always been a pool of people for whom voluntary service is a calling (the children of military members, for instance), and some young people have joined because they either could not find civilian employment or had no other meaningful options to military service. Peacetime, voluntary militaries have been the norm, as has conscription in times of great national distress. The United States drafted armed forces for the Civil War, the World Wars, and the highly armed Cold War because it needed much larger forces than those who would voluntarily agree to serve. The 1972 transition to an exclusively volunteer force was part of the national pattern.

Vietnam represented a sharp discontinuity in the previous national popular experience. America had fought wars with conscripts before, and it had fought wars that were not well supported previously. Except for the American Civil War in parts of the Union, all the previous wars requiring involuntary service had been overwhelmingly popular, making resistance to service minimal. Vietnam, however, became an unpopular war, and a major part of that unpopularity was because it was fought by conscripts who (along with their families) opposed the war. Conscription and an unpopular war were joined; the All-Volunteer Force was the mechanism to separate them.

The Vietnam War was never very popular among those forced to fight it, was not a victorious application of American force (it earned the aphorism, not entirely justified, as "the first war the United States lost"), and it was a conflict the purposes and winnability of which increasing numbers of Americans had come to question. A major cause of the war's unpopularity was the draft, which forced people into what they viewed as perilous personal service in a cause they opposed.

The solution to the post-Vietnam manpower problem was the All-Volunteer Force (AVF), which has been the basis of American military force procurement ever since. No living American who was not at least eighteen years of age on December 31, 1972, has faced the prospect of being forced to serve in the U.S. military. That means that nobody who is not in their sixties has experienced draft vulnerability: there are essentially three generations of Americans who have not involuntarily served or had to concern themselves with the possibility of forced service. Moreover, because of the way the draft ended, the idea of reinstating conscription (which is only a president's signature away from occurring) has never been a remote prospect.

The AVF military recruitment system has been a major success story. Virtually every affected group in the country supports it, if for different reasons. The military likes it, for instance, because it produced better, more motivated and disciplined soldiers than the conscript force of reluctant participants did, meaning a more competent, dedicated force that performs its tasks much better than a conscript force. Politicians love it because it relieves them of the possibility of voting for legislation that would force the sons (and probably daughters today) of their constituents unwillingly into military harm's way. Young people embrace the principle because it relieves them of the trauma of possible involuntary service.

Military personnel procurement is an important strategic concern, principally as a parameter setter on military capability and thus the strategic purposes for which forces can be raised and employed. In determining how much threat can be effectively nullified (how much risk can be reduced), a major determinant in capability is personnel availability: the "C" in the risk equals threat minus capability formulation. To this point, the "C" produced by the AVF has been adequate. The strategic question is whether this will always be the case.

The result has been a win-win situation for all concerned so far. There is, however, another, darker side to the manpower situation that suggests the very success of the AVF has not been without costs that could affect the country's national security situation in the future. The AVF is good, but it is expensive, it produces a limited-size force, and it may allow the country to become involved in some military engagements that a more service-vulnerable population might not allow. At the same time, it may also preclude the engagement of the United States in other military situations.

Perspectives on the Problem

The all-volunteer basis for providing service members for the armed forces is under no stress or serious political or geopolitical strain. It may have come into existence for less than pristine national security reasons—relieving opposition to continued forced military service in an unpopular war that was winding down anyway—but it has proven to be a flexible and durable means to keep the American military at an acceptable size and with more than adequate performance characteristics. The result is politically synergistic: the military has not needed to consider involuntary means of accession into its ranks, and potential conscripts who do not want to serve have not had to worry about the prospect they might be forced to serve.

The national security environment has also made the AVF viable. A major drawback of a voluntary force is that it is likely to be size-constrained when there is not a military emergency that causes a major surge in voluntary enlistment—a large *war of necessity* where the United States' national security is clearly in jeopardy unless a full mobilization occurs. Vietnam was treated as such a war, a designation significant parts of the draft-eligible base ultimately rejected, and there have not been potential contingencies where something like full-scale mobilization would seem justified. Instead, the military "opportunities" the United States has had, especially since the implosion of the Soviet Union, have been in smaller *wars of choice*, contingencies where American interests were arguably engaged but where a favorable outcome was not absolutely needed for national security and where major expansions in the force were not necessary to prosecute those conflicts.

Wars of choice, in other words, generally do not require the devotion of enormous forces to prosecute. They are involvements for which a military force with the size limits of the AVF is not a problem. It is axiomatic that volunteer forces are suited for smaller wars of choice than they are massive wars of necessity, for which they are likely to be too small. In the American experience, when the threat environment contained only small potential conflicts, volunteer forces have been adequate for the job; when the threats have been massive and deadly, those volunteers have had to be augmented by some other means of soldier procurement such as conscription. Nothing has fundamentally changed about that calculation.

One might object that the United States has, since 9/11, been in a conflict of necessity in its fight against terrorism. That observation is certainly true in one sense—combating and controlling or eliminating terrorism is clearly a vital imperative. It is, however, not true in the sense that the threat posed by terrorism creates a massive military task that requires the commitment of a large military force of the size, kind, or nature of the force that conducted World War II, for instance. It is not at all clear how such a force could confront and defeat the motley bands of terrorists that exist. The United States attempted such an approach on a limited basis in Iraq after 2003, and it did not work. In a sense, the United States has approached such a solution with its simultaneous wars against Iraq and Afghanistan since. That effort may have failed to accomplish its goals, and it has stretched the capacities of the AVF to their near limits but has not exceeded those limits. A simultaneous military use of the AVF in a similar conflict might force a rethinking of the voluntary basis of American forces and has been one of the arguments against employing American forces in places like Syria and against the Islamic State.

The use of the AVF in Iraq and Afghanistan has raised some residual questions about whether continuing it in its present form best serves the national security of the United States over the long haul. These questions are not immediate matters of policy concern given general satisfaction with the concept, but they do raise questions that could be important in the future. Two questions stand out. The first is the inherent limits of the size and capabilities of the AVF for the kinds of military uses the country might contemplate or be forced to confront in the future. The second is the detachment of the American public from the implications of a political environment where citizens do not believe they can possibly be personally affected by military decisions that are reached. It has allowed many Americans to suspend their concerns about how and where the country uses its forces in the name of national security.

The ambush of a U.S. Special Forces "A" team in Niger on October 4, 2017 (noted in chapter 13), provided at least a temporary glimpse at imperfections in the façade of the AVF-based military equation. In that tragic encounter, four of the twelve members of the team were killed in an ambush by Muslim terrorists as they were on patrol with members of the Niger military. The deaths were shocking and raised serious military questions. One question was whether the mission was a unique artifact of the AVF system and mentality.

Two concerns emerged. The fact that the victims were volunteers who the president artlessly said had signed up for the fate that befell them reminded the public that their defense and safety was entrusted to a very slender slice of the population—the 1 percenters, as they are sometimes known—who along with their loved ones bear the cost of that defense. There were ringing cries of gratitude for the Gold Star families who have lost members, but not much more.

There was also a geopolitical response. It turns out that inattention to how, when, and why forces are employed extends well beyond citizens unburdened by the personal consequences of these decisions to their elected members of Congress. In mid-October 2017, Senator John McCain, the late chair of the Senate Armed Services Committee, committee member Senator Lindsey Graham, and Senate Minority Leader Charles (Chuck) Schumer all professed they had no idea that the United States even had one thousand troops in Niger, much less what they were doing there. This episode may have qualitative implications: does the AVF produce enough of the "right" kind of forces?

Voluntary Forces as a Mission Inhibitor

Both voluntary and conscripted military forces have advantages and disadvantages and different impacts on the kind and quality of force a country possesses and the purposes for which these forces can be used. Generally, the advantages of one form of recruitment are disadvantages of the other. For circumstances where a "pure" method is unsatisfactory, a hybrid of mixed voluntarism and conscription is available.

The primary advantage of a volunteer force, as the preceding discussion has implied, is that it frees most citizens of the prospect of being forced into military service when they oppose that condition. As a practical matter, when a country "buys" its military force by offering adequate incentives that adequate numbers will volunteer, the average citizen is relieved of any practical concern with the possibility of being forced to arms. That has been the case in the United States since 1972, and most Americans (including virtually everyone who reads this book) have never known a time when they had to worry about being forced to become soldiers. In a conscript system, a much broader part of the population is vulnerable to being called, depending on the size of the force needed and what population segments are exempted from service (historically females, who would almost certainly be included in a future draft, being the major exempt category).

The bottom line is that there is a size tradeoff involved depending on how forces are procured. Volunteer force size is physically limited by the number of people who will volunteer for military service, and that number is finite and basically inelastic. It can be manipulated by things like increasing monetary and other incentives to join or raising or lowering entrance requirements for membership. A conscript force is much more flexible and expandable, since it can compel as many eligible (e.g., physically able) members of the population as it needs for its task to become members. There is not hard data on how large a force can be recruited for voluntary service, but there are upper limits that can easily be reached. Adding additional volunteers is difficult and quite expensive: AVF members must, for instance, be paid competitive wages and given commodious living conditions, beyond those provided for conscripts. An alternative method has been to use private contractors to do some military tasks, but this practice is controversial for a variety of reasons, including command and control issues over private operators and much higher costs associated with these services. The bottom line is that although a volunteer force may be very politically popular, it has limits in terms of size and the scope of tasks it can perform and in terms of the costs it incurs.

The AVF Compromise

The AVF thus creates a tradeoff of sorts for the country that tries to reconcile two factors that are not always compatible. Those factors are, of course, the aversion many Americans have toward military service and the need for adequate-sized and effective armed forces to fulfill the country's national security needs. In the relatively non-threatening environment since 1972, America's interests have not been imperiled to the extent that large armed forces have been necessary, and so there has been no need to have to consider augmenting those forces with involuntary accessions (conscripts). The size force that the AVF produces is not, however, probably adequate to deal with a major military contingency, and so the United States is capability constrained in thinking about using force in these very big ways for very large purposes. The force size, in other words, constrains the kinds of military contingencies the country might contemplate. Not everyone thinks this is a bad thing, because the constraint prevents the serious consideration of military operations that might be imprudent because the possible force implications of a given option preclude the adventure.

This constraint is not inconsiderable and provides an arguably valuable governor against imprudent force employment. There have been, for instance, periodic assertions that the United States might commit ground forces in the volatile and violent politics of the Middle East in places like Syria and against the Islamic State. One of the major constraints on such suggestions was whether the country, especially after the long and draining deployments to Iraq and Afghanistan, had the physical capability to do so without degrading the force, and this consideration helped to reinforce geopolitical restraints on "sending in the Marines." The other side of this argument is that if the country suddenly needed very large forces to fend off a military threat or action, it is not clear forces would be readily available in adequate numbers to do so. AVF-imposed force size limits effectively influence risk and risk reduction in these cases.

Voluntary Recruitment and Political Detachment

The military personnel question gets intertwined with other political considerations as well. One of the conceptual virtues of a force that includes conscripts is that it is more of a "people's" force than is the AVF, because using force means putting some citizens in harm's way who may not want that to happen. That personalizes the political decision to invoke force and, in effect, makes the decision a kind of popular referendum on whether Americans support a military course of action enough to put their own loved ones in harm's way. Conscription, in other words, personalizes military employment to the population in a way and to a degree that the deployment of volunteers does not. If you are exempt from the prospect of personal sacrifice in military action, does this make it easier to support courses of action that might give you pause if your life might literally be on the line if such a decision is made?

This quandary affects both political and military questions. One can argue that the current All-Volunteer Force effectively shields American citizens and their elected leaders from military decisions and especially their consequences, which are not personal for either. The average young American does not have to consider the personal consequences of committing troops into harm's way, because that decision has no personal effect on him or her: there is "no dog in the hunt" for most Americans most of the time. One result is that such decisions and the debates leading to them are not personal and thus not as large a limiting influence on decision-makers. Political leaders, even if most of them have personal military experience, realize this. George H. W. Bush, after all, was the last active military veteran to serve as president. It may mean that they can reach decisions without fearing citizen backlash that they might not make if doing so might create spirited opposition, even electoral peril, and they may not even realize the personal dilemmas decision-making in those circumstances entails. In that circumstance, is it easier to reach the decision to put Americans at risk in military conflict, knowing that few constituents are either aware of the issues or are personally affected by them? From a military vantage point, can operations be considered and advocated that might not be put forward if one knows there will be fewer popular objections than there might have been if voters and their loved ones might personally be affected? Would the Niger incident have come as such a surprise if some of the American troops on the ground were conscripts and thus constituents?

This is not a dynamic that Americans have faced for nearly a half-century, but it is potentially important. In addition to advocating the AVF to dampen opposition to the Vietnam conflict, the decision also meant there would not be loud protest about another conflict that might become a Vietnam-style quagmire. When Vietnam first arose, most Americans trusted the judgment of their elected officials about the wisdom of the action, but the course of that war destroyed much of the faith that had allowed it. Should another similar proposal occur in a conscript-manned force, would public opinion support it? Would, for instance, the Bush administration have been able to justify the war in Iraq against the objections that would have been raised if Americans would have had to be drafted to fight it?

Would constraint on decision-makers' ability to decide effectively to go to war without an informal, draft-based public referendum be a bad thing? Such constraint would not mean the public would preclude using force when it was clearly in the national interest to do so. When true national emergencies have arisen in the past, popular support has not been a problem. As the world wars impended, for instance, increasing numbers of Americans volunteered and the draft was not resisted in large numbers. During the Cold War, it was assumed that if World War III broke out, it would create such a concentrated orgy of violence that it would have to be fought with existing forces (what was called the "force in being"), because the war would be effectively over before a mobilization (raising and training) of an armed force could occur. As a result, conscription was tolerated, and even embraced by most of the few eligible young Americans who were drafted. If there is a constraint that a reinstituted draft would pose, it might be to preclude the questionable resort to military force in situations where there is not a compelling need to do so. That restraint is the true lesson of Vietnam and is arguably the most compelling reason to reinstitute the possibility of involuntary service.

Breaking the Clausewitzian Trinity

Carl von Clausewitz, the great Prussian military strategist of the Napoleonic era, maintained that the key element in sustaining military power was a synergistic relationship between three elements of society: the people, the government, and the army (military forces). If this "Clausewitzian trinity" of societal forces was mutually supportive, a country could maintain military operations, but if one or more elements was out of tune with the others, the ability to perform operations was compromised. The most critical element of the three, of course, was the people, since they were the source of personnel both for the government and the armed forces. In the contemporary American situation, it is possible to argue that the institution of the AVF has effectively severed the trinity by allowing (or promoting) a passive relationship between the military and the people. Military actions no longer have the meaningful impact of directly affecting most people intimately, and so they are not as concerned about them as they would be if they had a personal stake in the consequences of those acts. This divorce has been tolerable when there are not proposed uses of force that the people would oppose if they were involved. What, if anything, should be done about the possibility that imprudent conflicts, like largely unrecognized involvements in places like Africa, may arise?

Policy Options

The AVF concept is by no means under assault nor are there serious demands for its replacement in the short to medium run. It has worked in the sense of providing adequate numbers and quality of personnel for the country's needs since 1972. There are, however, two circumstances in which the return to some less than totally voluntary method of military recruitment might arise and threaten that condition. The first is a military contingency that could only be confronted with much larger armed forces than the AVF system has produced in the past and is likely capable of producing in the future. This has been the reason for turning to conscription in the past. The current geopolitical situation does not make this situation seem likely for now, but things can change. The second possible source of public disillusion could be expense: the AVF is expensive (see Pincus), and expansion using private contractors rather than conscripts adds to that expense. Some serious epiphany about the undesirability of growing deficits that goes beyond largely hollow current calls for deficit reduction would have to stimulate this concern, and advocates of the AVF would oppose such changes that entail defense budget reduction.

In these circumstances, consideration of alternatives to the AVF system thus fall in the general category of contingency planning—what could change and how would that affect the need for differently procured forces? The answer to the question of how the United States raises forces is likely to remain "from voluntary enlistments" for the foreseeable future. But what are the prospects moving ahead? Two stand out.

The Status Quo

The first, and most likely, is a continuation of the AVF basically as it now exists. The All-Volunteer Force has been durable and has basically fulfilled all the needs placed upon it admirably. Part of that success reflects that since 1972 circumstances have not put stress on its numerical or qualitative adequacy. Almost all the military contingencies the country has faced have been small in terms of their manpower demands, so that the limited size of the force has not been an impediment, and force multipliers like drones (see chapter 17) and Special Forces have removed the need for large numbers in some cases.

There was some quantitative stress during the middle 2000s, when the United States had reasonably large commitments in both Iraq and Afghanistan, and the result was strain on the active duty force that took the form of multiple deployments of individuals and units, the extensive mobilization and repeated use of reserve units, and the recourse to expensive, often hard to control private contractors. The situation was relieved by the drawdown of forces in both countries and especially the total withdrawal from Iraq after 2008. The military recognized the strain this contingency created, and one of the reasons there has been reluctance to engage U.S. forces in places like Syria and against IS has been to avoid a repeat of this experience. Capability limits arising from size have affected strategy.

The Iraq-Afghanistan experience illustrates the limitations of the AVF in application. To deal with those two simultaneous contingencies, the force was extended to arguable overextension, and only mechanisms such as not permitting soldiers to leave the service when their terms expired (so-called "stop loss") kept the force at adequate levels. It is not clear the force could have conducted another sizable simultaneous deployment, especially somewhere else in the world. The AVF's inelastic size limited the flexibility of potential uses in ways that may or may not be acceptable in the future.

Unless an overwhelmingly stressful contingency arises, the continued reliance on the AVF as the sole means of personnel procurement seems likely. The disadvantage is the inability of this approach to increase force size meaningfully in other than times of national emergency. The only way to increase the pool of people who might enlist otherwise is to increase the opportunities for groups not currently optimally represented (e.g., allowing women to volunteer for more combat-related positions) or by relaxing standards (e.g., not requiring enlistees to have a high school diploma). Whether these options are attractive depends on perceived need for a larger force.

The Conscription Option

The second option, which is in place but not publicized widely, is to upgrade and make it easier to reinstate involuntary accession in times of need. The old Selective Service system was not dismantled entirely, and it still operates in the sense that eighteen-year-olds must register for possible induction. This effort, beyond creating a registry that is basically not updated after initial registration, would be inefficient in raising a sizable force, and it would require an action by Congress to upgrade its authority to its former ability to induct people. If the country does not face imminent threats that make a compelling case for a quick-acting draft mechanism that would hang ominously over the heads of young Americans, it is hard to see how its authorization could become politically viable.

If one assumes the recourse to a full-scale conscription system is unlikely enough not to merit serious consideration, this alternative would entail reinstituting a streamlined, improved Selective Service System that would be available for activation whenever the possibility of manpower shortfalls might arise. A new conscription system would have to deal with deficiencies in the old system such as a series of deferments that made some people (notably the more affluent) significantly less vulnerable to being drafted and provisions to incorporate women into the involuntary system. One could expect both political and military resistance to change: politicians because it would put the progeny of constituents at risk of forced service, and the military because it is no longer well equipped to deal with the problems associated with conscripts (e.g., discipline and more difficulty training) and because it could dilute force quality.

The case for this alternative, however, is also political and military. The political attraction is that it would aid force expansion in times of perceived need even if very few young Americans were physically drafted. In the pre-1972 environment, for instance, manpower quotas were partially filled by what used to be called "draft-induced enlistment," which meant that draft-vulnerable individuals would volunteer for service to avoid being drafted into undesirable military "jobs" such as the infantry, as well as by volunteers.

A force that incorporates or threatens to add an involuntary component could visibly change the political calculation of military usage. At a minimum, it would mean that strategists and decision-makers would have to include likely public reaction into deployment decisions in ways they have not had to consider since 1972. Would the invasion of Iraq have been affected by the likely opposition of vulnerable young Americans who might have been forced to fight and die there? Moving away from the AVF would likely inhibit military activism. Would that be good or bad?

Consequences: What to Do?

Compared to other problems chronicled in these pages, military manpower is less immediate or pressing than most. The military is currently adequately populated with well-trained and motivated personnel that are adequate quantitatively and qualitatively to meet the country's defense needs. The country's most basic national security needs (e.g., survival of a hostile military action) are not endangered. The exception may be nuclear attack, for which manpower concerns are largely irrelevant anyway. The point in military terms is that the geopolitical environment makes all-volunteerism feasible. For as long as America's military needs are confined to personnel-bounded deployments of choice where policy and less-than-vital (LTV) interests do not dictate larger forces, the trade-off of constrained forces will continue to be acceptable. The reminder is that if this situation changes either because of an emergent threat or a decision to engage in a larger military contingency, compulsory service could return.

It is this last possibility that motivates consideration of personnel acquisition alternatives. The arguably most pernicious effect of the All-Volunteer Force is on the integrity of the Clausewitzian trinity. It weakens the links between the people and the government regarding decisions to use force, because it removes the potential personal consequences of such actions from voters and, by extension, from political authorities who might be affected by popular opposition to proposed courses of military action. The possibility of political fallout from the prospect that a military decision will force unwilling American citizens (and voters) into conflict is a limitation that politicians have faced in the past but do not today when "somebody else" (the AVF) does the "dirty work" for us. It also weakens the link between the people and the army. When there are conscripts in uniform, the armed forces are truly a "people's" force. The AVF is composed mostly of Americans citizens (some foreign nationals use joining as a pathway to citizenship), but it is a compartmentalized group of people who have agreed to take on that service as a profession.

The political effect of returning a conscription element to the manpower equation could be to change the quality and content of national debates and decisions about the use of American force by requiring those who make decisions about sending forces into harm's way to ask in a serious manner "what will the

American people think about this?" If the decision potentially means involuntarily impressing Americans in the name of that decision, the result could be a very different debate with different outcomes about when the United States uses force. What effect would such a consideration have on the calculation of interests, risk management, and strategies and policies designed best to protect the country's most vital interests—the heart of national security? What do you think?

Study/Discussion Questions

1. What have the historic methods of military personnel recruitment been for the United States? What has the historic pattern been? How did the Vietnam War upset this pattern? Describe.

2. What is the All-Volunteer Force (AVF)? How does it relate to national security concerns raised throughout the text? How has it worked in these terms since 1972?

3. How did the wars in Iraq and Afghanistan raise questions about the potential adequacy of the AVF for meeting military needs in the future? Include the question of costs in your answer.

4. What is the pro-conscription argument that reinstituting some form of draft vulnerability might produce greater hesitancy about putting U.S. forces in harm's way? How important and compelling is this argument?

5. How would you feel about the prospect of adding a conscription element to military personnel procurement, both personally and as a matter of national security policy? Why do you feel this way? Justify your position.

Bibliography

"The All-Volunteer Force: After 10 Years of War, It's Time to Gather Lessons." *Armed Forces Journal* (online), October 1, 2011.

Bailey, Beth. *America's Army: Making the All-Volunteer Force.* Cambridge, MA: Belknap Press, 2009.

Bickster, Barbara A., Curtis L. Gilroy, and John T. Warner (eds.). *The All-Volunteer Force: Thirty Years of Service.* Washington, DC: Potomac Books, 2004.

Clausewitz, Carl von. *On War.* Revised ed. translated and edited by Michael Howard and Peter Paret. Princeton, NJ: Princeton University Press, 1984.

Donovan, G. Murphy. "The All-Volunteer Military: Too Much from Too Few." *American Thinker* (online), July 2, 2015.

Engbrecht, Shawn. *America's Covert Warriors: Inside the World of Private Military Contractors.* Washington, DC: Potomac Books, 2010.

Flynn, George Q. *The Draft: 1940–1973.* Lawrence: University of Kansas Press, 1973.

Griffith, Robert K., Jr. *The U.S. Army's Transition to the All-Volunteer Force: 1968–1974.* Army History Series. New York: CreateSpace Independent Publishing Platform, 2015.

Hannigan, W. J. "Special Operations: Inside the New American Way of War." *Time* 190 (24) (December 11, 2017), 44–51.

Pincus, Walter. "Paying for the All-Voluntary Military." *Washington Post* (online), January 14, 2013.

Ricks, Thomas E. "Opinion: It's Time to Toss the All-Volunteer Military." *Washington Post* (online), April 19, 2012.

Rostker, Bernard. *I Want You: The Evolution of the All-Volunteer Force.* Santa Monica, CA: RAND Corporation, 2006.

Schaub, Jr., Gary, and Ryan Kelly (eds.). *Private Military and Security Contractors: Controlling the Corporate Warrior.* Lanham, MD: Rowman & Littlefield, 2016.

Segal, David R. *Recruiting for Uncle Sam: Citizen and Military Manpower Policy.* Modern War Series. Lawrence: University of Kansas Press, 1989.

Snow, Donald M. *The Middle East, Oil, and the U.S. National Security Policy: Intractable Problems, Impossible Solutions.* Lanham, MD: Rowman & Littlefield, 2016 (especially chapter 2).

———. *Thinking about National Security: Strategy, Policy, and Issues.* New York and London: Routledge, 2016 (especially chapter 5).

Stanley, Bruce E. *Outsourcing Security: Private Military Contractors and U.S. Foreign Policy.* Washington, DC: Potomac Books, 2015.

Taylor, William A. *Military Service and American Democracy: From World War II to the Iraq and Afghanistan Wars.* Modern War Studies. Lawrence: University Press of Kansas, 2016.

Wright, James. *Those Who Have Borne the Battle: A History of America's Wars and Those Who Fought Them.* New York: Public Affairs Books, 2012.

16

Cybersecurity
The Newest Frontier

Aconcern with information, its uses, its protection, and its exploitation for national security and other purposes is nothing new. Adding the prefix *cyber* changes how these tasks are done, not what is done. The national security question is how it should be handled in the contemporary scene. What difference does *cyber* make?

An example from World War II illustrates the role of cybersecurity without the computer-generated and -stored information that frames the contemporary debate. During the American island-hopping campaign in the Pacific, a major problem was how to deprive Japanese defenders of information about American military actions. The Japanese routinely intercepted Walkie-Talkie communications between American units, allowing them to discern U.S. troop movements. It was a cyber protection problem, and the Americans solved it by "encrypting" their communications. The medium was to employ 420 Navajo Marine "code talkers," who communicated exclusively in Navajo, a language with which the Japanese had no familiarity. The Japanese were never able to break the encrypted code. Much of the cyber problem of today is finding a new Navajo-like language to protect against the challenges presented by the cyber age.

The problem of protecting information, which is the core of cyber concerns at all levels, was both created and made more difficult by the very processes it has created. It is pervasive. Once information enters electronic systems that are the habitat of cyberspace, it becomes part of the vast cyber territory where, unless aggressive actions are taken to protect it, it is prey vulnerable to exposure or theft unintended by the source of the information. Cybersecurity is the dynamic enterprise that attempts to secure computer-generated or -processed information from those whom the original producer did not authorize or desire that access. The information can be individual data like Social Security or credit card numbers or corporate proprietary science which, if exposed, would undercut a product's comparative advantage in the marketplace. In the public realm, the information could be voter preferences in elections or private communications between political figures. In national security, it may involve protecting secrets that can reinforce or compromise the country's safety. The national security possibilities are, of course, the focus here.

Especially since the highly publicized and debated intrusion on the 2016 election process in the United States by Russian hackers (probably commissioned and directed by the Russian government), the problem of cybersecurity and even the possibility of cyber*war* has intruded into the American political debate, and the prospect that interference would be attempted in the 2018 midterm election kept this problem in the public eye. The war analogy, generally vaguely drawn and unfocused on any specific set of events or prospects, has extended the rapidly evolving technology of things "cyber" into the national security debate. Unlike other topics contained in these pages, the subject does not focus on traditional national security problems and solutions, is difficult to conceptualize in familiar national security constructs, and has a slightly ethereal aura that makes it difficult to grasp and around which to fashion strategy and policy.

The problem begins conceptually. National security, as it is normally thought of and as it has been depicted throughout this volume, centers on maintaining the physical safety of countries (or groups within states) from harm or extinction. Implicit in this formulation is that the major threats come from hostile others and contain a military element that provides the substance of the threat to be thwarted. Cyber formulations may involve threats to the state and its people, but those threats arise from different bases, notably electronic networks and virtual reality. The core concentration is thus on the technologies that compose the computer revolution and actions that hostile others may take to interrupt, steal, or subvert that information and formulations. Given the ubiquity of electronic, computer-based or -extended activities within society, this encompasses a very wide range of activities and operators. As one considers all the actions that can fall under the label of "cyber," the list is almost infinite, and when it is combined with the subjective nature of what threatens different people, becomes almost unwieldy, leading the authors of a RAND Corporation study on cybersecurity to conclude the "term is applied too inclusively."

The medium in which cyber activity takes place, cyberspace, only adds to the confusion. The heart of cyber concern is information technology, which is a pervasive part of modern social interaction. The breadth of concerns that attach to the information revolution provides fertile ground for speculation and the building of a virtually infinite array of potential threats, some of which frighten some people more than others, but also diffuses any systematic, focused delineation of the threat and thus the priority that should attach to solving it. The apparent Russian electronic interference in the 2016 election is an example of the nature and difficulty of dealing with cyber activity as a national security problem.

Perspectives on the Problem

It was probably inevitable that the complex of activities and ideas that share the cyber moniker would find their way into the national security conversation. The electronic revolution, including the information accumulation and transmission that is at its heart, represents the kind of magnet toward which the national security community is drawn: a new technological, scientific endeavor the prospects of which are not known but which could include applications that could produce military advantages in some ways. That motivation is normally double-edged, meaning scientists in the national security community asked themselves both how these technologies could be applied for military advantage and how they could ensure that those applications could not successfully be used against the United States. This endeavor exists in an environment of considerable uncertainty since, by definition, one cannot know what one will discover and how it might be applied until the discovery is made and its implications explored. This is as true for non-defense applications of cyber technology with which the reader may be more familiar as it is for national security applications. In either the national security or civilian sectors, the process is ongoing, dynamic, and changing.

Understanding the cyber phenomenon begins by trying to come to grips with its unique vocabulary and concepts. These involve using familiar national security terms with somewhat different meanings than are attached to those terms in more conventional analyses. This exercise in turn makes it possible to describe the kinds of cyberthreats that exist and to place them in the traditional national security framework.

Cyber Terms and Definitions

The root term in the discussion is *cyber*. It is the adaptation of an old Greek term that referred to space, and it has been adapted to the electronic revolution of the last quarter-century or more. Universal agreement about what exactly is encompassed by the term does not exist, although the *Oxford Dictionary* offers this definition: "relating to electronic communications networks and virtual reality." The heart of cyber phenomena is thus computers and their major "products," information technology and virtual reality. As it has been adapted to the national security debate, cyber refers to attempts to manipulate the processes and products of information technology to either intrude on the cyberspace of individuals or national security systems that use information technology as part of their operating base.

It is a slippery term, because it depicts an evolving phenomenon in the national security environment. Is, for instance, cyberspace intrusion a distinct form of activity, or is it a component of other forms of activity? Klimburg, for one, suggests that it is both. "It is difficult to take the measure of cyberconflict," he argues, "because it is now a part of every other form of conflict; it affects everything while deciding very little on its own, at least so far." It is also not the exclusive province of any group.

National security concerns and actions usually involve the actions of foreign actors, especially national governments or sub-national groups, but that is often not the case in cyber activity, which as often as not is conducted by individual "hackers" either acting on their own or with some mysterious, hidden relationship to a sponsor, most problematically a foreign government or movement whose intent is to weaken components of a more conventional national security concern. The practical effect is to muddy even more the identification and priority one assigns to cyber actions. "A cyberattack could be the work of almost anyone," Parker argues, and this makes the subject even more difficult: "a larger problem with cyberwarfare is uncertainty. How does a government respond to an invisible attacker?" This ephemeral quality of intrusion into hyperspace leads to some colorful evocations. Slaughter, for instance, refers to anonymous hackers as "the invading hordes of the twenty-first century." This description may be hyperbolic (which is true about much of the speculation that surrounds cyber actions), but it creates the dilemma that, as Parker points out, "A cyberattack could be the work of almost anyone."

Much of the discussion of cyber phenomena is directed at how the United States can protect itself from hostile cyber actions against it, and this is certainly the valid concern of American national security planners. It implicitly suggests a kind of victimization that probably leaves too much of an impression of American innocence in this area. A great deal of the computer revolution at the heart of cyber actions is, after all, American, and a significant part of the networks and manifestations of information technology were products of American science and technology, often generously sponsored and funded by the U.S. Department of Defense (especially the Defense Advanced Research Projects Agency or DARPA, which provided much of the funding and direction for the internet, among other parts of the information technology complex attempting to contribute to its solution).

The basic term to describe what former director of the National Security Agency General Michael Hayden has called the largest unregulated and uncontrolled domain in the history of mankind is the idea of *cyberspace*. Definitions, of course, vary, but the heart of the idea is that cyberspace is the internet environment through which ideas flow and the domain of information technology structures. The U.S. national security information collection, control, and dissemination effort is part of this environment (which it helped create) and has designated it a part of the country's "critical infrastructure." This network has developed in a basically unplanned, random, and chaotic manner to a size and complexity that is difficult to understand and even more difficult to regulate, as General Hayden's depiction suggests.

The Center of Concern: Cybersecurity and Cyberwar

The most common term used in the national security context is *cybersecurity*. Like other cyber concepts, it is a compound word with a compound meaning. Its heart is the security of its domain, which in the case of cybersecurity, is largely the protection of computer-based information and applications in cyberspace that harm the entity that needs protecting. Security, as described in chapter 1, refers to safety and a sense or feeling of safety. In traditional national security calculations, the safety that is sought is normally physical and expressed in terms of safety from physical harm and, at worst, extinction. Controversy surrounds the secondary use of the terms as a "sense" of security, since different situations frighten different people in different ways and thus differentially create fear and threat that must be countered with varying degrees of urgency.

This basic distinction applies to the cyber area. Definitions are abundant, but they all emphasize actions and methods designed to protect electronic information from being stolen, compromised, or successfully attacked, and it is usually attached to notions of computer security, since that is the medium in which most of the information is stored and transmitted. The security aspects of cybersecurity relate to stealing or distorting information in cyberspace for personal, commercial, or national advantage. The aspects of cybersecurity most interesting to national security are those with direct political or geopolitical applications, from the theft of government military secrets, the compromise of military technologies the applications of which are computer dependent, to more traditional geopolitical activities like interference with the internal politics of target countries or regions within countries.

Cybersecurity can be both an offensive or a defensive tool. Most of the discussion of the problem tends to focus on the defensive aspect: what can be done to deny access to information, its manipulation, and uses to which it can be put. For personal users, the most obvious example is the use of passwords to protect access to personal information, and it extends to familiar actions like encryption of data, firewalls, and the like. Vulnerability exists for any entity with information stored or transmitted on computer networks, which is a very broad net of potential targets. Efforts to engage in the development and application of technologies designed to thwart cybersecurity breaches, of course, tend to vary depending on the degree of threat different entities possess and on resources to engage in counter-technology efforts. Individuals fall at the bottom of this pyramid of concern; national governments trying to protect their national interests are at the apex.

Efforts to reinforce cybersecurity are compromised by a conundrum familiar to all scientific phenomena. Knowledge with applications to controlling or channeling the use of scientific advances is not abstract but is dependent on the existence of problems that can be remediated. Countermeasures presume measures to be countered, and this means that those who want to exploit scientifically based mischief are always a step ahead of those who seek to rein in those applications. For better or worse, the development of countermeasures has generally received less priority than the burgeoning discovery of new applications in the cyber world, and this makes it more difficult to devise technologies that enhance security of the systems themselves and how they can be used.

The concept of *cyberwar* presents a particularly dramatic and potentially traumatic example of this problem. Like cybersecurity, the term is used in a different way than "war" is used in the traditional military context. The core of definitions of war is that they involve armed conflict between hostile political units, with their key element being hostile armed conflict to subdue or destroy the other side's will or ability to resist the imposition of politically defined terms, up to and including physical subjugation (see Snow and Drew for a detailed discussion).

War in the cyber context lacks the employment of organized forces in combat, unless one stretches the meaning of combat to include electronic means and counter-means to protect or subvert the computers, control systems, and networks of one side (which may or may not be engaged in traditional war at the same time). Rather than being direct instruments of war, cyberwar capabilities are generally conceptualized in supportive roles to aid the pursuit of goals by adversaries. These activities include espionage, sabotage, and propaganda.

Libicki offers a useful distinction in types of cyberwar, what he calls strategic and operational cyberwar. In his view, strategic use consists of "a campaign of cyberattacks one entity carries out on another," while operational cyberwar "involves the use of cyberattacks on the other side's military in the context of a physical war." Operational cyberwar is closer to traditional notions and conduct of military actions in support of physical security, since it can involve actions like interrupting communications between weapons systems being aimed at enemy targets and those who control the attack. Directing drones to targets (see chapter 17) is an area where this activity could apply, just as cyberwar capabilities can have responsibility for aiming the weapons in the first place. The 2016 Russian election campaign interference is an example of the strategic application of cyberwar concepts.

The use of the term *war* suggests the furtiveness, level of effort, and the seriousness with which cyber activities in the national effort are viewed, but it is not a literal description that can be translated from one domain to the other. Cyberwar is a part of an increasing number of military purposes and capabilities, but it is in a supportive, capabilities-enhancing role, not a physical warfighting role. Computers and their operators may clash on virtual battlefields where the object is to make one electronic device outperform the other, but they do not literally fight and kill one another. But things change in the cyber world, and one cannot discount the prospects of what will be possible. When the classic 1950s movie *1984* was filmed, the technology only allowed depiction of intrusions on personal and private behavior through crude cardboard "eyes" watching the population. The author of the book on which the movie was based, George Orwell, would have been shocked that the ability to monitor and intrude today is a routine part of the physical capacity of governments and others.

The Cyber Problem

The ubiquity of the cyber phenomena makes it so difficult to grasp and solve. It is all part of the domain of cyberspace. It is not the exclusive, "sovereign" province of any political jurisdiction in the way that physical intrusions into the atmosphere above national territory are. No country or body has exclusive or effective power to regulate cyberspace or to enforce violations of norms and regulations which, by and large, do not exist anyway. Much cyber activity is private in nature, conducted by individuals who may be violating some domestic laws for which they can be prosecuted if they are caught, but the ephemeral nature of cyberspace makes apprehension more difficult than catching someone who holds up a convenience store, and jurisdictions are less defined anyway. When nefarious activity is conducted by governments trying to conceal their role, it is often difficult as well to determine the locus of behavior that travels through cyberspace. It is not impossible to do so, but the "forensics" of cyber crime are far less developed than those covering domestic criminal behavior.

The task is made even more difficult because cyberspace is used to conduct some of the hidden business that governments have historically conducted against one another. The most famous act of cyber aggression for Americans is Russian interference in the 2016 presidential election, discussed in the next section. The manipulation of cyberspace to hack into the election process is the unique characteristic of that intrusion, but the idea of interfering in the electoral processes of other countries is a long practiced but officially illegal violation of the national sovereignty of states. The United States, principally in the Western Hemisphere but also in more remote locations like Iran, has long interfered to promote or defeat candidates it opposed. (Kinzer's study of U.S. intrusion into the 1954 Guatemalan elections is a particularly vivid depiction.) What is unique about the 2016 (and 2018) elections is that the United States was the victim rather than the perpetrator and that the intrusions were committed in cyberspace rather than by CIA personnel engaging in espionage.

Policy Options

The determination of policy options surrounding cyber phenomena is contextually different and more complicated than other areas of policy. The complex of challenges in the cyber arena certainly affects the safety of those whom cyber areas touch, but they are also more diverse and represent different constituencies, different substantive problems, different solutions, and different groups that must devise and implement solutions. In some cases, there are points of overlap, but in others there are not.

Cyber Levels and National Security

There are two levels at which cyber problems manifest themselves. The first is the individual level, where the major security issue is the sanctity of personal efforts and entities to devise and implement solutions to that safety. The Facebook crisis of 2018 is a very public manifestation of that problem. Both individual parties, who must do a better job of protecting things about themselves that are detrimental if exposed, and the cyber industry, which has apparently invested far less in protecting the information explosion it has enabled than in providing users a secure environment, are part of the problem and its solution. Personal information stolen by hackers or others may create individual security issues, but as such they are not high on national security agendas.

The problem of interconnectivity of cyber problems can begin at this level. The second level is public and private information that may not have a direct national security content. Industrial espionage can be accomplished against firms by domestic and foreign competitors or governments for their comparative advantage at the expense of American companies, or aggressive and antagonistic actions like sabotage may be easier to obscure by using cyberspace. The ability of cyber warriors to obscure their nefarious behaviors is a prime objective of those who must thwart national security–based attacks. This problem can only be handled effectively by the federal government (if by anyone), and more specifically by military agencies within the national security community. The Chinese are particularly adept at these activities as part of their theft of intellectual property.

The problems created by the cyber revolution are not so much unique additions to the things that countries do to one another as they are about new ways that states attempt to accomplish traditional political actions against one another.

The challenges are consequential because of the extent to which the operation of society has become based in information generation, exchange, and protection. The cyber revolution has not produced a game-changing military technology and capability like nuclear weapons did seventy years ago. The cyber phenomenon is, however, a driving part of the scientific revolution that is changing life generally, and so even that limit on the impact of cyber capability may change as well.

The 2016 Russian Election Interference Controversy

The Russian electronic interference in the 2016 presidential election in the United States was both a unique and simultaneously thoroughly traditional event in the ways in which states intrude on one another's sovereignty. It was unique in the sense that it was conducted by manipulating cyberspace by so-called cyber warriors and that it represented a large-scale effort to interfere with an *American* election. It was a thoroughly traditional, if extra-legal, event in that states interfere with the politics of other countries all the time.

The unique aspect is that the election intrusion was conducted by hackers who found ways into files of the Democratic National Committee (DNC) and the private files of certain Democratic politicians, notably presidential candidate Hillary Clinton. The American intelligence community investigated these intrusions, and their unanimous conclusion was that the hackers were Russian and were probably employed in some manner by the government of Vladimir Putin. The Russian president, of course, has consistently denied the perpetrators were Russian or that his regime was in any way linked to this theft.

The signature contribution of cyber dynamics comes from the methods used to generate the materials that were stolen and the difficulty of finding a "hard" evidence trail that could definitively link the Russians to the intrusion. The files that were stolen were obviously not theft proof. The intrusions that occurred required some sophistication on the part of the hackers, but they were actions that dedicated hackers—from paid Russian operatives to President Trump's four-hundred-pound lone wolf—could have carried out. This process left no literal "paper trail" of evidence about how the hacks occurred, making it difficult to prove cupidity and easy to deny legal responsibility. The certitude of the American intelligence community about who committed these acts, however, suggests there are classified methods available to allow conclusive detection and presumably penetration that are available to the government. These techniques were clearly unavailable to or not utilized by the DNC.

The opacity of hacking creates a dilemma with national security implications that goes far beyond the substantive case. A cyber attack, Parker points out, "can be the work of almost anyone," and this creates a "larger problem of cyberwarfare. How does a government respond to an invisible attacker? How can a state prevent cyberattacks without attribution?" This difficulty extrapolates into the problem of how you can punish an intruder whose guilt you know about but cannot prove. This has been a problem of American attempts to deal with Russian actions, and the answers are not clear. As a result, however, it may be that foreign hackers and propagandists are unafraid to launch attacks against the United States in and through cyberspace as effectively as in a real theater of war. RAND analysts translate this into a Defense Department mandate to "figure how to deter foreign actors in cyberspace as effectively as in nuclear and conventional war." Ramo suggests a strategy of "hard gatekeeping" to make penetration of hardened networks impossible.

This question of penetrability is the unique national security contribution of this episode. It has gained continuing traction because of its connection in time to the 2016 presidential election, the possibility that the Russians sought to undermine the election prospects of the Democratic candidate by their actions, and that the Trump campaign may have had some involvement in the plot. All of these are important political concerns, and the fact that the Russians felt they could carry them out against the United States adds to the outrage that surrounds the episode.

Some of the concern about Russian violations of American sovereignty is disingenuous, if not openly hypocritical. Although the principle of sovereignty suggests the impenetrability and unacceptability of trying to influence politics—including who wins elections—it is a process in which states routinely engage. The United States has been a consistent historical intruder in other nations' politics, including those of Russia (the United States was an open supporter of Boris Yeltsin after the fall of the Soviet Union). In his May 8, 2018, announcement removing the United States from the JCPOA with Iran, President Trump openly suggested the Iranians replace their government. The Russians did the same thing covertly, while the president was on global TV. Americans may (and do) dislike others turning the tables on them, but their indignation is hardly heartfelt. The real challenge of the 2016 incident (beyond possible internal political ramifications) lies in the challenges of finding ways to detect and thwart cyber attacks and of unambiguously identifying perpetrators and punishing them.

Consequences: What to Do?

The entire domain of cyber activity has a strong link to national security. The exploitation of the potential of computers and computer networks has been influenced greatly by defensive concerns: how cyberspace can be translated into increased cybersecurity for the United States and what military and other national security potential capabilities can be created and need to be protected from. One of the unique characteristics of the information technology revolution, especially from a security vantage point, has been effectively to "democratize" the exploitation of cyberspace for good and not so good ends: individuals and small groups of people can manipulate access to the information and processes of cyberspace, and this creates a thriving enterprise both among those who wish to breach sources of information and those who try to protect those sources.

Clearly, the process is dynamic. In recent decades, efforts aimed at expanding access to cyberspace have outdistanced efforts to contain and channel that access. This is certainly true in "civilian" access, as shown by the activities of organizations like WikiLeaks or the casual ignoring of potential privacy invasion through cyberspace exploiters like Facebook.

The problem is different in the national security area. Government national security–related organizations like the highly secret National Security Agency (NSA) expend great effort and resources both learning how to deny access to vital information by those who would use it to the detriment of the country and devising methods to penetrate the equivalent kinds of efforts by others. For those in the private information "business" the emphasis is on maximum information collection, and the primary issues are about the privacy of personal and proprietary information. For government, the emphasis is on the protection of privileged or secret information with potential value for enhancing or undermining the security of the country. For both groups, there are legitimate common concerns about what should and should not be protected and who should and should not have access to information.

At this point in time, cyberspace use in the national security environment has been derivative, not basic. Clearly, the information process has the discovery of new information with scientific—and by extension—military applications as a major by-product. The prototype of the internet, after all, was the product of a DARPA grant the purpose of which was to allow university research laboratories to communicate scientific findings among themselves more efficiently, thereby enhancing the speed of scientific discovery. Some of those findings inevitably had military applications, which was part of the rationale for the effort.

In the publicly available contemporary environment, cyberspace and its dynamics are difficult to isolate and to assign or attribute solutions to. Cyber capabilities provided the method by which Russian 2016 hacking occurred; the motivation came from nefarious Russian political motivations. The problem is acute wherever cyber activity occurs. Billionaire Warren Buffett, addressing Berkshire Hathaway's annual shareholders' meeting in May 2018 (he owns the insurance company), warned that "cyber is uncharted territory and it's going to get worse, not better," adding it "will get more intense as time goes by." He was talking specifically about the insurance business, but do his comments apply to national security concerns? Is what we see of cyber potential the tip of the iceberg of the national security future? What does all this say about the cyber phenomenon and how it should be handled? What do you think?

Study/Discussion Questions

1. What does it mean to talk about cyber phenomena? What are the basic cyber concepts? How do they compare to the same concepts outside the cyber context?

2. Are the various cyber concepts basic national security problems, or are they examples of the application of cyber capabilities to traditional national security concerns?

3. What is the cyber "problem?" Is it something new or the latest way in which traditional problems are manifested? Cite examples of how problems like protecting intelligence and interfering with other countries have been accomplished in the past.

4. Discuss the 2016 case of Russian interference in the American pres-

idential election. Is it primarily an example or an illustration of how cyber phenomena can be applied to more traditional national security concerns?

5. Can or should the United States have a discrete cyber strategy, or is cyber a part of various aspects of strategy? How does this distinction affect how we think about cybersecurity in the broader context of national security?

Bibliography

Brodie, Bernard, and Fawn M. Brodie. *From Crossbow to H-Bomb: The Evolution of Weapons and Tactics of Warfare.* Bloomington: Indiana University Press, 1973.

Buchanan, Ben. *The Cybersecurity Dilemma: Hacking, Trust, and Fear Between Nations.* Oxford, UK: Oxford University Press, 2017.

Buffett, Warren. "Cyber Is Uncharted Territory." *Yahoo Online,* May 5, 2018.

Clarke, Richard A., and Robert Knake. *Cyber War: The Next Threat to National Security and What to Do About It.* New York: ECCO Books, 2011.

Flynn, Stephen. *The Edge of Disaster: Rebuilding a Resilient Nation.* New York: Random House, 2007.

Futter, Andrew. *Hacking the Bomb: Cyber Threats and Nuclear Weapons.* Washington, DC: Georgetown University Press, 2018.

Harris, Shane. *@ War: The Rise of the Military-Internet Complex.* New York: Mariner Books, 2014.

Hennessey, Susan. "Deterring Cyberattacks: How to Reduce Vulnerability." *Foreign Affairs* 96 (6) (November/December 2017), 39–46.

Isikoff, Michael, and David Korn. *Russian Roulette: The Inside Story of Putin's War on America and the Election of Donald Trump.* New York: Twelve Books, 2018.

Jarmon, Jack A., and Pano Yannakogeorgos. *The Cyber Threat and Globalization: The Impact on U.S. National and International Security.* Lanham, MD: Rowman & Littlefield, 2018.

Kaplan, Fred. *Dark Territory: The Secret History of Cyber War.* New York: Simon and Schuster, 2017.

Kinzer, Stephen. *The Brothers: John Foster Dulles, Allen Dulles, and Their Secret World War.* New York: Times Books, 2013.

Klimburg, Alexander. *The Darkening Web: The War for Cyberspace.* New York: Penguin Books, 2017.

Kramer, Franklin, Stuart H. Starr, and Larry Wentz (eds.). *Cyberpower and National Security.* Washington, DC: Potomac Books, 2009.

Libicki, Martin C. *Cyberspace in Peace and War.* Annapolis, MD: Naval Institute Press, 2016.

Nez, Chester, and Judith Schleiss Avila. *Code Talkers: The First and Only Memoir by One of the Original Navajo Code Talkers of WWII.* New York: Penguin Books, 2011.

Parker, Emily. "Hack Job: How America Invented Cyberwar." *Foreign Affairs* 96 (3) (May/June 2017), 133–38.

Perkovich, George, and Ariel E. Levite (eds.). *Understanding Cyber Conflict: Fourteen Analogies.* Washington, DC: Georgetown University Press, 2017.

Ramo, Joshua. *The Seventh Sense: Power, Fortune, and Survival in the Age of Networks.* New York: Little, Brown, 2016.

Rid, Thomas. *Cyber War Will Not Take Place*. Oxford, UK: Oxford University Press, 2017.

Rosenzweig, Paul. *Cyber Warfare: How Conflicts in Cyberspace Are Challenging America and Changing the World*. Westport, CT: Praeger Security International, 2013.

Scharre, Paul. *Army of None: Autonomous Weapons and the Future of War*. New York: W. W. Norton, 2018.

Segal, Adam. *The Hacked World Order: How Nations Fight, Trade, Maneuver, and Manipulate in the Digital Age*. New York: Public Affairs Books, 2016.

Singer, P. W., and Allan Friedman. *Cybersecurity and Cyberwar: What Everyone Needs to Know*. New York: Cambridge University Press, 2014.

Slaughter, Anne-Marie. "How to Succeed in the Networked World: A Grand Strategy for the Digital Age." *Foreign Affairs* 95 (6) (November/December 2016), 76–89.

Snow, Donald M., and Dennis M. Drew. *From Lexington to Baghdad and Beyond*. Third Ed. Armonk, NY: M. E. Sharpe, 2010.

Springer, Paul. *Cyber Warfare: A Reference Handbook*. Contemporary World Issues. New York: ABC-CLIO, 2015.

———. *Encyclopedia of Cyber Warfare*. New York: ABC-CLIO, 2017.

Steinnon, Richard. *There Will Be Cyberwar: How the Move to Network-Centric War Fighting Has Set the Stage for Cyberwar*. London: IT-Harvest Press, 2015.

United States Senate, Select Committee on Intelligence. *Russian Interference in the 2016 Election*. New York: CreateSpace Independent Publishing Platform, February 19, 2018.

17

Force Multiplication
Drone Warfare or Drone Terror?

Technology's impact on warfare, as on so many things, is often both ambivalent and dynamic, and the impact of drone aircraft has been no exception. Arguably, human lethal inventiveness has had a greater effect on war than virtually any other factor that affects how humans organize to impose their will on others by deadly force. As Bernard and Fawn Brodie captured in their richly titled *From Crossbow to H-Bomb*, the major impact of technology has been to make organized armed violence enormously more deadly and impersonal. Individual combatants and groups have become increasingly efficient at decimating other groups of humans to the point that it is at least theoretically possible for appropriately armed combatants to destroy mankind in a fiery thermonuclear apocalypse without seeing the victims.

Drones are a current part of increasing force effectiveness introduced in the previous two chapters on military personnel and cyberwarfare. Military personnel policy crafted in the AVF era has as one of its purposes attracting and training better quality, more capable soldiers whose skills make them more effective in military roles, and thus more valuable assets than previous combatants. Cyberwarfare both aims to make forces more effective and to nullify similar efforts by opponents. Drones are another example of this process, known generically as force multiplication: making killing an enemy more effective while minimizing one's own losses.

The attempt to make individual fighters more effective compared to those with whom they must compete in the lethal environment is central to the Brodies' analysis. The heart of military technology has been to increase the likelihood of prevailing over whatever enemy one faces, so multiplying the effectiveness of the forces one has always has been a theme of that process. A major subtheme of military inventiveness is that it tends to produce new lethal capabilities more rapidly than it does norms about how to employ and to counter new killing means. Drones are just the latest example: there have been countless others; there will be many more.

One way that human societies have sought to deal with quantum leaps in lethality is through the articulation of increasingly elaborate post facto sets of rules governing where, when, under what circumstances, and against whom death and destruction are permissible. The distinctions that have emerged are found in their most elaborate form in the so-called Geneva Conventions on War that were codified starting in the early part of the twentieth century. Among the things they deal with in the greatest detail are the rules of engagement (ROEs) governing the use of force multipliers like drones, the set of rules that specify (among other things) who can be killed and under what circumstances by combatants. A basic distinction has been made between combatants (designated and identified members of combatant armed forces) and noncombatants (people who do not play a formal combatant role and who are often referred to as "innocent" civilians). Combatants are generally fair game for attack and death in warfare (with some limits on how this can occur), and noncombatants are not legitimate targets. Indeed, the laws of war make the purposeful killing of noncombatants a war crime. It is a distinction that is decreasingly made in modern hostilities.

Modern warfare has diluted these distinctions and in the process added ambiguity and even hypocrisy to the distinctions applying to the conduct of hostilities. Indeed, since the early 1900s the percentage of noncombatants killed in war has risen greatly; in contemporary conflicts, as many as 90 percent of war-caused deaths are to civilians. Much of the cause of this change can be attributed to force multipliers like drones.

This trend has been accentuated by at least two factors. First, modern technology has made it much easier to attack an enemy civilian population than it used to be. In earlier times, assaults on civilian population and environments required that one combatant defeat the other's armed forces in battle, because a primary purpose of armies was to protect their populations from attack. Heavier-than-air flight, originally by airplanes but now by a growing variety of flying machines, erased that need and the distinction underlying it. Attacking targets using drone aircraft is the latest technological example, and it is a rapidly evolving set of capabilities for war making. Second, the sacrosanctity of the combatant-noncombatant distinction has been rejected by increasing numbers of war-making entities. Part of this assault reflects technology that makes institutions like war-making industries a prominent part of war and their interruption a necessary aspect of military success. Are, for instance, workers in factories that manufacture the weapons with which soldiers fight combatants or "innocent" civilians? What about the scientists and engineers who discover and apply new principles that produce novel military capability and lethality? Or the remotely located "pilots" of drone aircraft?

The more prominent source of assault on the distinction has been conceptual. Increasing numbers of warlike entities argue that all members of the opponent's society are in fact combatants and that thus everyone is a legitimate target in war: there are, in other words, no "innocent" bystanders. This position is most pronounced in the philosophies of terrorist organizations and is used to justify terrorist attacks against civilians. It also widens the menu for those employing force multipliers, because terrorists, even if they are part-time fighters, consider themselves soldiers and are thus "fair game."

When the two influences are conjoined, they bring together, among other things, the technological innovation of drones and the question of whether using a drone is a terrorist act or a legitimate act of war. The answer is not unambiguous, and depending on the answer one accepts, it has serious implications for the ROEs that attach both to the use of drones and means by which to obviate that usage as well as future efforts at force multiplication. Is the subject of drone warfare a military or a terrorist topic—or both?

Perspectives on the Problem

In 2017, fiction writer Kirk Russell published a novel titled *Signature Wounds.* It was a crime procedural wherein the protagonist, an FBI agent, was pursuing terrorists who had blown up a family party in a Las Vegas nightclub and seemed intent on further mayhem. Although the book's scenario was hardly unique in structure, what made it different was that the terrorist initiative was aimed at the American military drone program, much of which is concentrated in the Las Vegas area. Most of the victims at the party were drone pilots whose job it is to direct military drones to targets in the Middle East and to dispense deadly ordnance to kill them. Attacking drone pilots in their remote Nevada habitat was arguably an act equivalent to shooting down pilots of more conventional aircraft. The climactic terrorist purpose in the novel was to capture drones located in the area and to use them against American military facilities.

The Advantages of Drones

The book casually refers to the jihadi attackers as terrorists, but the situation it portrays has deeper philosophical implications. Drones have been among the most successful force multipliers for the United States in its pursuit and decimation of terrorists in Middle Eastern locations. They were a prominent element in the strategy followed by the Obama administration in seeking to weaken organizations like Al Qaeda (AQ) and the Islamic State (IS) by selectively locating and attacking and killing terrorist leaders and concentrations of operatives. Reports began to surface in 2017 that one of the major causes of the purported weakening of IS had been that a great deal of their leadership ranks had been targeted and killed and their organization's effectiveness severely disrupted by successful drone action, and that their leadership ranks had lost much of their cohesion as a result. Probably the most famous victim of an American drone attack, ironically, was the American-born Al Qaeda leader Anwar al-Awlaki, who was killed in a drone attack in Yemen in 2011.

From an American perspective, drones have some distinct advantages as weapons in the war against terror in the Middle East region. First and foremost, they are currently a virtually indefensible weapons platform against an opponent who may be adroit at manipulating the internet but does not have the technological wherewithal to identify and defend against the death from the sky that drones mete out. Once a target is located (possibly by drones, but also by traditional intelligence means), drones can be dispatched over long distances to the target area in a very short amount of time. They fly high and very quietly, meaning a target probably does not know they are coming, can "loiter" over territory for extensive periods of time to make sure the target is on the scene, and are small and quiet enough that visual or auditory recognition of their presence is virtually impossible. They can be armed with large ordnance (bombs) capable of very effective target destruction or with more discreet explosives. Moreover, they can fly over territory that, if ground or other air forces were dispatched to carry out their missions, would violate the national sovereignty of the country to which they were dispatched, a problem that is mitigated by denying the drones (which fly back to their bases after missions) were involved in the operation, a convenient fiction for both the United States and the government of the "host" country. Finally, they represent an "antiseptic" form of warfare for the United States, since the drone "pilots" (the people who direct them electronically to target) generally do so from remote places in the United States, where they are safe from personal retaliation. Removing their invulnerability is one of the subtexts of the Russell novel.

The capability of drones creates some of the controversy that surrounds them. From the viewpoint of the United States, they are part of the technological advantage the country's military seeks to establish for conducting military business with the greatest effect and minimal dangers to its military personnel. No one can, after all, "shoot down" a drone pilot, because that individual is operating from a secure computer terminal on American soil. Were war a contest in which one of the values was fairness, in this case the symmetrical vulnerability of attacker and attacked to personal harm, one might easily conclude the use of drones is unfair, violating rules of mutual competition, but that is not the case in war. Military planners are not motivated by abstract notions of fairness; rather, their value is defeat of the enemy by whatever means are legally available. A major part of that calculation is force multiplication that minimizes or eliminates harm to one's own forces; drones do that.

A century or more ago, there was an analogous military situation. In the early days of submarine warfare, for instance, existing versions of the Geneva Conventions required that before a submarine could attack a surface vessel, it had to surface itself, warn the target of its intent, and have provisions to take aboard survivors of the attack. These standards were impractical: early submarines were so small they could not accommodate many survivors, for instance. The requirement to surface would also leave the submarine highly vulnerable for destruction, as their armor and surface weaponry were minimal. Germany was the first country officially to embrace the idea of unrestricted submarine warfare, particularly against transatlantic naval activity in World War I, and negated these restrictions by ignoring them. It temporarily abandoned the practice in 1915, after a U-boat sank the British (Canard Line) luxury liner *Lusitania*. There were 128 Americans who perished in the attack, creating a spirited U.S. demand that Germany abandon the practice. The Germans feared the failure to comply with existing norms would bring the United States into the war on the Allied side and thus suspended the practice. It was resumed in January 1917 to stem the flow of American war-related materiel to Britain and contributed to the U.S. decision to join the Western Allies.

One of the bases for opposing unrestricted submarine attacks was the effective terrorism they represented. If the U-boats remained submerged and provided no warning as required under existing naval prize rules, there was no warning of an attack, and before anti-submarine warfare was developed during the interwar years, no effective means to ward off the attack or to mitigate the deadly effects. These attacks were, for the victims, an earlier equivalent of terrorist attacks made worse because they occurred on the ocean, from which rescue of the victims was usually impossible. For those who suffer drone attacks, there is an arguably parallel sense of vulnerability and helplessness.

Drone Controversies

As is the case with the introduction of most force multiplying weapons innovations into war, drone use is comparably controversial. Drones have been used prominently against suspected terrorists, raising two particularly noteworthy dilemmas. The first is the problem of collateral damage: injury or death to noncombatants who happen to be in an area being attacked but who are not members or supporters of the group under attack. This is also slippery moral and legal ground. It is not unusual for asymmetrical warriors to hide among civilian populations to avoid attacks, thus making themselves invisible to their enemies and activating inhibitions based in the fear of killing innocent noncombatants (so-called collateral damage). Attacking such targets is always controversial and results in accusations of atrocity. Doing so may alienate otherwise friendly residents and drive them into the arms of the terrorists being attacked. To avoid such unfortunate outcomes, great care is taken to make attacks as precise as possible to avoid or minimize civilian casualties, but they inevitably cannot be eliminated altogether. Using drones against remote enclaves where terrorists seek sanctuary may be militarily effective and efficient, but it can do so at the cost of alienating reluctant host populations.

The second problem derives from the first. Regardless of the rhetorical or physical care that attackers may exercise, some victims will inevitably view drone attacks as terrorist in nature. Like torpedoes launched from underwater submarines, a drone attack is a surprise attack that is launched from the sky without warning and with deadly consequences. It would likely not be effective otherwise: just as it destroyed all the advantages of submarine attacks to surface and inform the targets of what was to occur, advanced notice of drone attacks would render them ineffective, because the warning would allow both the targets and the innocent victims to take measures to avoid them. Since drone attacks must ignore these dynamics to succeed, it is almost certain that local populations will oppose the policy of drone use. They will also probably complain to their national government to have drone attacks suspended when they do occur. This has clearly been the case in Pakistan, where many terrorists hide and where drones have been used often. One can try to be very selective and responsible in launching drone attacks, but they inevitably kill people not directly culpable as well as targeted victims.

Policy Options

The extensive use of drones as a primary tool in the campaign against terror is largely an artifact of the Obama presidency. Obama recognized the need to take lethal action against IS, Al Qaeda, and similar organizations, but he also opposed the use of large numbers of American service personnel in the effort. This opposition came partly from his belief that the United States had overextended itself militarily in Iraq and Afghanistan (see chapter 15) and that a direct American military presence was likely to result in open-ended, inconclusive operations such as those undertaken by his predecessor in the wake of 9/11. This conviction was reinforced by the fact that the terrorists had established effective sanctuaries in places like Pakistan, Yemen, and, with the advent of the IS caliphate in 2014, in parts of Iraq and Syria. An American ground presence in any of these places would be opposed by the natives and would run the risk of creating new quagmires for the United States. Moreover, success in one venue would likely simply lead to the terrorists moving to new sanctuaries in places like North Africa. None of the scenarios appealed to Obama or those around him.

The campaign was opposed by many elements both within the United States and abroad. There was considerable partisan opposition on the basis that such an emphasis would be too pusillanimous and weak to produce desired results, a sentiment shared (mostly privately and anonymously) by many military leaders. At the other ideological extreme, some liberals viewed the campaign as morally objectionable, since its core tactic was what were essentially sneak attacks against targets (including noncombatant citizens) who could not possibly defend themselves when bombs from the drones began to fall on them.

President Obama ultimately decided that drone warfare would be the centerpiece of his lethal efforts against IS/AQ, rejecting more direct U.S. military efforts in the process. The decision was based on several elements, presented in no special logical sequence or order of importance.

The Lure of Drones

The first attraction was that drones were a relatively cheap way to deliver military power to remote, largely inaccessible target areas such as the sanctuaries from which IS and other terrorists operated. Exact figures on how much a military drone costs to build, operate, maintain, or replace are, of course, classified, and those costs vary considerably depending on how the drone is configured and used—for reconnaissance or for bombing targets, for instance. Estimates suggest that the cost may be as high as that for a fighter jet (a not inconsiderable amount), but since they are reusable and, in current circumstances, virtually impregnable, their use is relatively inexpensive, particularly since they do not put human pilots' lives at risk (a major reason the U.S. Air Force began developing them in 1959). Indeed, the protection of American service members is one of the principal virtues of "unmanned aerial systems" (UAS) as they have been known in official circles since 2005. Further, like other aircraft, they can overfly hostile territory to attack otherwise inaccessible targets and can do so without being detected.

There are other military advantages. Military drones can fly long distances to targets and "loiter" over them for extended periods undetected, thereby aiding target acquisition and precise location, and they can carry a considerable bomb load that can be delivered against that target without its foreknowledge, a considerable advantage against terrorists who are adept at fleeing assaults they see coming. There are currently very few, if any, effective defenses against the drones, and evolving technologies like "drone swarms" (where multiple small drones are used to confound radar detection) make it likely that advantage will continue. These kinds of advantages made drones quite popular first with the Central Intelligence Agency and more recently the Defense Department against terrorists in places like Pakistan, Afghanistan, and Yemen.

The Obama administration set out guidelines to minimize the negative impact of drones on target areas. These included "near certainty" intelligence that the targeted enemy was present and that civilians would not be killed, that drone attacks were the only effective option if local forces could not or would not capture the terrorists, and that there were no feasible alternatives. These rules were designed to make drone attacks more palatable where they are employed, but they have not entirely succeeded. This form of warfare is particularly disliked both by the people who have become victims of it and by their governments.

The major objection to the attacks in target zones like the Federally Administered Tribal Area (FATA) of Pakistan along its border with Afghanistan arises from the terroristic effect of the actions among population members who experience them. Gen. Stanley McChrystal (ret.), former commander of U.S. forces in Afghanistan, summarizes the emotion: "The resentment created by the American use of unmanned strikes . . . is much greater than the average American appreciates. They are hated on a visceral level, even by people who've never seen one or seen the effects of one." The major source of terror, of course, is the fear of being part of the collateral damage from an attack, and it has caused many natives in affected areas to demand a suspension of the practice. These objections are generally phrased in terms of unauthorized violations of territorial sovereignty (the atmosphere above a country is legally considered part of its sovereign space). These objections are voiced most loudly by the countries who suffer the most attacks, notably Pakistan, which is the sanctuary for the largest number of terrorists and where support for those terrorists is often highest. It should be remembered that Osama bin Laden hid openly in the Pakistani city of Abbottabad (home of Pakistan's military war college and retirement destination of many Pakistani military) for several years without interference from Pakistani authorities.

Another reason potential victims dislike drone warfare is their absolute inability to defend themselves or to fight back. One's village can be leveled by a drone-delivered bomb, and there is nothing the villagers can do either to prevent the effects or to strike back and punish those who carried it out. The virtues of drones as an attacking weapon thus are a major part of the frustration that victims experience—whether they are terrorists or innocent peasants who become collateral damage—because of the practice. A Yemeni activist quoted in the Friends Fact Sheet summarizes the impact: "what radicals had previously failed to achieve in my village . . . one drone strike accomplished in an instant: there is now an intense anger and growing hatred of America."

Consequences: What to Do?

Like most innovations in war, the development and employment of drone technology against America's enemies is not an unambiguous virtue or evil. For the United States, drones provide a unique weapons platform that allows it to contemplate and carry out military options against unconventional, elusive enemies in a part of the world hostile to many American interests and where the physical environment would make historic military practices impossible or hopelessly expensive in terms of blood and treasure. It is probably fair to say that there is no effective alternative to drone warfare for the United States in its policy goal of destroying the leadership ranks of organizations like IS and AQ in their developing-world sanctuaries. If it proves true that drone attacks have indeed killed much of the leadership of IS and to the point of making it a less potent opponent in the "war" against terrorism, it has served as a useful tool in the military kitbag. Drones, in that sense, are instruments of war for the United States, even if they appear to be instruments of terror to people in the areas where they are employed.

The effects of drone warfare, however, go beyond conventional conceptualizations of war. Like so much of modern warfare, drones are also instruments of destruction that kill civilians, as defined under the Geneva Laws of War, who are supposed to be exempt from attack as well as combatants—soldiers—who are fair game for killing. In a sense, the situation is indeed analogous to the early twentieth century, when German submarines were the "stealth" weapons of their day. The purpose of unrestricted submarine warfare was military: to intercept supplies intended for the Allies and send them to the bottom of the Atlantic Ocean. People who might be aboard were the collateral damage of their day. Just as a Yemeni peasant may be inconsolably alienated when a drone attack kills not only AQ combatants like al-Awlaki but also his relatives and friends, so too were German torpedoes the source of anger and alienation against the Germans.

The analogy does not completely hold, of course. The Allies demanded and received from Germany an agreement to suspend unrestricted submarine attacks in 1915 after the sinking of the *Lusitania*, because they had geopolitical leverage: the German fear that if they did not meet American demands to quit sinking vessels without warning, the United States would join the fight and help bring Germany to its knees. This fear worked for two years until it became clear that the policy was too costly in economic terms, at which point the self-abnegation no longer served its purpose and the practice was resumed. Those who support the terrorist organizations have no equivalent leverage over the United States except for the alienation the attacks cause in the target areas. Most Americans are unaware of these effects and probably would not respond to them in a decisive way if they did. The situations are simply not analogous.

Instruments of War or Terror?

This brings the discussion back to the initial example and question raised in the subtitle: is the use of drones an example of legitimate warfare or an instrument of terror? Or is it both? And in what circumstances could it be either?

The situation portrayed in *Signature Wounds* provides a framework within which to consider the dichotomy. In a general sense, attacking a target on American soil is certainly an act of terror, which is how the novel portrays it. The novel contains two parts of the terrorist scenario, however, and by separating them, the certitude of the assertion becomes less obvious. Attacking a party where drone pilots are in attendance is the first scenario and seems the most obviously terrorist. But is it? From the viewpoint of the terrorists, it can be argued that killing the pilots is qualitatively no different than using the drones the pilots "fly" to attack their leaders in places like Yemen. In both cases, combatants are targeted and killed, but in each, there are other victims—non-pilot partygoers or villagers— both of whom are arguably collateral damage. Both involve sneak attacks against which the victims cannot defend, and each is an indirect way to retaliate against terrorist attacks and operations intended to diminish the ability of the opponents to carry out further attacks. There may be some distinction in terms of how hard one side or the other tries to prevent the deaths of innocents and whether terrorizing the target population is an explicit mission, but structurally, are the different forms of attack fundamentally different? Is one form of attack terror and the other an act of war? Most Westerners would say they are different in a legal sense, and most terrorists would deny the comparison.

The second scenario in the novel—its climactic scene—is the attempt to capture drones in the Nevada desert and turn them against the bases from which they operate. The methods by which this assault is mounted were illegal (hijacking drones) and almost certainly violated the rules of conventional warfare, but is that so different than sneaking a Navy Seal team into Pakistan to capture or kill bin Laden? The terrorists broke American laws in what they viewed as a military operation; American forces in Pakistan also broke local laws in their assault.

The purpose of this comparison is not to disparage or to justify either form of activity. Drone warfare may be the only effective way by which to reduce the leadership cadre of terrorist organizations to defeat these enemies, but problems like sovereignty violation and collateral damage make it neither a morally nor legally pristine activity. If terrorist bombings in European cities are reprehensible because they take innocent lives, how is that different than when a Middle East villager is collateral damage in a drone attack? Are these two forms of ROEs fundamentally or tangentially different?

Implicit in this discussion are two confounding, ambiguous elements. One is the relationship between scientific discovery and application in the form of force multipliers and the regulation of their use. In this relationship, scientific progress inevitably precedes regulation, because it is impossible to anticipate what should be regulated and how regulations should be enforced when both the discovery and its application do not exist. There is always a lag time involved. The other element is the relationship between new weapons and the purposes for which they are intended and used: the link between capabilities and national security interests and strategies. Scientific discovery and applications are often serendipitous, making it difficult or impossible to know how strategy is affected before a capability emerges.

Warfare is always a messy business in which moral and practical concerns can come into conflict. From a military viewpoint, the basic purpose of drone warfare is to increase the ability to accomplish military tasks that could not otherwise be carried out successfully without endangering American lives (force multiplication). In a sense, the terrorist action in the *Signature Wounds* scenario represents an attempt to reduce part of the advantage created by weapons by reducing the invulnerability of the drone operators. Is this kind of retribution terrorism, or war, or some hybrid value? If attacks by drones represent terror, should they be outlawed? If so, should the employment of drones against targets containing both enemies and innocent people also be circumscribed? Or, should we simply admit that calling one side of the equation terror and the other war contains an element of hypocrisy? Is the use of drones a practice that represents war or terror? Maybe the dilemma will solve itself: the ambiguity surrounding submarines was largely rendered moot by advances in anti-submarine warfare (ASW) that made submarines vulnerable to attack and destruction. Will this happen to drones? What do you think drones effectively are: instruments of war or terror—or both?

Study/Discussion Questions

1. What is force multiplication? Why do the militaries of countries pursue it? How and why is it often both beneficial and controversial?

2. What is unrestricted submarine warfare? Why was its practice controversial in World War I? How is its employment parallel to the use of drone aircraft today? How was the legal problem of unrestricted use of submarines resolved? Is there a parallel with drone aircraft usage?

3. What are drones? What do they do? What are their contemporary military applications?

4. What are the major advantages and controversies surrounding contemporary applications of drone aircraft in military roles, particularly in antiterrorist missions in the developing world? Elaborate.

5. Are drone aircraft instruments of war or instruments of terror, or both? Is the distinction meaningful or meaningless? Is the kind of response to drones in the novel *Signature Wounds* a more or a less legitimate action than the use of drones against civilian populations that house terrorists? Defend your position.

Bibliography

"Barack Obama Defends Just War Using Drones." *BBC Online,* May 24, 2013.

Benjamin. Medea. *Drone Warfare: Killing by Remote Control.* Revised and Updated. London: Verso, 2013.

Brodie, Bernard, and Fawn M. Brodie. *From Crossbow to H-Bomb: The Evolution of Weapons and Tactics of Warfare.* Revised and Enlarged Ed. Bloomington: Indiana University Press, 1973.

Drew, Dennis M., and Donald M. Snow. *Making Twenty-First Century Strategy: An Introduction to Modern National Security Processes and Problems*. Maxwell Air Force Base, AL: Air University Press, 2006.

Gusterson, Hugh. *Drone: Remote Control Warfare*. Cambridge, MA: MIT Press, 2016.

Hasian, Marouf. *Drone Warfare and Lawfare in a Post-Heroic Age*. Rhetoric, Law and the Humanities. Tuscaloosa: University of Alabama Press, 2016.

JAG Legal Center and School (U.S. Department of Defense). *Textbook on History and Framework: Geneva Conventions, War Crimes, Human Rights, Comparative Law*. Washington, DC: U.S. Department of Defense, 2012.

Kaag, John, and Sarah Kreps. *Drone Warfare*. London: Polity Press, 2014.

Parks, Lisa, and Caren Kaplan (eds.). *Life in the Age of Drone Warfare*. Durham, NC: Duke University Press, 2017.

Rae, James De Shaw. *Analyzing the Drone Debates: Targeted Killings, Remote Warfare, and Military Technology*. London: Palgrave Pivot, 2014.

"Retired General Cautions Against Overuse of 'Hated' Drones." *Reuters* (online), January 7, 2013.

Rogers, Ann, and John Hill. *Unmanned: Drone Warfare and Global Security*. London: Pluto Press, 2014.

Ronzitti, Natalino. *The Law of Naval Warfare: A Collection of Agreements and Documents with Commentaries*. Leiden, Netherlands: Martinus Nijhoff, 1988.

Russell, Kirk. *Signature Wounds*. Seattle: Thomas and Mercer (Amazon), 2017.

Shaver, Andrew, and Jacob N. Shapiro. "The Military Costs of Civilian Casualties: Why Minimizing Harm During Conflict Is Also Good Strategy." *Foreign Affairs Snapshot* (online), August 22, 2017.

Snow, Donald M., and Dennis M. Drew. *From Lexington to Baghdad and Beyond: War and Politics in the American Experience*. Third Ed. Armonk, NY: M. E. Sharpe, 2010.

"The U.S. Drone: A Fact Sheet." Washington, DC: The Friends Committee on National Legislation, 2012.

Williams, Brian Glyn. *Predator: The CIA's War on Al Qaeda*. Washington, DC: Potomac Books, 2013.

CONCLUSION

18

Quo Vadis

Facing the National Security Future

The Latin term *quo vadis*, which was used as the title of a 1951 biblical movie, translates literally as "whither goest thou?" In more contemporary parlance, it means "where are you going?" It is a good question to ask about most future conditions, and the subject of national security is no exception. Since the future has not happened and is thus a matter of speculation, it is a difficult task. In a subject with the gravity and potential consequences of national security, it is also a critical concern.

The preceding pages have suggested two apparently contradictory truths about the process of extrapolating the national security past and present into the future. The first impression arises from the ability to depict that process as a rational application of the national security model developed in chapter 1 and applied in subsequent chapters. The other impression, which is an inevitable consequence of examining actual case applications, is that the process is a good deal less neat and more idiosyncratic than the model suggests, with sufficient exceptions in the "real world" that a straight-line extrapolation from the present and past into the future is a perilous enterprise.

Each element has relevance for the question. The development of strategy in a systematic and comprehensive manner adds order and predictability to the process and its outcomes. At the same time, it is most applicable in a world environment where all the members have basically similar values and interests. Since this is clearly not the case, the superimposition of a framework is a difficult if not impossible task in actual situations and with different states. The other end of the spectrum suggests that the idiosyncratic nature of different situations may be so great that any framework must be so broad and vague as not to offer concrete guidance in achieving U.S. interests. From this perspective, the nature of the world situation may be such that the only sensible solution is to treat all situations on an ad hoc basis.

A sensible way to view national security policy prospects lies somewhere between the extremes. Individual, and in some cases, regional world situations are sufficiently different that a universal standard like communism versus anti-communism (the shibboleth of the Cold War) does not clearly apply, or at least may need to be modified so that it does overlay a given U.S. national security situation at any specific place on the globe. At the same time, the United States (as well as other countries) starts from certain personal national values like democracy promotion and different ideas about how much it can and should act to promote those values at different places, a determination combined with an assessment of the resources that can and should be marshaled in different situations.

The United States, like other countries, has not had a sustained agreement on exactly how it should face the world since the end of the Cold War. During times of great national stress and peril (e.g., World War II, the height of the Cold War) a consensus emerged around how Americans must act to protect the country, but these periods represent the historical exception, not the rule. When the parameters of threat are less sharply drawn, the population loses its focus and tends to divide on national security priorities. Although the threat of international terrorism provided a national focus in the years immediately after 9/11, that flame has faded, and disagreement has returned to the debate. The current distinction is the partisan nature of the division.

There are two major, contrasting traditions, each with some internal variations. Both traditions, introduced in chapter 14, have reflected the geopolitical worldview of different administrations in this century. At the operational level, they suggest the levels and quality of national security preparation the country should be willing to undertake and sustain, as suggested in chapter 14. They also represent the basic orientation the country has toward its interaction in the world in the future, which is their role in this preview of the future.

The two basic orientations are internationalism and interventionism. As already noted, the internationalist position is generally associated with liberal political philosophies. At the international level, it tends to emphasize multilateral cooperation and solutions to national security problems in which the United States seeks out and incorporates the ideas and participation of other like-minded countries in seeking solutions to international difficulties. As such, it consciously tries to avoid unilateral actions that may place the country at odds with others whenever possible. An important consequence is that the threat or recourse to military force, especially without the direct support of friends and allies, should be a last resort and only when vital interests are at stake. It does not deny the need for military force, which always remains a possibility, but it is less militarily activist. Force is a contextual reality which the internationalist will remind opponents is available; but it is not an aggressive weapon to be brandished in other than unusual cases.

The interventionist position differs in two important regards. First, it tends to be more unilateralist, believing the country must be willing to pursue and secure its interests through the threat or employment of U.S. military force in contravention to the positions of others when it feels the pursuit of those interests require the country to act "on its own." This predilection tends to result in others characterizing the position as more narrowly nationalist than does internationalism. The "America First" idea is a prime example. Second, it tends to be more militaristic than internationalism. This tendency is manifested in a willingness to elevate military threats and solutions above the nurturing of broad international support for positions and possible actions.

As should be obvious, the two positions tend to be partisan, and since both parties have been in power in this century, both orientations have characterized different presidencies. The interventionist position burst on the policy scene in the reaction to the 9/11 terrorist attacks under Republican George W. Bush. It was closely associated with the so-called "neo-conservatives" who were imbedded in the national security establishment. A remaining prominent "neo-con," as they were known, is Trump national security advisor John Bolton. They were particularly associated with a policy of promoting "regime change" in national leaderships of which the United States disapproved. Their most prominent action under Bush was the invasion and occupation of Iraq in 2003. The interventionist position has largely been reinstated by Trump; the most obvious example of its implementation was Trump's 2018 removal of the United States from the Iran nuclear deal, accompanied by a barely veiled invitation by the president for the Iranian people to engage in regime change. Both Bush and Trump emphasized the need for a robust, and expensive, military establishment.

The Obama administration, following general Democratic preference, was explicitly internationalist in its orientation toward the world. Obama promised to extricate the United States from its de facto wars in Iraq and Afghanistan, goals which he was only partially successful in achieving. On a broad range of international issues, the Obama administration sought to build broad multilateral support for policies it favored. Support for the Paris climate change agreement and American participation in the Iran nuclear deal, including the JCPOA, are prime examples. This orientation requires less emphasis on the threat or use of American military force than does interventionism, and it tends to be opposed by Americans who prefer a more robust American military component to national security policy.

Perspectives on the Problem

Regardless of the underlying philosophical position one prefers, that orientation toward national security matters is framed by two additional considerations. One of these is the breadth of matters that one thinks of in national security terms, and it can be characterized as either traditional or extended, generally to include so-called humanitarian concerns. The other is geographic and refers to the various physical parts of the world (and sub-areas within them) where one assigns greatest emphasis. The two concerns help narrow and focus where national security efforts should be preferentially directed. They also occasionally overlap, as demonstrated by the problem of the Rohingya in Bangladesh and Myanmar.

Traditional Concerns

When one thinks about national security, the immediate matters to which one is drawn are the promotion and protection of American interests and the means one would use to deal with challenges to various interests. In turn, the assessment reflects the self-image the country has of itself—as a leader by example and principle, for instance, as opposed to a leader that imposes its will with military force or the threat to employ force. At the same time, the assessment also reflects some judgment about the country's ability and willingness to embrace the mantle of global leader—how much leadership of what kind can the country afford.

The traditional American post–World War II view has been expansive. Prior to that conflict, the United States did not seek nor accept an active world leadership role politically or militarily, and in the postmortem of the period leading to the second global conflict of the twentieth century, many agreed that a more assertive American leadership and physical effort might have prevented the war or made its outcome less difficult to achieve. Given the growing Cold War military confrontation with the Soviet Union, there was necessarily a major—arguably *the* major—emphasis on military force as the primary guarantor of the peace.

The result was a consensus that had two primary components. The first was to define national security in basically military terms and thus to make the maintenance of a robust military capability across the spectrum of possible warfare the bedrock of national security strategy and policy. Given the structure of competition with a heavily armed Soviet opponent, the threat clearly dictated that stance. When the Cold War ended, most of that threat structure evaporated with the demise of the Soviet opponent. There has, however, been very little questioning of translating that change into any different structure or philosophy for protecting American interests. When the sequester was effectively lifted in 2018 (as discussed in chapter 14), there was virtually no discussion of whether a changed threat meant a need for lesser, or at least different, force size and structure. Instead, President Trump trumpeted the occasion as an opportunity to rebuild the armed forces to (presumably) something like their Cold War prowess.

The second part of the consensus was that the United States should work in concert with its friends and allies: it was explicitly internationalist. Whether it was the rebuilding of the international economic system centering on the Bretton Woods system or military security in the form of the North Atlantic Treaty and other multilateral or bilateral arrangements, the United States consciously chose a burden-sharing approach in which it would be the leading force but in which it would consult and coordinate activities with friends and allies. Such an approach seemed necessary in the face of expansionist communism; it has been seen by some as less crucial in the contemporary, less focused national security environment.

The internationalist consensus centering on military strength and multilateral consensus has eroded. Part of the reason is that the old structure of threats to the United States and its international partners is no longer as pressing as it once was, making the burden-sharing emphasis on mutual consultation and decisions less compelling than it was in the face of the communist threat. The successor central threat of terrorism, while not insignificant, is much more diffuse and less concentrated, making multilateral policy determination and application less compelling and looser forms of cooperation more acceptable than before. A united front is, in other words, not so clearly necessary as it was before. At the same time, the quantitative aspects of the threat have also receded. It is no longer clear where a major military challenge to American security might occur, and thus where the help of other countries would be necessary. The United States, after all, has engaged in several military adventures since Operation Desert Storm in which it has acted unilaterally or essentially on its own. In Iraq and

Afghanistan, the effort was officially multilateral, but most of the "heavy lifting" was American. Does the United States truly need international consensus and participation in its national security efforts?

Changed circumstance has allowed for the spirited advocacy of more unilateralist postures and actions. The campaign and early presidency of Donald J. Trump has been the cutting edge of the assault on traditional internationalism. The foreign policy premise of the Trump candidacy was "America First," a recurring theme in American history the premises of which include a retreat from global leadership, a concentration on the unilateral promotion of American interests even when they come into conflict with those of other countries (including friends), and the willingness to use force and major diplomatic effort unilaterally. Given the role of the United States since the middle of the twentieth century, the turning inward of American pursuit of its national security has been disconcerting to many of the country's major collaborators. Whether the Trump gambit will prove to represent an enduring change in U.S. national security policy or an aberration that will be supplanted by a return to a more traditional internationalist role remains to be seen.

Unconventional Concerns

The primary example of unconventional national security concerns in the contemporary environment is represented by so-called humanitarian interests. The idea that there are situations occurring in various parts of the world that are grossly offensive to universal human rights and that there is a resulting moral and physical obligation of the international community to participate in ameliorating these conditions gained currency in the period between the end of the Cold War and 9/11. This period was geopolitically tranquil other than speculating about the successor structure of the Cold War confrontation and how the vacuum created by the disappearance of the Soviet Union would be filled. At the same time, grotesque human tragedies in places like Kosovo and Rwanda reminded the world that there were awful ongoing situations that the world was ignoring.

There were, and still are, sizable parts of Africa, the Middle East, and some other parts of Asia where the populations are physically repressed, and their most basic human rights denied. There are even cases of genocidal campaigns against unwanted members of groups. The United Nations Charter, to which virtually every country in the world is a signatory, has the protection of basic rights woven through it, and basic documents like the Universal Declaration on Human Rights, to which all members are nominally committed to honor but which are unevenly addressed or enforced. In some cases, violations of those rights are ignored or rationalized. Why?

There are several reasons (for a summary discussion, see Snow, *Thinking About National Security*, chapter 3). Probably the most important is that most of these events occur in isolated, geopolitically marginal parts of the world where the absence of remediation does not have major systemic national security consequences. In the contemporary environment, there is no more vivid example than the plight of the Rohingya, a Muslim ethnic group of an estimated 3.5 million who have been a persecuted and displaced minority that has lived for centuries in Myanmar (former Burma) and has been forced into exile in Bangladesh in what Human Rights Watch has referred to as a classic "ethnic cleansing" by the Myanmar government. Bangladesh lacks the resources to sustain the Rohingya, and the international community has offered scant assistance to the ethno-religious group, which continues to live in totally inadequate refugee areas in Bangladesh. There are no important geopolitical ties between Americans and the Rohingya nor much interest in the part of South Asia where the tragedy is occurring. Most members of the international community are unaware of the plight and wretched prospects of the Rohingya. Should they be?

The unconventional response is the advocacy of something known as *humanitarian vital interests.* The premise of this assertion is that basic humanity and the obligations under the UN Charter create for the states of the world a moral and legal obligation to ensure the minimal conditions of all humans. The term *vital* is crucial to this claim: it elevates the interest to a level concomitant to traditional national security interests. For its advocates, this translates into something called the Responsibility to Protect (R2P) that it believes should be incorporated as a basic tenet of national security policy for the United States and others.

This elevation has not occurred, of course, and at least two additional reasons underlie why not. One is a rejection of the premise of any universal obligation in other than a vague moral sense, and it is not clear that intervening in the affairs of even bad actors is an accepted part of American national security. This view is basically compatible with the Trump administration's "America First" policy. Advocates of R2P assert the obligation as essentially universal, suggesting an internationalist preference.

A further argument is that the proposition, however laudable in a hortatory sense, is too extensive and expensive in a world where there are many national security concerns to address and where there are simply not enough resources to extend to new and additional concerns. It is not coincidental, for instance, that the apex of popularity of the humanitarian interest movement was in the years leading to 9/11 and that the movement has been moved to the international backburner as attention moved to the challenge of terrorism, including military responses by the United States in Middle Eastern countries like Iraq, Afghanistan, and to a much more restrained extent, Syria.

Policy Options

From the general imperative that national security is the maintenance and promotion of the physical safety and well-being, it follows that policy should seek to implement and maintain that safety. These core values—safety and promotion of well-being—are the primary national interests that the United States (or any other country) hold most dear and necessary. All interests, however, are neither as intense nor important as others, and some interests are threatened to a greater degree than others.

National Interests Levels and National Security

The pursuit of a national security strategy begins by attempting to sort out the more important from the less important threats facing the country, which in turn allows one to see how threats to those interests can appropriately be secured. The basic distinction, introduced in chapter 1, is between *vital interests* (VIs) and *less-than-vital interests* (LTVs). The difference between the categories centers on the tolerability of securing or failing to secure American interests. Vital interests are generally considered those conditions that, if not realized, would be intolerable for the United States, whereas LTVs are situations that would inconvenience or displease the country but where that failure would not put the country at basic risk.

Some interests of the United States are clearly more important than others, and the realization or failure to secure different interests has greater consequences in some areas than in others. The basic VI-LTV division is conventionally thought of as the line that divides situations where the United States would use force from those where it would not. This distinction is controversial, partly because the point at which interests cross the VI-LTV line (in either direction) is controversial (reflecting the subjective nature of security) and because some national security analysts feel it is too restrictive in terms of permitting the commitment of American forces in conflicts.

Moreover, the distinction is muddied when one looks at it in different parts of the world where the interest-threat mismatch is at play. It is not, for instance, particularly helpful in developing contemporary American policy toward Europe. The security of Western Europe has been the most important (vital) overseas interest of the United States for more than a century, but that security is arguably the least threatened of any geographic area in the world. Although the United States would be more likely to defend Europe from military threat than any other place on the globe, it is probably the geographic area in which it is least likely to be called upon to do so. When one translates interests into military capabilities, what guidance does securing Europe provide?

Geographic Factors

The application of national security is strongly geographically influenced. This introduces the pure influence of geopolitics (international relations as influenced by geography) into the process and makes the proposing of a coherent national security strategy even more daunting than it would otherwise be. In terms of national interests, there are clear differences for American security that arise in different geopolitical parts and sub-parts of the world. Put another way, saying some parts of the world are more important to the United States than others is another way of saying American national interests are more important and more threatened in some places than others.

For convenience sake, one can divide American geographic interests among five regions, four of which have been partially examined in the cases in this volume (the exception is the Western Hemisphere). The other areas are Europe, East Asia, the Middle East, and Africa. Each provides a different interest profile for the United States, and there are different challenges within each region.

The problem with a geographical approach is the idiosyncratic nature of American global interests. Western Europe, followed closely by the Asia-Pacific region, has been where the most important American interests lie, but both areas present different mosaics of policy concern and national interest challenge. The United States' relationship with Western Europe has both political and economic components; maintaining the integrity of European democracies and market economic systems was the second most vital national security interest of the United States after the physical survival of the United States in the face of Soviet nuclear weapons during the Cold War. The end of that confrontation removed most of the threat, although a resurgent, expansionist Russia presents problems for the United States and its allies. Europe remains important, but in what sense and with what kind of national security mandate?

East Asia and the Pacific are similar. It is becoming clear that a more aggressive China wishes to strike an effective bargain wherein the United States acknowledges primary Chinese domain on the continent (thus their apparent interest in removing the American military presence from the Korean Peninsula), while ceding American primacy over the western Pacific. Such an arrangement probably relieves the North Korean threat as a major national security challenge, but it does not necessarily affect the growing economic competition and enmity between the world's two largest economies. Chinese-American competition is clearly the national security issue of the future, but what outcomes are tolerable and intolerable for Americans, and what are we prepared to do in areas where vital interests cannot clearly be achieved?

The other problematical area is the Middle East. It is the area in which the United States has been most active since 2000, because so much global terrorism emanates from regional sites. Oil used to drive U.S. policy there (see Snow, *The Middle East, Oil, and the U.S. National Security Policy* for a discussion), but now policy tends to center on Israel and the Palestinians, Israel and Iran, and the Syrian conflict, with lesser spinoffs like the plight of the Kurds, continuing instability in Iraq, and the inability to end American involvement in Afghanistan satisfactorily. Trying to sort out, and more importantly to rationalize the various strands of interest into a coherent regional policy encompassing them all, has proven so elusive that one rarely even sees a solution proposed.

This brief overview points to the difficulty and frustration of trying to formulate a national security strategy for the United States. American interests, vital or LTV, are so diverse and geographically disparate, that almost any overarching value or rationale one might propose will prove valuable for some places and make no sense in others. The result is that there really is no coherent strategy like containment during the Cold War to guide strategists and policymakers. That conclusion may be less than satisfying, but it reflects the messy reality in which policy and strategy must be devised and applied.

Consequences: What to Do?

It would be helpful to be able to reduce the national security into a neat set of theorems and corollaries that could be applied to all situations, but that is clearly not the case. National security is a multi-actor exercise that virtually assures disagreement and conflict. Different states have contradictory views of what constitutes their national security, and those visions may or may not be compatible to change when they fly in the face of contrary American assessments. At the same time, there are inevitably different visions in the internal politics of states that lead to different assessments and advocacies of different strategic directions. The interplay of those interests and their dynamic, changing nature is a dizzying process. The convoluted, twisted process of U.S.-DPRK relations in 2018 is a clear example. It is not alone.

There has been a recurring tendency in national security considerations in the United States that reflects basic political, national interest determinations. When the United States faces a clear and compelling threat with dire potential consequences, the country comes together and devises a national security strategy that is consensually supported. Defeating the fascist threat to the international order in World War II was such an occasion, as was facing down and defusing the existential threat posed by Soviet nuclear weapons during the Cold War.

The corollary is that when there is not a threat the nature and severity of which is agreed upon by nearly all Americans, a consensus rarely exists or can be sustained. Terrorism symbolized by 9/11 appeared to create such a situation in the years immediately after 2001, but the threat, while serious and dangerous, never rose to an intensity around which a similar consensus emerged. Americans agree the terrorist threat is dangerous and should be eradicated; that agreement is not so deep, however, that it has produced a consensus on how to go about solving the problem.

The United States is currently somewhere between consensus-producing threats and thus the compelling need for a unifying strategy and willingness to bear the sacrifices implementing such a strategy would require. There are clearly threats to American interests and values, some of which have been chronicled in this volume. Individually and collectively, they indicate a turbulent and challenging environment. At the same time, none has created a demand for a unifying strategy around which political elements do or must congregate. The result is that there is no clear national strategy that is much more than a string of platitudes. What is current U.S. national security strategy? Good question.

There are logically two ways to create the environment in which a new equivalent of containment might emerge. One is clearly undesirable: a new encompassing military or other threat the equivalent of fascism or nuclear-armed Soviet communism. The other is a broad political appeal that results in a determination to unite politically in support of national goals and how to achieve them. In the toxic partisan nature of contemporary American politics, this scenario seems naïve in the absence of a unifying threat.

Is there another approach? If so, what is it, and how can it be achieved? Alternately, is the ambiguous national security environment in which we find ourselves indicative of a satisfactory, if not satisfying, condition? What do you think?

Study/Discussion Questions

1. What are the basic orientations toward foreign and national security policy? Describe and contrast each, including apparent contrasts in the orientations of Presidents Obama and Trump.
2. What are the traditional concerns of national security policy? What has the American orientation been? Explain, citing relevant examples. How has President Trump challenged this approach?
3. What are humanitarian vital interests? Are they legitimate concerns of U.S. national security policy? How is the Rohingya crisis an example? What are the primary objections to this category of interests?
4. Discuss the national security policy options of the United States. Include in your response the VI-LTV distinction and geopolitical concerns. Why is it so difficult to develop an overall strategy except in times of severe national crises?
5. Does the United States have a coherent national security strategy? If not, why? How important a problem do you think this situation represents?

Bibliography

Bellamy, Alex J. *Responsibility to Protect*. Malden, MA: Polity Press, 2009.

Evans, Gareth. *The Responsibility to Protect: End Mass Atrocity Crimes Once and For All*. Washington, DC: Brookings Institution Press, 2008.

Farrow, Ronan. *War on Peace: The End of Diplomacy and the Decline of American Influence*. New York: W. W. Norton, 2018.

Fishel, John T. *American National Security Policy: Authorities, Institutions, and Cases*. Lanham, MD: Rowman & Littlefield, 2017.

Garrett, Stephen A. *Doing Good and Doing Well: An Examination of Humanitarian Intervention*. Westport, CT: Praeger, 1999.

George, Roger, Harvey Rishikoff, and Brent Scowcroft (eds.). *The National Security Enterprise: Navigating the Labyrinth*. Second Ed. Washington, DC: Georgetown University Press, 2017.

Jarmon, Jack. *The New Era in U.S. National Security: An Introduction to Emerging Threats and Challenges*. Lanham, MD: Rowman & Littlefield, 2014.

Kessler, Ronald. *The Trump White House: Changing the Rules of the Game*. New York: Crown Forum, 2018.

Meacham, Jon. *The Soul of America: The Battle for Our Better Angels*. New York: Random House, 2018.

Preble, Christopher A., and John Mueller. *A Dangerous World: Threat Perception and U.S. National Security*. Washington, DC: Cato Institute, 2014.

Reveron, Derek S., and Nikolas K. Gvosdev. *The Oxford Handbook of U.S. National Security*. Oxford, UK: Oxford University Press, 2018.

Snow, Donald M. *The Middle East, Oil, and the U.S. National Security Policy: Intractable Conflicts, Impossible Solutions*. Lanham, MD: Rowman & Littlefield, 2016.

———. *National Security*. Seventh Ed. New York and London: Routledge, 2020.

———. *Thinking About National Security: Strategy, Policy, and Issues*. New York and London: Routledge, 2016.

Suri, Jeremi, and Benjamin Valentino. *Sustainable Security: Rethinking American National Security Strategy*. Oxford, UK: Oxford University Press, 2016.

Weiss, Thomas G. *Humanitarian Intervention*. Malden, MA: Polity Press, 2012.

Index